The Voices of #MeToo

From Grassroots Activism to a Viral Roar

Carly Gieseler

ROWMAN & LITTLEFIELD
Lanham • Boulder • New York • London

Published by Rowman & Littlefield
An imprint of The Rowman & Littlefield Publishing Group, Inc.
4501 Forbes Boulevard, Suite 200, Lanham, Maryland 20706
www.rowman.com

6 Tinworth Street, London SE11 5AL, United Kingdom

British Library Cataloguing in Publication Information Available

Library of Congress Cataloging-in-Publication Data
Names: Gieseler, Carly, 1978- author.
Title: The voices of #MeToo : from grassroots activism to a viral roar / Carly
    Gieseler.
Other titles: The voices of [hashtag] MeToo
Description: Lanham : Rowman & Littlefield, [2019] | Includes bibliographical
    references and index.
Identifiers: LCCN 2019014919 (print) | LCCN 2019018243 (ebook) | ISBN
    9781538128022 (ebook) | ISBN 9781538128008 (cloth) | ISBN 9781538128015
    (paperback)
Subjects: LCSH: Sexual abuse victims. | Sex crimes—Prevention. | Social media. |
    Sexual harassment—Prevention.
Classification: LCC HV6625 (ebook) | LCC HV6625 .G54 2019 (print) | DDC
    362.883—dc23
LC record available at https://lccn.loc.gov/2019014919

∞™ The paper used in this publication meets the minimum requirements of
American National Standard for Information Sciences—Permanence of Paper for
Printed Library Materials, ANSI/NISO Z39.48-1992.

Contents

ACKNOWLEDGMENTS   v

AUTHOR'S NOTE   vii

CHAPTER 1. THE SOCIAL MEDIA ACTIVISM OF #METOO:
"THE SILENCE BREAKERS"   1

CHAPTER 2. THE PUBLIC AND PRIVATE FACES OF #METOO:
"WHEN MOVIE STARS DON'T KNOW WHERE TO GO,
WHAT HOPE IS THERE FOR THE REST OF US?"   27

CHAPTER 3. TARANA BURKE'S GRASSROOTS GOAL AND
THE IMPLICATIONS OF #METOO FOR WOMEN OF COLOR:
"SISTERS STILL MANAGED TO GET DIMINISHED OR ERASED"   47

CHAPTER 4. THE DOUBLE BIND OF SILENCED SEXUAL
VICTIMIZATION IN THE LGBTQ+ COMMUNITY: "MOST OF
US WERE NEVER TAUGHT THE LANGUAGE WITH WHICH TO
UNDERSTAND THE EXPERIENCES OF OUR YOUTH"   69

CHAPTER 5. GLOBAL RESPONSES TO #METOO: "THE FASTEST
WAY TO DISCREDIT ANY WOMEN'S RIGHTS STRUGGLE IS TO SAY
IT COMES FROM SOMEWHERE ELSE"   95

CHAPTER 6. THE OMISSION OF PEOPLE WITH DISABILITIES FROM
#METOO: "DISABILITY IS THE ONE MINORITY GROUP WE CAN
ALL JOIN"   123

CHAPTER 7. Toxic Masculinity and Male Responses to
#MeToo: "Perhaps All the Moment Requires Is for
Men to Shut Up and Listen"   141

Final Thoughts   169
Index   171

Acknowledgments

The journey of this book began with those two simple words: Me Too. Following the cascade of voices across digital spheres, into marginalized communities, and around the world has been one of the greatest privileges of my life as a scholar-practitioner and human being. Thank you to Tarana Burke, who changed the trajectory of healing. Thank you to all survivors and allies, as well as anyone still searching and learning. Words are not enough to express my gratitude to the many who shared their stories with me personally and with the world.

Many thanks to Elizabeth Swayze, executive editor of the Communication and Media Studies and Conflict Resolution Division at Rowman & Littlefield, for contacting me about this project. Her enthusiasm and guidance inspired me to transform my fledgling presentation piece into an entire book. I also want to thank assistant editor Megan Manzano for her detailed dedication in bringing this text to fruition. My deepest gratitude to the tireless efforts of assistant managing editor Janice Braunstein and copy editor Jo-Ann Parks; I am indebted to both of you for such careful and insightful readings of this manuscript. I consider myself so fortunate to have worked with such an invaluable team at Rowman & Littlefield. Also, much gratitude to my readers and reviewers for their time and consideration—their suggestions and insights strengthened this project immeasurably.

My home institution of York College within the City University of New York—and specifically my colleagues in the Department of Performing and Fine Arts—have fostered one of the most supportive, dynamic, and collegial spaces imaginable. While the labor of writing a book might seem a daunting task from the outset, any doubts were vanquished by my colleagues and friends in my department and across all disciplines and departments at York.

Further, my students—my many, brilliant, talented, generous, dedicated York College students—have been an unending source of inspiration. Every moment in every classroom, I am awakened by the insights, challenged by the questions, and awed by the remarkable sense of caring and collaboration demonstrated by this phenomenal group. While this book offers a philosophical overview of the #MeToo movement and its cultural impact at this historical moment, I hope that it helps build understanding, compassion, and communication that might shape a greater future for my students.

Finally, to being supported, nurtured, and loved by family and friends. My unending gratitude and all of my love for a December snowstorm holiday at "the nest" in South Dakota, typing away while Jinks (Susan-mom), Gomes (Mike-dad), Beans (Megan-sis), and the stampeding doodles (Ace and Syd) chimed in or let me work, to my furry assistant over Thanksgiving in Chicago (Lulu), and for my Newf (Mike) who raised my spirits with the vision of our cabin in the sky . . . where I write this now.

Author's Note

This text incorporates numerous online posts from Twitter and other cited sources. The majority of these comments were reproduced verbatim. In some cases, the author chose to correct spelling errors or typos for the sake of clarity. These minor changes were made with care to ensure that the edits would not fundamentally alter the original message.

CHAPTER 1

The Social Media Activism of #MeToo

"The Silence Breakers"

Women's March, Pennsylvania Avenue. *Vlad Tchompalov/Unsplash*

> If you've been sexually harassed or assaulted write 'me too' as a reply to this tweet.
> Me Too.
> Suggested by a friend: "If all the women who have been sexually harassed or assaulted wrote 'Me too.' as a status, we might give people a sense of the magnitude of the problem."
>
> —@Alyssa_Milano, October 15, 2017

Following the avalanche of sexual harassment and assault allegations against movie mogul Harvey Weinstein, a social awareness and activism project emerged as people took to Twitter to add their voices to the growing roar of the #MeToo movement. On the suggestion of a friend, on October

15, 2017 actor Alyssa Milano reached across the social media feed to ask anyone who'd experienced sexual harassment, abuse, and assault to respond with the #MeToo tweet. In using the #MeToo hashtag and Twitter as a medium of instantaneous response and public sharing, Milano sought to illustrate the scope of sexual violence and misconduct.[1] Twitter became a megaphone for public outcry as women and men, public and private citizens alike answered the call. Tweets varied from detailed stories of experiences to that simple message of "Me Too." The powerful, collective response to two small words spread to eighty-five countries with 1.7 million tweets within ten days. While the message originated on Twitter, it expanded across other social media sites including Facebook, which released statistics that the "Me Too" movement sparked over twelve million posts and comments in less than twenty-four hours.[2]

In the hours that drew immediate attention to the viral movement, it was soon noted that black feminist activist Tarana Burke originated the "Me Too" movement a decade prior to Milano's call to action in the trending hashtag.

> Shout out to my girl @taranaburke who has been advocating for assault victims & saying #MeToo for years. metoo.support
>
> —@BritniDWrites, October 15, 2017

> #MeToo. Thank you @TaranaBurke for bringing us this gift of #MeToo almost 10 years ago. Still powerful today.
>
> —@aliciagarza, October 16, 2017

Once aware, Milano acknowledged Burke's foundational work in the movement and asked followers to visit Burke and MeToo/#MeToo's[3] origin story. Regarding the resurgence of this message, Burke stated: "It wasn't built to be a viral campaign or a hashtag that is here today and forgotten tomorrow. It was a catchphrase to be used from survivor to survivor to let folks know that they were not alone."[4] As founder of several organizations including Just Be Inc. and Girls for Gender Equity, Burke created the original campaign as a strategy to communicate with sexual abuse, assault, exploitation, and harassment survivors. Burke's iteration was a specific effort to reach underserved communities and women of color (WOC). As Burke said, from its inception the movement was about "us talking to us."[5] She spoke of the conversation with a young girl that compelled her to create the movement in 2006. Working as a director at a youth camp, Burke recalled the day the girl followed her down the hall, asking:

> "Ms. Tarana, can I just talk to you for a second?" Everything in my spirit knew that she wanted to tell me this thing . . . she just opened up and started talking

about this stuff that her stepfather had done to her. And I cut her off. I was just like, "You know what? Baby, I can't help you." . . . I was still grappling with my own survival. . . . That just haunted me! And I kept saying to myself, "Tarana, if you could have just said 'me too.'"[6]

Burke's grassroots mission was to provide a safe space for sexual abuse victims to step away from shame and silence. She wanted to open a dialogue where these women might find their voices in empathetic concert with others. This was especially significant for the disadvantaged communities where, as Burke said, "rape crisis centers and sexual assault workers weren't going."[7] This reiterates how women of color and other marginalized populations experience sexual violence in different, intense, and often silenced ways.

Rather than continue the suppression or appropriation of marginalized voices, #MeToo might reveal how identity politics create a greater conversation regarding the intersection of dominant, violent forces against all oppressed communities. This book unravels the ideas and practices of activism throughout the #MeToo movement from its inception to its current viral moment. Detailing the mediated coverage, #MeToo conversation, and surrounding responses to that discourse provides context surrounding #MeToo and the potential for its impact in the future. This text assesses the experiences of marginalized communities and the urgency for #MeToo and all movements to recognize intersectional experiences as sources of empowerment and resistance against oppressive and abusive forces. In exploring these issues of social justice and intersectionality, we may begin to hear and amplify the voices that are often silenced in the louder, viral roar.

THE VOICES OF #METOO

Smashing the patriarchy is messy. Shit will get broken. Don't believe #MeToo is a fragile movement. That's what they want us to believe.
    The path forward won't be linear—there may be missteps—but there's no going back.

—@shannonrwatts, November 19, 2017

#MeToo is not the first social media campaign to augment stories of abuse against women. The #EverydaySexism campaign of 2012 serves as a living document of sexism and abuse; British feminist writer Laura Bates established the project as an open forum for individuals to share their stories of sexism from the wildly offensive to the benevolent or normalized forms. The #YesAllWomen hashtag of 2014 garnered attention after Elliot Rodger killed six people and injured fourteen more near the UC Santa Barbara campus in the Isla Vista shootings. When media uncovered Rodger's online misogynist

rants and manifesto threatening women for rejecting him, #YesAllWomen
galvanized as a direct response.[8] Early into the #MeToo hashtag flurry, Debbie Kilroy asked "Why can't men say #Ihave for the sexual harassment &
sexual violence they have perpetrated? Time for men to take responsibility &
name it" (@DebKilroy, October 16, 2017). Many men responded with the
#IHave hashtag, admitting past violations, transgressions, and complicity.
These movements exemplify how open-access platforms offer compelling
forums for social justice projects.

Digital spaces create perpetual conversations, especially for marginalized folk who use social media as an access point they are often denied
in live communication. #MeToo opens an online dialogue focused on
survivor stories, rather than the mediated attention to salacious details and
controversial perpetrators such as Weinstein.[9] While the level of celebrity
involved in the Weinstein allegations may raise the profile and attention
from mainstream media, the grassroots activism of #MeToo reiterates the
reality and commonality of sexual abuse, harassment, exploitation, and
assault for women (and many men) everywhere. The power of a movement
like #MeToo is how it spotlights silenced issues of oppression, begins the
conversation about these experiences, and transforms the dialogue into a
movement. Gilbert wrote, "unlike many kinds of social-media activism,
it isn't a call to action or the beginning of a campaign. . . . It's simply an
attempt to get people to understand the prevalence of sexual harassment
and assault in society."[10] Voices are now populating the decades of silence
enshrouding sexual abuse in all forms. The #MeToo movement has digitally
opened a space for these voices.

Drawing from the personal narratives of sexual assault, harassment, and
exploitation survivors, #MeToo builds volumes on testimonies of inspiration and trauma. Clark-Parsons alludes to the strategic power of hashtag
feminism as a processual event beginning with a breach of social norms
that "escalates to the level of crisis, during which actors contest social meanings, and ending with a reintegration period, during which the movement's
interpretive framework is rejected, adopted, or revised."[11] The intricate
digital steps constructing these frameworks expand possibilities for greater
inclusion and diversity, etching a blueprint for future acts of organization
and resistance. As Stache notes, "hashtags in particular continue the conversation beyond the originating dialogue by creating an identifier or tag for
fellow activists."[12] The visual cues of hashtag activism mark movements of
social justice, increasing recognition and participation.

Challenges of Change

As with any cultural phenomenon, after the initial praise for #MeToo,
critics began adding their voices to the conversation. These concerns in-

cluded the efficacy of hashtag activism; the spectrum of abuse; the problematic "trial by media"; and the risk of overexposure or misogynist threats.

Unless women are going to name names, enough with the slacktivism.

—@MazzPokrivac, October 28, 2017

#MeToo has opened debates about social media activism, its capabilities in enacting real change, and its ideological challenges. Many label these movements "slacktivism"—humorously chastising those who participate in activism from the safety of their homes. The interrogation of hashtag activism finds fault with the self-satisfaction generated by online activist experiences that seemingly have little to do with action on the ground.[13] Critiques surrounding hashtag activism correspond with the notion of lazy or conformist thinking that ignores the significance of grassroots organization. Yet Gilbert's appraisal of #MeToo suggests otherwise: "For all the frequent grumbles about the passivity of most forms of Twitter activism, this was a moment in which the form fit perfectly with the message."[14] Twitter provided the equal access and instantaneous sharing that captured the zeitgeist of survivors forging a collaborative network of support and resistance.

Different degrees of sexual transgressions necessitate consideration insofar as oppressors—much like the oppressed—are not monolithic but multiple and complex. Mediated coverage and social justice movements often conflate the experiences of sexual violence and misconduct to lend credence to the larger cause. Graham suggested the #MeToo call intended to illustrate the vast spectrum of violence and misconduct yet "'harassment' in the colloquial sense encompasses a vast range of misbehavior."[15] Generalizing all misconduct and perpetrators is dangerous, but regarding compartmentalized offenses and offenders as concrete also opens a treacherous discourse. Solnit reasserts the tendency for treating "violence and abuse of power as though they fit into airtight categories . . . it's a slippery slope."[16] Recognizing the specificities of sexual violence and misconduct is important, yet it is also necessary to "acknowledge that a spectrum of behaviors, from verbal harassment to sexual violence, emerge from the same culture of sexism."[17] Transformative social movements often forgo categorizing the acts and perpetrators, instead choosing to dismantle the forces upholding these slippery slopes entirely.

My issue with the #metoo movement is its overuse, the fact that it's clearly a "Hollywood" thing since I don't see anyone using it for victims of the Ohio state coach or pedophilloic priests . . . and this delusion that people must be believed without evidence. That's dangerous.

—@KaneGeorgina, August 21, 2018

Social media movements also attract criticism as many are accused and tried in the court of public opinion. While this trial by social media poses a problem for due process, there are also severe consequences for protecting public figures from media scrutiny. In the UK, strict libel laws have prevented media sources from reporting without concrete evidence surrounding public figures. In these cases, public figures are often afforded special protection because of both these laws and their positions. This sustains a culture that protects perpetrators like famed BBC host Jimmy Savile, who amassed over seventy allegations of sexual misconduct that went unreported until his death in 2011.[18] Similar cases unfurl around the world, even in places absent of libel laws that might chill the media's watchdog role. The decades-long trajectory of accusations against entertainment icons Bill Cosby and Michael Jackson or venerated journalists Matt Lauer and Charlie Rose reveals the tragedy of rape culture. It may take one perpetrator to commit these acts, but it takes an adoring village to protect him or her.

Hashtag activism and #MeToo carries risks of exposure, oppression, and further victimization for its participants. Much as social media has contributed to the emergence and spread of activism and advocacy, so too has it enabled a resurgence of more regressive ideologies. Performances of toxic, hypermasculine, and hegemonic masculinities have been studied for their strident articulation and support across social media.[19] The anonymity of social media platforms enables and often encourages antagonistic or even illegal masculine performances that remain unregulated in the online sphere. For example, survivors of sexual violence and misconduct might also face online abuse and threats from misogynist trolls across the "manosphere"; thus, hashtag activism can create a double victimization.[20]

Other components of backlash involve labeling the movement a "witch hunt," "mob mentality," or "hysteria."[21] Doubting and blaming the victim also looms in the online discourse surrounding sexual violence and misconduct, recalling the horrifying tradition of implying that someone "asked for it." Additional critique of #MeToo comes from the executive or corporate sphere. On opposite ends of the discourse, motivational speaker Tony Robbins and Facebook COO Sheryl Sandberg spoke to this issue. At a speaking event, Robbins discussed the impact of #MeToo, using the example of a CEO friend who confided that he would no longer hire women for prominent positions for fear of crossing any lines. Audience member and survivor Nanine McCool challenged him on this and captured the ensuing exchange.[22] After reiterating that he was not mocking #MeToo as a movement but mocking victimhood, Robbins stated that some "use the #MeToo movement to try to get significance and certainty by attacking and destroying someone else."[23] These comments and the viral video incited the following Twitter responses:

The confidence of a large, attractive white cis man who has never weathered oppression telling those that have to get over it/stop leaning on it. Thanks for your contemplative insight, dad-bro.

—@MariaHeinegg, April 8, 2018

Crashcourse@TonyRobbins:
1. @MeTooMVMT is NOT about victimization it's about SURVIVORS.
2. Women are not to blame for the deep-seated misogyny that you and men like your "friend" are mired in.

—@TaranaBurke, April 7, 2018

Sandberg also discussed the impact of #MeToo on corporate discourse. While acknowledging the strides made by the movement, Sandberg noted that systemic, enduring change must begin in this moment of awareness and recognition. In a viral Facebook post, Sandberg wrote that much more must be done to end the structural inequity across industries, especially because a backlash is afoot: "I have already heard the rumblings. . . . 'This is why you shouldn't hire women.'"[24] Sandberg reiterated that this entrenched attitude was precisely why more women must be given equal opportunities and representation in the first place. Gender equality in representation may also translate to representation of gender in workplace policies. While greater visibility of marginalized others would not solve all problems of oppression or abuse, "many fewer people would be groped and worse while trying to do their jobs. And that would be a major step in the right direction."[25]

Additionally, anxiety surrounds any social media movement that might emphasize its political cause over the privacy or vulnerability of survivors.

Reminder that if a woman didn't post #MeToo, it doesn't mean she wasn't sexually assaulted or harassed. Survivors don't owe you their story.

—@apbenven, October 16, 2017

As Burke noted, "the viral moment is great but the amplification of that— I worry about disclosing their status as survivors en masse and not having space to process."[26] The movement must remain a space for survivors to heal themselves and each other. This illustrates how the magnitude of the victims' voices, amplified through social media forums, blurs borders between liberation and exploitation.

Meeting the Challenge

The focus on #MeToo aligns this analysis accordingly to various critiques of hashtag activism.[27] The attendance to the potential flaws of this form of advocacy reasserts its significance as a site of study. Hashtag feminism specifically has become "so widespread in recent years as to merit its own digital archive, *hashtagfeminism.com*, curated by digital media analyst and commentator Tara L. Conley."[28] The narrative structure of #MeToo illustrates the dramaturgical elements of this wildly successful form of activism in the social media age.

Twitter and hashtag activism are often maligned as ineffectual or frivolous, "collective whining over unimportant issues vocalized by a sea of coddled youth, incapable of exerting concrete change in the offline world."[29] Criticism suggests that the conflation of political identity with social media currency endangers the altruistic goals of social justice projects. Yet the profound and irrefutable impact of movements like #BlackLivesMatter, #WhyIStayed, and #MeToo write a counternarrative to this obfuscation of personal testimony and selfish concern. In addition to the digital calls, disruptive acts of protest on the ground emerged in greater numbers precisely because of the shared spaces of hashtag activism.[30] These social media movements have united the voices of those traditionally silenced, galvanizing collective agency.

Considering #MeToo as a discourse that operates in large part within the digital sphere, Vandiford suggests that "it's difficult to pinpoint which individual organizers are responsible . . . it's harder to determine what drives different trends in the #MeToo movement and the faces behind it."[31] While the relative anonymity of online forums has engendered mass criticism for its uncontested nature, it might also open access for marginalized individuals to combat systemic oppressions through shared narratives and support. This reiterates the potential for sociopolitical transformation that does not depend on supporting systems entrenched in hegemonic or capitalist ideologies.[32] Hashtag activism that utilizes free social media platforms enables and encourages subordinated individuals and interests to reach larger audiences.

Through hashtag activism, digital communication and social media have provided historically marginalized communities with powerful modern platforms. This form of resistance incorporates the elements of social drama, compelling larger audiences through the power of narrative. As Clark-Parsons suggests, "hashtag feminism's ability to initiate sociopolitical change depends upon the many contingencies that exist between dramatic actors and their audiences."[33] Hashtag activism links the past and present, memory and empowerment. Fang notes that hashtag activism "powerfully mixes the teaching of history with self-expressive acts of political resistance."[34] Envisioning the hashtag as a shorthand for political disruption illustrates how sharing ideas digitally is its own form of radical resistance.

Logical and survival imperatives often give rise to backlashes and countermovements. Confronting the status quo of sexual violence and misconduct remains a challenge, especially for those in privileged or quasi-privileged positions. Rather than relinquish this power, many doubt allegations, individuals, and supporting movements. While these responses emerge in denial, shame, or anger, the silencing effect keeps us from questioning our own complicity within a system of power and oppression. This discourse illustrates the dynamic between those opposed to and in support of the strengthened voices within social media movements. While debating the merits of social media activism or the difference between raunchy jokes and sexual assault remains integral to the larger discussion, it might also prevent a thorough appraisal of the movement afoot and the strategies necessary to enact lasting change. #MeToo raises difficult issues yet tears down the patriarchal bulwark, penetrating cultures of toxic and dominant masculinities and revealing how social constructions are fallible and fluid, changeable and challengeable. Situating the #MeToo movement within the context of historical activism and collective action, social media movements, and intersectional identities and oppressions illustrates the significance and potential of this moment at its zenith and with an eye toward the future.

A History of Collective Action

Defining "collective action," Postmes and Brunsting refer to "actions undertaken by individuals or groups for a collective purpose, such as the advancement of a particular ideology or idea, or the political struggle with another group."[35] While much scholarship alludes to the alienating impact of social media interaction, collective action online becomes possible as participants depend on group membership and social identities to legitimize involvement. When individual or independent forms of activism unite many to achieve a shared outcome, these protests and actions become collective in nature.

Historically, theoretical approaches to sociopolitical movements provide foundational understanding while reframing the potential for future research. Activist research through the 1960s employed crowd-based theories, illustrating how crowds or "mobs" generated their own dynamics at the core of protest actions—often based on emotional responses as opposed to the structured logic of institutions and systems. Goodwin and Jasper stress that "the portrait of emotions in these traditions was flawed in many ways."[36] Much of this literature projected anxieties onto the "illogical" or "irrational" mobs threatening the security of the status quo.

Moving to structuralist approaches to activism that emerged in the late 1960s and early 1970s, sociologists employed rational models and organizational theory. Structuralism eliminated emotion altogether, positioning activists as solidly rational citizens acting after assessing benefits or risks of participation. Creating an oppositional tension between rationality and emotion, "resource mobilization and political process theorists missed powerful springs of collective action."[37] While earlier scholarship depicted activists as emotional to further emphasize irrationality, structuralism attempted to emphasize rationality by eradicating the discussion of emotion altogether.

As activism rose again in the 1990s, researchers took a cultural studies approach to understanding protests and protestors as influenced by customs, identities, beliefs, values, artifacts, rituals, and symbols. Emerging scholarship on "framing" also illustrated how culture shapes understanding against interpretive schemata that simplifies and condenses complex issues by encoding events, identities, objects, and ideologies. The potent yet simple condensation of experiences with sexual abuse, assault, harassment, and exploitation into a hashtag response of #MeToo illustrates how framing was successfully used in this movement.

Assessing sociopsychological models toward collective action, three factors contribute directly to protest participation: anger over perceived injustices, shared social identification, and faith in collective efficacy and impact.[38] When shared interests or narratives are established as overarching themes, individuals experiencing injustice begin to strongly identify with the collective group that might allow them to express their anger, frustration, and hurt while contributing to a larger movement. In exploring van Zomeren, Postmes, and Spears's social identity model of collective action (SIMCA),[39] Jost and colleagues note the insight and elegance of the model yet push this framework further to assess ideological and system-level factors in protest participation.[40] Advancing this model helps analyze protest participation at the ideological levels while interrogating how collective action reveals attitudes of the sociopolitical system. Ultimately, this consideration of system-justification theory articulates the strategies that defend and justify systemic forms of status quo.[41]

Epistemic, existential, and relational motivation factors all contribute to this phenomenon, further integrating a model of collective action that considers social identification, moral outrage, and beliefs about group efficacy in addition to ideological and systemic factors.[42] Epistemic motivation emerges from the sociopsychological need for certainty and control. Considering existential motivation, most people justify and uphold the social system because it addresses essential drives for safety and security. The third factor of relational motivation emerges in desires to affiliate with similar others and construct a shared reality. While these factors might hinder protest participation, a social media movement like #MeToo operates on these motivations yet upends the cycle upholding the status quo and instead engenders greater participation than ever before. Sexual violence and misconduct are considered issues of power, control, and hegemony. Thus, epistemic motivation contributes to the collective need to wrest control of the narrative surrounding these traumas. Existential motivation often reified the social system and status quo through promises of safety and security; however, #MeToo indicates the widespread hazards surrounding the system as it stands and thus challenges the status quo of oppression and abuse. Finally, #MeToo cultivates and emphasizes the factor or relational motivation specifically, issuing a call for shared experiences and group membership. This engenders a revision of the dominant narratives of sexual violence and misconduct told for much of history. Instead, #MeToo's force of relational motivation ensures that the affiliated voices of the movement construct a shared reality affirming belief, support, and progress.

While moral outrage is commonly articulated as an antecedent of protest participation, it becomes mitigated and rationalized against various systemic frameworks. For example, as noted by Becker and Wright,[43] women enduring hostile misogyny rejected gender-specific justifications of that supporting system. Women exposed instead to subtle forms of sexism more readily accept system justification. In fact, "system justification mediated the dampening effect of benevolent sexism on women's support for feminist collective action."[44] System justification might then undermine not only activist participation but support for social justice movements combating oppression. Thus, while group-based anger and protest efficacy may motivate forms of resistance for advantaged and disadvantaged groups within the status quo system, it seems that a greater awareness of others' commitment and group status, ideological motivation, and emotional expression may create sustained forms of collective action.

Social media has become a focus of the intersecting frameworks structuring digital activism and advocacy, especially concerning marginalized and oppressed communities. These platforms have expanded discourse surrounding social justice movements, criticism and "call-out" strategies, and group alliances and discord. Traditional grassroots organizations are no longer the only viable forms of protest. Thus, it becomes necessary to explore the growth of social media movements and the collective activism of #MeToo.

Social Media and #Intersectionality

Digital spaces are creating entirely new ways of constructing meaning, primarily through the open dialogue between private and public discourse. Social media power organizes around a multidimensional, multiaccess network that, while offering specific spaces for individuals, continues to underscore dominant sociopolitical interests. As our social networks virally transmit information in real time, this knowledge and communication becomes polysemic, fragmenting and fracturing across its non-hierarchical network of power and influence.

The distinction and debate structuring the bridge between earlier forms of feminism and social media projects illustrates the growth and continuity of activism and advocacy. Hashtag activism and social justice movements often begin as spaces for marginalized communities to express frustration and anger over oppression and abuse. These spheres of engagement subsequently invite participation across online platforms, which generates a dramatic uptick in collective activism and advocacy. The dynamic interaction involving agents from diverse sociopolitical cultures and communities furthers the discourse; these online interactions "are especially conducive to the formation of feminist hashtag protests, given the movement's historical emphasis on discourse, language, and storytelling."[45] Drawing on concepts such as Turner's social drama,[46] McFarland's reiteration of dramatic importance in activism,[47] and Shaw's discursive activism,[48] Clark-Parsons structures an ideal perceptive framework to analyze hashtag feminism in the social media era.

Turner articulated social drama as a paradigm to comprehend the performative nature of ritualized, collaborative actions that simultaneously reify the structure in place and highlight the potential of disruption within it. The digital reproductions of collective experiences and knowledge-sharing through merged voices sustain a communitas of collective sharing and longing for connection and ritualized performance. McFarland's reiteration of Turner's work crafts a new framework that might deal directly with performance, ceremony, and drama—key ingredients for dynamic social media activism and communication.[49] Intrepid journalists and courageous survivors instigated the breach of social order sustaining systemic sexual violence and misconduct. Citing perpetrators like Weinstein and a corrupt structure protecting and enabling his violence, the social drama began in response to this breach. As the breach of the social order escalated, a crisis manifested in the ensuing allegations against multiple perpetrators and amplification of survivors' stories through #MeToo. At this stage, international activist responses began in earnest, as advocates and allies joined survivors to reframe the discourse and ensure recognition and respect for their cause.

Shaw posited that discursive activism articulates new vocabularies and frameworks that might invite individuals and communities to actively engage and converse in response to the movement. Much as previous forms of feminism failed to acknowledge the intersectional and marginalized identities within their movement, hashtag feminism now sits at a historical and cultural crossroads reminiscent of these debates. This resonates in the oppressive and silencing legacy of "white, middle to upper class, college-educated women who historically dominated feminist organizations at the expense of feminists occupying various intersections of difference along axes of gender, race, class, sexuality and ability."[50] Applying Kimberlé Crenshaw's edicts of intersectionality directly to the current context of social media platforms and access illustrates the potential for continued discourse and activism.

Crenshaw articulated intersectionality while exploring the various forces shaping oppressions in identity politics and institutional oppressions within antidiscrimination doctrine.[51] Antidiscrimination doctrine often ignores the intricacies of oppressions, stereotypes, and prejudices in shaping the relational positions of survivors and perpetrators. Responding to the limiting language of the legal system in protecting the civil rights of women or persons of color, Crenshaw posits intersectionality as a strategy to reframe identity politics as encompassing multiple oppressions and identities. When gender, sexual orientation, race, class, religion, embodiment, and various other intersectional aspects structure someone as potentially vulnerable, less credible, or unharmed by acts of sexual violence and misconduct based on contextual circumstances, it disregards potential moves forward for survivors. While #MeToo has much ground to gain in refocusing its attention on intersectionality and marginalized communities, it has been one of few sites committed to opening a safe and continuous space for sharing these experiences.

Intersectionality has been restructured and repurposed, following Crenshaw's articulation of the concept as transitional and fluid. As theorists and advocates continue broadening the terrain of intersectionality, the expansive possibilities rise to meet the increasing multiplicities of oppression. As Hutchinson suggests, "multidimensionality offers a compelling response to essentialist scholars who reject intersectional analyses on the ground that such work is relevant only to those individuals who endure multiple forms of domination."[52] This is particularly significant because it prevents the advocates of essentialist thought from invoking exclusionary practices. Cultivating Crenshaw's intersectional discourse, theorists developed concepts such as gendered racism and multidimensionality to reassert how identities juxtaposed at intersecting forces of privilege and oppression experience vacillating forms of subordination and domination.

The forces of intersectional identity or multidimensional subordination render marginalized communities especially vulnerable to tactics prioritizing essentialist thought. For social media movements like #MeToo, essentialism targets and reframes progressive social projects as potentially competing or opposing perspectives. Rather than envision a space of "separate spheres" in thinking through identity, "post-intersectionality" or "multidimensional" paradigms move to "examine forms of subordination as interrelated, rather than conflicting, phenomena."[53] The sedimentary impact of oppressive essentialist thinking emerges not only because of direct opposition but because there remains insufficient evidence or research on the specifics of intersectional identity and multidimensional oppression. Further, as privileged individuals and communities favor or align with certain sociocultural identifiers over others, the reassertion of a dominant hierarchy structures all other identity politics.

The relational dynamics between patriarchy, ableism, racism, class oppression, heteronormativity, and binaried thought continue extending the scholarship and activism already situated in intersectionality. Intersectional and multidimensional approaches illustrate how various aspects of identity and oppression are assessed within networks of power. This challenges essentialism in privileging or subordinating individuals based on single-identifying advocacy. As race-sexuality scholar Valdes suggests, multidimensionality might "promote awareness of patterns as well as particularities in social relations by studying in an interconnected way the specifics of subordination."[54] Rather than continuing the tradition of categorizing and generalizing, multidimensionality or intersectionality reiterates the importance of assessing a problem originating with limited perspectives of representation and visibility.

Research races to match the rapidly growing intersection of digital technology and social movements; in a constantly evolving field, it has proven challenging (if not impossible) to capture any snapshot within a theoretical framework. This is made more difficult as the sociopolitical implications of these moments become increasingly fleeting. Activism in the social media age grants greater access and visibility, illustrating the hegemonic structures undermining everyday experiences. Social justice movements subsequently require understanding of the enduring discourse that shifts seamlessly from online to face-to-face and back again, and again, and again. Acknowledging this particular form of activism—which shows signs only of growing, not disappearing—illustrates how social media movements have recognized the significance of shared personal action frames in galvanizing collective identity and action—or connective action.[55] This theory "highlights the mechanisms through which tweets, despite their brevity, can, via hashtag networks, become the building blocks for collectively constructed, thematically linked narratives in 140 characters or less."[56] This activism emanates from the networks of communication and discourse as opposed to traditional organizational frameworks.

Twitter as a platform and tweets as communicative modes collectively structure narrative spaces that build alliances for further activism and advocacy. In the context of online activism and media coverage, "less confrontational actions—which actually appear to be more dominant forms of online collective action in terms of number of participants (certainly) and number of actions (possibly)—tend to be less prominently covered."[57] While media coverage might have focused on the divisive elements of #MeToo, the voices of the movement reframed the conversation as one of narrative sharing and support. This was reinforced by the participatory nature of social media activism and more specifically, Twitter. The ability to galvanize millions internationally has shifted the narrative of sociopolitical history. Further, the potential to participate anonymously and outside the reach of traditional media creates a new protestor for the digital age. The media smokescreen focusing on particularly visible, disruptive, and confrontational forms of activism may thus have concealed the persuasive yet pacifist transformation in activism evolving across social media platforms all along.

Considering hashtag activism generally or hashtag feminism specifically, Twitter unites spectators and participators alike, floating across the digital spheres of private and public platforms and experiences while engaging audiences that might be passive, active, or any combination at any time. In the face of collective activism, cultural institutions and governmental bodies around the world have responded in varying degrees. Yet in articulating and revising legislative acts or cultural practices, the redress of human rights injustices inevitably fails to establish or maintain equality for all groups seeking justice. Although identity politics generate collectivities through identification of the intimate publics, it is often through the acts of reallocation and reparation that international institutions contribute to polarization within these larger movements, splintering factions among interest groups.

Social engagement and grassroots activism have taken place through the many-to-many forums of social media more than at any other point in history.[58] As this phenomenon grows, discourse arises regarding the socioeconomic possibilities and pratfalls of mediated and social networks. These platforms "radically change the way in which public communication takes place and provides an electronic agora to allow for alternative issues to be raised, framed and effectively debated."[59] In dispersing traditionally concentrated hierarchies of media and communication, these horizontal networks instead enable and encourage viral participation and representation at all points of access. To explore the context of #MeToo, a mixed-methods content analysis emphasizing intersectionality shares the story of this multiplicity of participation and representation.

INTERSECTIONAL APPROACHES

The interdisciplinary applications of intersectionality hold implications not only for academics as a theoretical lens or activism as an afterthought. Intersectional thought creates an intricate and dynamic network of oppressions and identities that reflect the lived experiences and power negotiations of everyday existence.

Culling from standpoint theory articulated by feminist scholars such as Dorothy Smith, Nancy Hartsock, and Patricia Hill Collins, postmodern feminists asserted that in socially constructed gender identities, it is impossible to essentialize or generalize the experiences of women. Standpoint feminism illustrates how in addition to sexism, women's unique experiences of inequality relate to homophobia, racism, ableism, classism, and colonization—to name a few categorical oppressions. Further, subordination, appropriation, and victimization do not emerge from one primary source in one recognizable form. Much as intersectionality structures identity, multiple oppressions collude to create specific, intricate webs of injustice. As Crenshaw suggests, "battering and rape . . . are now largely recognized as part of a broad-scale system of domination that affects women as a class."[60] The recognition of systemic sexual violence characterizes identity politics for women, people of color, the LGBTQ+ community, and other marginalized individuals. These communities have drawn on the experiences of intersectional identity as a source of lone and group survival and activism. Yet as Crenshaw notes, identity politics often become negated or sacrificed for broader social justice movements. In considering #MeToo, this book reasserts the necessity of recognizing and appreciating intersectional experiences as sources of empowerment and resistance against oppression.

According to Gramsci, in moments of cultural or sociopolitical crises, aspiring groups might attain hegemonic status by challenging the dominant ideologies of the ruling group while conforming to the needs of other marginalized groups.[61] It is possible then to counter the traditional use of hegemonic masculinity in exploring #MeToo and its impact on gendered relations. For example, #MeToo upended the status quo yet may continue striving for positions of power and leadership in the cultural and sociopolitical structure. At this precipice of technological advance and historical import, the movement might continue forging a path based on equitable support and alliance. Yet it could also implement strategies similar to those deployed by the hegemonic structure. Or, the incorporation of intersectional experience and oppression may provide an alternate route to implode the hegemonic power structure entirely.

Theories of intersectionality have been critiqued for a lack of any explicit methodological mapping or guidance.[62] Analyzing the interactions and themes operating across hierarchical networks, intersectionality can neither be isolated nor uniformly applied. An intersectional analysis must focus on the methodological significance of context, specifically in determining how ableism, gender, sexuality, class, race, or various other sociopolitical systems may have predetermined or shaped the outcome of the study. As Mutua argues, intersectionality "requires observation and thick (detailed and relatively comprehensive) description of context, together with the acquired knowledge about and experience with these systems and identity categories."[63] These intertwined categories and systems constitute the multiple forces diffusing and distributing power. Even as intersectional approaches recognize the patterns emerging throughout these hierarchies, sociopolitical dimensions must be interrogated based on context.

Intersectionality frames the dynamics and interactions within a situation, highlighting the cultural expectations, practices, productions, and structures informing that context. As a metaphor and tool to analyze identity, intersectionality remains the flexible, broad theoretical framework that speaks to and addresses multiple critiques and challenges. Much as Crenshaw envisioned in early iterations of the concept, intersectionality has revised accordingly with critiques. The intersectional turn reasserts how individuals might occupy and relinquish positions of power and subordination—often simultaneously—based on the fluidity of identity. #MeToo alternately embodies the experiences of the dominant and oppressed, while media casts its own spotlight on the faces that gain traction in the public eye. This text's intersectional approach reveals the both/and of experience for the privileged and marginalized within one of the most critical conversations of the social media era.

Moving beyond traditional empirical studies of academia, this book offers a philosophical overview of #MeToo while drawing on the scholarship of activism, social media, and identity politics. Intersectionality remains the central theoretical force of this project; however, in turning to hear the voices of each marginalized community, additional theories will be implemented to better assess the ongoing discourse of activism and identity. A mixed-methods approach emphasizing the qualitative strains of content analysis, phenomenology, and performativity appraises the mediated coverage of #MeToo; #MeToo posts and responses over the first year of the movement; and Twitter projects built by marginalized communities. While this text remains primarily qualitative in approach, the incorporation of quantitative statistics and studies in several chapters provides context to assess the impact of sexual violence and misconduct within these communities. Each chapter stands as a piece in an overall puzzle of intersectional identity and marginalized voices; these diverse theoretical approaches reassert the overarching goal of the book to understand the significance of intersectionality in activism and advocacy.

Mapping the Margins

The book opens by tracing the complicated, intersectional genealogy of the #MeToo movement—arguably one of the most successful social media projects in recent history. Exploring intersectional identity politics in #MeToo reveals how marginalized voices are engaged or silenced in the social media roar. I turn to conversations within diverse communities facing issues of racism, classism, ableism, homophobia, transphobia, biphobia, ethnocentrism, binaried ideologies, toxic masculinities, and systemic oppression. In addition to addressing the critical appraisal and backlash concerning social media activism and ideological content, this chapter previews the implications of #MeToo including the dual forces of public and private citizens driving #MeToo; the appropriation and silencing surrounding identity politics and grassroots activism for people of color; the double bind of oppression and dismissal for the LGBTQ+ community; the varied responses to #MeToo around the developed, developing, and underdeveloped world; the unique experiences and challenges facing citizens with disabilities in discussing #MeToo; and, the discussion of destabilized masculinity for hetero, cisgender men living in the #MeToo moment.

The second chapter of this book reframes the question asked in *Time* magazine's "Silence Breakers" issue:[64] "When movie stars don't know where to go, what hope is there for the rest of us?" When *Time* named its 2017 Person of the Year as "The Silence Breakers," it featured everyday survivors alongside the famous faces of #MeToo and #TimesUp. This inclusion of private citizens reiterated the prevalence of sexual abuse and harassment for individuals in public and private spheres alike. Much of the #MeToo discourse correlates with the feminist critique of what Keller and Ringrose call "celebrity feminism—made visible recently by young celebrity women eager to publicly claim a feminist identity."[65] Yet this also illuminated a blind spot in social media movements—the discourse beyond public figures. While digital movements like #MeToo have raised the visibility of sexual violence and misconduct, a conflict remains because privileged positions must first gain attention for everyday survivors to achieve legitimacy. As Peters suggests, "the experiences survivors claimed happened were no less true before these high-profile takedowns occurred. It's only after they've occurred, though, that we're starting to take them at their word."[66] It remains disheartening that despite abuses that have gone unnoticed for much of human history, it took the "Weinstein effect climate" and those in the most privileged and visible positions to come forward for everyday survivors to find legitimacy in their claims.

As #MeToo gained international attention, it led to a rediscovery and recuperation of Burke's decades of work. Despite starting the conversation, women of color often find themselves ignored and displaced from a dialogue they created for their specific lived experiences, thus echoing the white infiltration and appropriation of black culture for the "greater good" or "umbrella movement." The third chapter of the text considers the implications of #MeToo for women of color, examining the legacy of grassroots activism for minority populations. While the level of celebrity involved in this cavalcade of allegations against public figures may raise the profile and attention from mainstream media, as Burke stated, "somehow sisters still managed to get diminished or erased in these situations."[67] Burke and the community of oppressed black feminist activists use practice as philosophy to reclaim the both/and of knowledge and activism. Rather than continue the silencing or appropriation of their voices, the moment of #MeToo might provide a springboard to revisit how identity politics reveals a greater conversation regarding the intersection of oppressive, violent forces against women of color and all oppressed communities.

As discourse shifts to the nature of consent and communicative dynamics between men and women, many communities have yet to see their #MeToo moment. With the exception of public figures such as alleged perpetrator Kevin Spacey and survivor Terry Crews, the discussion of same-sex sexual violence has been relatively quiet. Yet LGBTQ+ communities often face even higher rates of rape, physical violence, or harassment.[68] Despite the staggering statistics that nearly half of transgendered individuals (47 percent), bisexual women (48 percent), and gay (40 percent) and bisexual men (47 percent) have experienced sexual violence, there remains a culture of silence surrounding these experiences. To address this, the fourth chapter of this text focuses on the intricate negotiations of sexual victimization in the LGBTQ+ community. Segalov states that stifled conversations surrounding consent correlates with the lack of vocabulary: "most of us were never taught the language with which to explain or understand the experiences of our youth."[69] In addition to educational voids, the silencing practices surrounding LGBTQ+ identity can create a double bind in which sexual victimization adds another layer of oppression. Outside the typical narrative of the heteronormative, cis, white female victim, all other experiences are robbed of visibility, language, and representation.

While #MeToo and #TimesUp have had unparalleled recognition in the United States, the global impact of these movements has varied drastically. The fifth chapter of this book highlights the international responses to #MeToo. Issues of access, backlashes, and divisive feminist factions have transformed the acceptance of the U.S.-born movement. Moreover, the largely prominent, privileged voices have led to criticism and skepticism, with some coining the hashtag #WeFew in response. Developing and underdeveloped countries are plagued not only by systemic violence and oppression against women but acceptance of that violence. In these nations, feminists are often excluded from the global sweep of movements like #MeToo. Much as white feminism often misses or ignores the intersectional identities and experiences of women of color, Western feminisms have further diminished the significance of women and feminisms indigenous to developing countries and diasporas. Women in the developing world perceive Western feminism as tied to understanding based solely on oppressions of race, class, and heteronormativity. This dialectic emerges from postcolonial and Afrocentric feminist populations seeking to enlighten Western women about experiences beyond their specific spaces.

Mainstream attention to #MeToo has largely failed to address the disabled and differently abled survivors of sexual violence and misconduct.

This is of particular concern as acts of abuse and assault perpetrated against this community are reaching epidemic heights. Misconceptions and stigma surrounding disabled and differently abled folk as sexual citizens has created a hazardous lack of education and conversation. With a void of specific education and access, support, and security emphasizing healthy sexual, romantic, and physical relationships, there is further risk that differently and disabled folk will endure abusive, exploitative, and violent experiences. Visibility, voices, and support remain instrumental to a movement for communities repeatedly silenced and shamed. As shown in the sixth chapter, for a community overlooked entirely in terms of their sexual embodiment, or marginalized and victimized because of that ignorance, the #MeToo movement cannot hesitate to include disabled and differently abled folk.

While #MeToo and #TimesUp have given voice to sexual victimization, there may also be an opportunity to address those trapped in the discursively produced binaried opposition—hetero, cisgender men. The seventh chapter of this book explores the culture of toxic masculinity and the multiple male responses to #MeToo. The dual emergence of toxic masculinity and popular feminism have garnered widespread attention from critical and cultural perspectives. After decades of "feminism" and "feminist" being shunned as divisive "F-words" for girls and women to embody and boys and men to rally against, the current social media moment has rearticulated the significance of these movements and the necessity of equality in discussions of gender, race, sexuality, class, religion, and various other social categorizations. While it is true that dominant voices have held the stage for far too long, there are opportunities for men to learn from those who finally have a turn at the microphone. #MeToo—along with the U.S. election of a president who brags about sexual assault—helped to shred the illusion of infallible masculinity, exposing a state of destabilization. Thus, one of the most teachable moments for men is that this crisis also creates an opportunity to redefine what it means to act and think as healthy, positive humans.

Not a Moment, But a Movement

Against this backdrop, interdisciplinary studies of gender, culture, and social media possess one of the most pivotal roles, asking how we arrived at this moment and how we move forward. Interdisciplinary work must revisit its roots in activism, its recognition of oppressive and divisive practices, and its legacy of articulating new and transformative opportunities for uniting across academia, culture, and the world. These diverse threads weave throughout this book, revealing how marginalized voices and digital platforms open spaces for oppressed populations to engage in intersectional dialogue and activism.

As Hutchinson notes, "when progressive theorists do not acknowledge the relationships between various forms of subordination, they place progressive movements in tension with one another."[70] When individuals are faced with the choice to participate in social movements, they are often forced to silence certain aspects of their identities and experiences in favor of others. Movements like #MeToo create opportunities to expand the limited representations and voices of activism and advocacy, reaching across communities and pushing for widespread social change.

The discursive force of social media justice projects has generated a flurry of academic and mediated criticism. #MeToo confounded many of these trajectories; it opened a platform for speaking about the unspeakable, granting voice to the silenced. As touched upon throughout this book, #MeToo has built upon the groundwork laid by multiple communities—invisible and visible. From #YesAllWomen to #WhyIStayed, numerous hashtag activist movements have long fought rape culture and its attendant victim-blaming discourse. Yet there remain limitations to the reach and power of these movements, especially considering hegemonic oppressions at the local, regional, and global levels.

Identity politics and politicized identities generate only a relatively recent body of scholarship—much of this arising from second-wave feminism and its articulation that "the personal is political." Identity politics stems from responses to broader movements like feminism and civil rights as the intersectional experiences of individuals chime from the larger chorus. Considering tendencies to reduce social movements—specifically feminism in its waves—to monolithic movements surrounding one unified goal, #MeToo again faces a challenge that it is yet to become another wave, sweeping away the intersectional experiences of everyone within its wake. When Crenshaw spoke of how intersectionality illustrates the multiple ways that oppressions intersect, and Judith Butler[71] argued that gender is performative and distinct from biological sex, these were theories that arose in the 1980s yet continue to sustain relevance in the current moment of #MeToo.

Valenti posited that the fourth wave of feminism could catch fire not on the streets but online.[72] While digital activism has certainly become a hallmark of this suggested "fourth wave" through movements like #MeToo, #BringBackOurGirls, #YesAllWomen, or #YouOkSis, this is also true of the sweeping online justice projects of #BlackLivesMatter, #NODAPL, or #Kony2012. These forms of activism might take place on the streets or online, yet much of the work originates and organizes across digital platforms. Considering this, Grady suggests that this fourth wave emerged "around 2008, when Facebook, Twitter, and YouTube were firmly entrenched in the cultural fabric and feminist blogs like Jezebel and Feministing were spreading across the web."[73] Considering the second-wave force of sociopolitical,

grassroots organization and third-wave appreciation for individual expressivity and intersectional experience, #MeToo—and the multiple hashtag
movements of the past decade—may embody these aspects on a digital
platform with the greatest global reach yet.

While media and academic coverage continue the debate surrounding
which wave of feminism #MeToo is embodying, rebelling against, or
pissing off the most, it is perhaps far more useful to move past the notion
of "waves" and embrace a sea change that invokes the past, present, and
future. As #MeToo continues its resistant awakening, "as record numbers
of women seek office, and as the Women's March drives the resistance
against the Trump administration, feminism is reaching a level of cultural
relevance it hasn't enjoyed in years."[74] Placing the subsequent framework
of traditional media coverage over the stories of #MeToo illustrates how
general audiences might also validate or reject the emergent politics of
social media activism and advocacy, despite limited or nonexistent interaction with those conversations. When audiences are forced into choosing
sides, the dramaturgical elements posited by Turner reemerge. Further, the
processual events in this social drama create a blueprint that—despite its
intricate specificities (i.e., #WhyIStayed vs. #MeToo)—offers a historical
framework to understand future events and experiences. These perspectives help galvanize greater narratives of resistance for future social media
movements, strengthened by the accomplishments and alliances made in
this digitally fleeting time line.

The stages of "breach, crisis, and reintegration" key to collective activism
and advocacy align with the "plot elements of beginning, middle, and end
. . . well suited for studying online feminism, whose discursive tactics often
call on participants to collectively build narratives of resistance."[75] Hashtag
or twitter activism and feminism might then create a potent new discursive
and interpretive framework that reiterates and responds to the immediacy
of the digital media era. Tweets are aggregative in nature and thus provide
analytical ground to explore the contextual moment of resistance in relation to #MeToo.

Khoja-Moolji suggests that in moving past the individual use of social
media to analyze collective hashtag activist practices, it is possible to "ob-
serve the emergence of a publics that engages in epistemic violence against
women and girls."[76] The power of #MeToo in all its manifestations is that
it reaches across borders where other words and phrases dissipate. As Burke
said, "somebody had said it to me and it changed the trajectory of my
healing process."[77] The small phrase has built into a collective, inescapable
roar. At the crossroads of gender, sex, race, embodiment, technology, and
activism, greater recognition of intersectionality, grass-roots organization,
and identity politics might write a new chapter in an inclusive conversation
of activism and change.

NOTES

1. Cassandra Santiago and Doug Criss, "An Activist, a Little Girl and the Heartbreaking Origin of 'Me Too,'" *CNN*, October 17, 2017, http://www.cnn.com/2017/10/17/us/me-too-tarana-burke-origin-trnd/index.html.

2. Andrea Park, "#MeToo Reaches 85 Countries with 1.7M Tweets," *CBS News*, October 24, 2017, https://www.cbsnews.com/news/metoo-reaches-85-countries-with-1-7-million-tweets. Analytics company Talkwalker compiled a graphic incorporating updates on its own twitter feed to illustrate how #MeToo spread around the world.

3. Noting the distinction between Burke's original "Me Too" campaign and the #MeToo resurgence on Twitter, this text refers to the overall movement as #MeToo for clarity unless specifically designated in the text for emphasis.

4. Zahara Hill, "A Black Woman Created the 'Me Too' Campaign Against Sexual Assault 10 Years Ago," *Ebony*, October 18, 2017, https://www.ebony.com/news/black-woman-me-too-movement-tarana-burke-alyssa-milano.

5. Alanna Vagianos, "The 'Me Too' Campaign Was Created By A Black Woman 10 Years Ago," *Huffington Post*, October 17, 2017, https://www.huffingtonpost.com/entry/the-me-too-campaign-was-created-by-a-black-woman-10-years-ago_us_59e61a7fe4b02a215b336fee.

6. Tarana Burke, "The Real Woman Behind 'Me Too,'" *Root*, December 6, 2017, video, 3:16, https://twitter.com/theroot/status/938427427096793090?lang=en.

7. Hill, "A Black Woman."

8. Samantha C. Thrift, "#YesAllWomen as Feminist Meme Event," *Feminist Media Studies* 14, no. 6 (2014): 1090–92.

9. Park, "#MeToo Reaches."

10. Sophie Gilbert, "The Movement of #MeToo," *Atlantic*, October 16, 2017, https://www.theatlantic.com/entertainment/archive/2017/10/the-movement-of-metoo/542979.

11. Rosemary Clark-Parsons, "'Hope in a Hashtag': The Discursive Activism of #WhyIStayed," *Feminist Media Studies* 16, no. 5 (2016): 788–804, https://doi:10.1080/14680777.2016.1138235.

12. Lara C. Stache, "Advocacy and Political Potential at the Convergence of Hashtag Activism and Commerce," *Feminist Media Studies* 15, no. 1 (2014): 162–64.

13. Sherri Williams, "Digital Defense: Black Feminists Resist Violence with Hashtag Activism," *Feminist Media Studies* 15, no. 2 (2015): 341–44, https://doi:10.1080/14680777.2015.1008744.

14. Gilbert, "The Movement."

15. Ruth Graham, "Why the #MeToo Moment Is Liberating, Dispiriting, and Uncomfortable All at Once," *Slate*, October 17, 2017, http://www.slate.com/blogs/xx_factor/2017/10/17/why_the_metoo_moment_is_liberating_dispiriting_and_uncomfortable_all_at.html.

16. Rebecca Solnit, *Men Explain Things to Me* (Chicago: Haymarket Books, 2014), 9.

17. Maryam Omidi, "The Many Faces of the #MeToo Backlash," *Public Seminar*, January 18, 2018, http://www.publicseminar.org/2018/01/the-many-faces-of-the-me too-backlash.

18. "Savile and Hall: BBC 'Missed Chances to Stop Attacks,'" *BBC News*, February 25, 2016, https://www.bbc.com/news/uk-35658398.

19. Sarah Banet-Weiser and Kate M. Miltner, "#MasculinitySoFragile: Culture, Structure, and Networked Misogyny," *Feminist Media Studies* 16, no. 1 (2016): 171–74, https//doi:10.1080/14680777.2016.1120490.

20. Banet-Weiser and Miltner, "#MasculinitySoFragile"; Nathian Shae Rodriguez and Terri Hernandez, "Dibs on That Sexy Piece of Ass: Hegemonic Masculinity on TFM Girls Instagram Account," *Social Media Society* 4, no. 1 (2018): 1–12, https://doi:10.1177/2056305118760809.

21. This is a particularly concerning term considering the antiquated Freudian diagnoses of "hysterical" women—those who speak out or express emotions.

22. @nowthisnews, April 6, 2018, https://twitter.com/nowthisnews/status/98238 9487836778496.

23. Amir Vera, "Life Coach Tony Robbins Issues Apology after Comments on #MeToo," *CNN*, April 9, 2018, https://www.cnn.com/2018/04/09/us/tony-rob bins-apology-metoo/index.html.

24. Caitlin Gibson, "Abusive Men Are Falling; Women Are Replacing Them. But Will This 'Reckoning' Spark Real Change?" *Washington Post*, December 9, 2017, https://www.washingtonpost.com/lifestyle/style/abusive-men-are-falling-women -are-replacing-them-but-will-this-reckoning-spark-real-change/2017/12/08/833e 7c9a-db76-11e7-b1a8-62589434a581_story.html.

25. Sheryl Sandberg, Facebook, December 3, 2017, https://www.facebook.com/ sheryl/posts/10159569315265177.

26. Santiago and Criss, "An Activist."

27. Caitlin Gunn, "Hashtagging from the Margins: Women of Color Engaged in Feminist Consciousness-Raising on Twitter," in *Women of Color and Social Media Multitasking: Blogs, Timelines, Feeds, and Community*, ed. Keisha Edwards Tassie and Sonja M. Brown Givens (Lanham, MD: Lexington Books, 2015), 21–34.

28. Clark-Parsons, "Hope in a Hashtag," 788.

29. Jenn Fang, "In Defense of Hashtag Activism," *Journal of Critical Scholarship on Higher Education and Student Affairs* 2, no. 1 (2016): 140.

30. Stache, "Advocacy"; Williams, "Digital Defense."

31. Hannah Lee, "LGBTQ Voices Aren't Included in the #MeToo Movement," *UNC Media Hub*, May 3, 2018, http://mediahub.unc.edu/lgbtq-voices-arent-includ ed-metoo-movement.

32. Frances Shaw, "The Politics of Blogs: Theories of Discursive Activism Online," *Media International Australia* no. 142 (2012): 41–49.

33. Clark-Parsons, "Hope in a Hashtag," 801.

34. Fang, "In Defense," 138.

35. Tom Postmes and Suzanne Brunsting, "Collective Action in the Age of the Internet: Mass Communication and Online Mobilization," *Social Science Computer Review* 20, no. 3 (2002): 290–301.

36. Jeff Goodwin and James M. Jasper, "Emotions and Social Movements," in *Handbook of the Sociology of Emotions*, ed. J. E. Stets and J. H. Turner (Boston: Springer, 2006), 611–35, https://doi:10.1007/978-0-387-30715-2_27.

37. Goodwin and Jasper, "Emotions."

38. Nicole Tausch, Julia C. Becker, Russell Spears, Oliver Christ, Rim Saab, Purnima Singh, and Roomana N. Siddiqui, "Explaining Radical Group Behavior: De-

veloping Emotion and Efficacy Routes to Normative and Nonnormative Collective Action," *Journal of Personality and Social Psychology* 101, no. 1 (2011): 129–48.

39. Martijn van Zomeren, Tom Postmes, and Russell Spears, "Toward an Integrative Social Identity Model of Collective Action: A Quantitative Research Synthesis of Three Socio-psychological Perspectives," *Psychological Bulletin* 134, no. 4 (2008): 504–35, https://doi:10.1037/0033-2909.134.4.504.

40. John T. Jost, Julia Becker, Danny Osborne, and Vivienne Badaan, "Missing in (Collective) Action," *Current Directions in Psychological Science* 26, no. 2 (2017): 99–108, https://doi:10.1177/0963721417690633.

41. This conceptualization correlates with the decision not to protest anything that might threaten that same system, regardless of one's disenfranchised positionality within it.

42. Jost et al., "Missing."

43. Julia C. Becker and Stephen C. Wright, "Yet Another Dark Side of Chivalry: Benevolent Sexism Undermines and Hostile Sexism Motivates Collective Action for Social Change," *Journal of Personality and Social Psychology* 101, no. 1 (2011): 62–77, https://doi:10.1037/a0022615.

44. Jost et al., "Missing," 102.

45. Clark-Parsons, "Hope in a Hashtag," 90.

46. Victor Turner, *From Ritual to Theatre: The Human Seriousness of Play* (New York: PAJ, 1982).

47. Daniel A. McFarland, "Resistance as a Social Drama: A Study of Change-Oriented Encounters," *American Journal of Sociology* 109, no. 6 (2004): 1249–1318.

48. Shaw, "Politics of Blogs."

49. McFarland reasserts Turner's social drama in a context of activism in the following process: (1) a breach of social order occurs, initiating social drama; (2) the breach escalates and spreads, creating a crisis for competing interpretations of the breach; (3) activists and advocates enter the fray, engaging in a processual reframing to earn support for their specific side.

50. Clark-Parsons, "Hope in a Hashtag," 792.

51. Kimberlé Crenshaw, "Mapping the Margins: Intersectionality, Identity Politics, and Violence Against Women of Color," *Stanford Law Review* 43, no. 6 (1991): 1241–99.

52. Darren Lenard Hutchinson, "Identity Crisis: 'Intersectionality,' 'Multidimensionality,' and the Development of an Adequate Theory of Subordination," *Michigan Journal of Race & Law* 6 (2001): 312.

53. Hutchinson, "Identity Crisis," 290.

54. Francisco Valdes, "Beyond Sexual Orientation in Queer Legal Theory: Majoritarianism, Multidimensionality, and Responsibility in Social Justice Scholarship or Legal Scholars as Cultural Warriors," *Denver University Law Review* 75 (1998): 1415.

55. W. Lance Bennett and Alexandra Segerberg, "The Logic of Connective Action, Digital Media and the Personalization of Contentious Politics," *Information, Communication & Society* 15, no. 5 (2011): 739–68.

56. Clark-Parsons, "Hope in a Hashtag," 793.

57. Postmes and Brunsting, "Collective Action," 292–93.

58. Fang, "In Defense"; Michael A. Peters and Tina Besley, "Weinstein, Sexual Predation, and 'Rape Culture': Public Pedagogies and Hashtag Internet Activism,"

Educational Philosophy and Theory (2018): 1–7, https://doi:10.1080/00131857.2018
.1427850.

59. Mark Wheeler, "The Mediatization of Celebrity Politics through the Social Media," *International Journal of Digital Television* 5, no. 3 (2014): 223.

60. Crenshaw, "Mapping," 1241.

61. Antonio Gramsci, *Selections from the Prison Notebooks* (New York: International, 1971).

62. Jennifer C. Nash, "Re-Thinking Intersectionality," *Feminist Review* 89, no. 1 (2008): 2–3.

63. Athena D. Mutua, "Multidimensionality Is to Masculinities What Intersectionality Is to Feminism," *Nevada Law Journal* 13, no. 341 (2016): 354.

64. Stephanie Zacharek, Eliana Dockterman, and Haley Sweetland Edwards, "Person of the Year 2017," *Time*, December 18, 2017, http://time.com/time-person-of-the-year-2017-silence-breakers.

65. Jessalynn Keller and Jessica Ringrose, "'But Then Feminism Goes out the Window!': Exploring Teenage Girls' Critical Response to Celebrity Feminism," *Celebrity Studies* 6, no. 1 (2015): 132.

66. Lucia Peters, "*Time* Included Non-Celebrity Women in Its 'Silence Breakers,' and It Helps Address a Major Problem in the #MeToo Movement," *Bustle*, December 6, 2017, https://www.bustle.com/p/time-included-non-celebrity-women-in-its-silence-breakers-it-helps-address-a-major-problem-in-the-metoo-movement-7376675.

67. Hill, "A Black Woman."

68. Michele C. Black, Kathleen C. Basile, Matthew J. Breiding, Sharon G. Smith, Mikel L. Walters, Melissa T. Merrick, Jieru Chen, and Mark R. Stevens, "National Intimate Partner and Sexual Violence Survey (NISVS): 2010 Summary Report," Atlanta, GA: National Center for Injury Prevention and Control, Centers for Disease Control and Prevention.

69. Michael Segalov, "Why Hasn't the Gay Community Had a #MeToo Moment?" *Guardian*, March 7, 2018, https://www.theguardian.com/commentisfree/2018/mar/07/gay-community-metoo-moment-conversation-consent-sexual-assault.

70. Hutchinson, "Identity Crisis," 297.

71. Judith Butler, "Performative Acts and Gender Constitution: An Essay in Phenomenology and Feminist Theory," *Theatre Journal* 40, no. 4 (1988): 519–31; Judith Butler, *Gender Trouble* (New York: Routledge, 1990).

72. Jessica Valenti, "Fourth-Wave Feminism," interview by Deborah Solomon, *New York Times*, November 13, 2009, https://www.nytimes.com/2009/11/15/magazine/15fob-q4-t.html.

73. Constance Grady, "The Waves of Feminism, and Why People Keep Fighting Over Them, Explained," *Vox.com*, July 20, 2018, https://www.vox.com/2018/3/20/16955588/feminism-waves-explained-first-second-third-fourth.

74. Grady, "The Waves."

75. Clark-Parsons, "Hope in a Hashtag," 794.

76. Shenila Khoja-Moolji, "Becoming an 'Intimate Publics': Exploring the Affective Intensities of Hashtag Feminism," *Feminist Media Studies* 15, no. 2 (2015): 347.

77. Vagianos, "The 'Me Too' Campaign."

CHAPTER 2

The Public and Private Faces of #MeToo

"When Movie Stars Don't Know Where to Go, What Hope Is There for the Rest of Us?"

Alyssa Milano, U.S. Congressperson Carolyn Maloney, and the ERA Coalition call for ratification of the Equal Rights Amendment (H.J. Res 33) at a press conference in front of the Fearless Girl statue in New York City. *MediaPunch Inc./Alamy Stock Photo*

> So @TheAcademy has voted to expel Harvey Weinstein. Good. A reminder that Roman Polanski and Bill Cosby are still members. Keep going.
>
> —@ReignOfApril, October 14, 2017

Time magazine's 2017 Person (People) of the Year celebrated "The Silence Breakers" of #MeToo and #TimesUp. The article illustrated the relational participation and motivation between the public faces and private citizens who had galvanized these movements. Stephanie Zacharek, Eliana Dockterman, and Haley Sweetland Edwards coauthored the annual special issue, connecting the experiences of these seemingly disparate groups. As they write of the assumed differences between the private and public citizens involved in the movement: "In the most painful and personal ways—movie stars are more like you and me than we ever knew. . . . Actors and writers and journalists and dishwashers and fruit pickers alike: they'd had enough. What had manifested as shame exploded into outrage. Fear became fury."[1] In this sense, #MeToo and its famous, recognizable faces have emboldened people of all races, occupations, classes, and nationalities. The degrees of difference between these figures varied vastly yet the collective spoke to the shared narrative of sexual abuse, harassment, and assault.

Additionally, the *Time* article illuminated a blind spot in many movements—the correlating discourse beyond public faces and mediated voices.[2] While justice projects like #MeToo have raised the visibility and awareness surrounding sexual misconduct and violence for all citizens, the movement and its attendant cultural attention reifies a common theme. When public faces occupying privileged positions gain attention first, it often validates the experiences of everyday survivors. Despite the hegemonic structure allowing acts of abuse and misogyny for much of human history, this creates a perception that the most visible and famous figures must first speak up in order for private citizens to gain legitimacy in their lived experiences.

The unique marriage of public and private citizens within the #MeToo movement underscores the value of what celebrity studies scholar Brockington refers to as celebrity advocacy.[3] The question is not whether celebrity advocacy functions, but how it speaks to and for public and private citizens united through increased awareness and shared narratives. While a great deal of literature discredits celebrity advocacy for its privilege, self-interest, or inability to enact change, this chapter explores the mediated coverage and communicative dynamics of public and private citizens united in social movements like #MeToo. Brockington argues that "we need to create the space to explore the muted, and non-responses, to attempts to engage people through celebrity."[4] For many public figures, activism has grown as important—and in many cases, superseded—their chosen careers. To better understand how the lines between celebrity and politico have eroded in the past few decades, this chapter explores sociocultural theories that assess celebrity advocacy and its impact on causes, the critiques surrounding consumerism and reductionism involved in public activism, the impact of social media in negotiating the public/private divide of #MeToo, and the performative aspects of activism.

THE CELEBRITY MACHINE

With the rapid growth of mediated and technological communication, the reach of celebrity advocacy has expanded globally. Exploring the machinery supporting and producing public figures reveals the nature of personal influence and the function of celebrity in advocacy and activism.

The celebrity industry has experienced a shift; William Morris, Creative Artists Agency, and United Talent Agency have all created foundations to promote charities to their famous clients in the past two decades. Cataloguing celebrity advocacies and causes has also supplemented this transition in publicizing the link between famous figures and their causes and charities. The media coverage of public figures and their activism had already shifted and thus provided a large spotlight and stage for the public and private intervention of #MeToo. The systemic and organized relationship between charitable causes and the celebrity industry has increased in its professionalism, outreach, and recognition. This transformation now involves three major constraints: understanding the uncertainty of celebrity lives and professional commitments, negotiating between colleagues with little understanding regarding the lives of public figures and those celebrities, and the recognition of the unequal or elitist power structure dictating communication between celebrities and their causes.[5] Rather than racing to critique celebrity culture and advocacy, the levels of discourse can instead be assessed for the ways in which celebrity advocacy and presence within a social movement operates.

Celebrity studies scholarship has often been critiqued for its Western bias. Several scholars have noted the position of celebrity throughout vastly different regions, sociopolitical contexts, and developing or underdeveloped communities. While celebrity cultures vary drastically around the world, the primary goal of this chapter is to explore the public/private realms generating interest in #MeToo.[6] Using a comparative perspective to comprehend how celebrity advocacy—specifically in the #MeToo movement—operates differently within diverse cultures and nations illustrates the significance of specific historical, technological, and globalized access and connection.

As mass mobilization shifts from participatory activism toward a post-populist style of third-party politics and interventions, the celebrity role is resituated to cultivate awareness.[7] Considering the reassignment of public figures to cultural advocacy positions, Brockington and Henson advocate for a lens of post-democracy[8] as developed by Colin Crouch.[9] This framework interrogates politics marked by public disconnection and elite dominance. While critiques of celebrity advocacy inevitably emerge in those privileged positions and elite status, it might also be understood as a strategy to reignite public engagement. As Brockington and Henson note, "most people supported the charities that they supported because of personal connections in their lives and families which made these causes important, not because of the celebrities."[10] Despite their own indifference to celebrity involvement as a motivating factor, the focus groups involved in the study believed that others were persuaded by celebrity and that their own lack of interest was atypical. The framework of post-democracy helps explain this paradoxical belief in the power of celebrity advocacy. The disengagement between private citizens and public advocacy emerges as a focus on celebrity itself rather than the movement or project that figure attempts to support. One example emerges as the rise of celebrity advocacy correlates with increased opportunities for elite donors to meet famous people. This exemplifies how activism might shift toward these elite-oriented approaches that work effectively within hierarchical systems.

Scholarship assessing celebrity advocacy critiques the structural inequality and elitism that buttresses this type of activism. Kapoor's critique asserts that only a Marxist revolution might eliminate inequality and injustice, provocatively equating celebrity activists with sadists relishing their own privilege within an unequal world.[11] Yrjölä also relegates celebrity activism to an inherently capitalist or commodified enterprise propped up by the injustice of all philanthropic organizations.[12] Other literature addresses the positive intentions of celebrity advocacy, yet rearticulates how public figures often become center-stage distractions rather than behind-the-scenes boosters for these causes.[13] Further, the alignment with specific campaigns might strengthen the bond between public figure and corporate interests, rather than highlight the source of these social inequalities and injustices. In a slightly different approach, Brockington and Henson posit that moving beyond symbolism and inequality enables an investigation of audience response to celebrity advocacy and how that might bolster the overall movements.

Despite the lack of qualitative-oriented celebrity studies scholarship, these approaches are especially useful in exploring the meaning of consumption practices and processes—integral to understanding how celebrity is employed and deployed. Heeding calls for increased methodologies and international expansion of celebrity studies,[14] consumer interaction with celebrity through qualitative, mixed methods research might build on the foundations of quantitative and U.S.-rich scholarship already in circulation. Qualitative approaches explore how celebrity advocacy operates across different communities in terms of identity and meaning construction for public and private citizens.

Revisiting the cultural shift in activist studies as shaped by beliefs, values, and attitudes applies to the elevation of celebrity advocacy. Celebrity advocacy often emerges in the most visible aspects of culture, specifically as media and cultural studies gather, condense, and encode intricate issues and ideas into familiar representational models. The Western preoccupation with celebrity and the historical regard for rebellion and protest creates dual narratives that embody these ideologies.

Critical Mass

Celebrity affiliations have become established within many charitable associations and social justice projects. Public figures from sports, entertainment, and politics advocate for various causes, although the level of commitment is enacted and portrayed differently for each individual. Some celebrities—such as Oprah Winfrey, Bono, and Angelina Jolie—have become instantly recognized (and in some cases sharply criticized or mocked) for their philanthropic personas. Poniewozik calls these forms of celebrity advocacy "charitainment"[15] as the cause and public figure become inextricably linked.

While hashtag activism and celebrity advocacy continue to face criticism, these public productions and pedagogies provide "information sharing, action coordination, crowdfunding, citizen analysis of government statistics, the archiving and coordination of personal narratives, monitoring of legislation, the basis for research communities, and publicity and public awareness campaigns."[16] In social media, the controls of agenda setting and gatekeeping may be subverted to enact multiple strategies of change. The horizontal power structure of social media movements increases awareness and connection between those very famous figures and the multiple everyday citizens united under that shared experience of #MeToo. The stories of humiliation, exploitation, threats, violence, and judgment create rallying cries against the hegemonic rape culture that has traditionally silenced women. If the battleground of rape culture works to isolate and prevent survivors from speaking publicly, #MeToo is powerfully equipped in its alignment with figures already armed with public platforms and audiences.

Despite inherent conflicts, celebrity advocacy generates success in and of itself: supporting public status while increasing visibility and amplifying the voices of those without the same elite platform. Celebrity advocacy creates a new sociopolitical framework to enact change through fundraising or lobbying acts. Moreover, direct participation and narrative exchange enhances celebrities' public images and raises awareness of the issue. To gauge the impact of celebrity advocacy in the #MeToo movement, this text turns to the scholarship of celebrity studies that explore how "celebrity is constructed and consumed, how celebrity texts are read, how fans behave and so on."[17] As advocacy works as a strategy to elevate recognition and invite participation, reviewing celebrity scholarship aids in assessing the public impact on private citizens' engagement with sociopolitical issues.

Consumerism

When public and celebrity figures are introduced or positioned as champions of a cause, commercialization imbues the overall message or movement. This invokes branding techniques that play on the symbolic link between the glow of celebrity and its promotional power. This bond of market and morality plays on the dual levels of famous faces and everyday citizens to elevate the overall cause. Chouliaraki notes that this does not necessarily emerge from the work of the public figure but rather because market interests commonly infiltrate humanitarian communication.[18] Thus, celebrity advocacy becomes an easy mark for criticism of this commercial imperative.

The economy of celebrity culture is sustained by the admiration and loyalty between consumer/audience and media attention. As Tsaliki, Frangonikolopoulos, and Huliaras note, "celebrity activism and charity may be interpreted as part and parcel of this symbiosis, whereby the celebrity persona is this all-round individual who . . . takes active interest in 'heavy artillery' matters."[19] As publicity machines focus on the activism of the figure, this attention also lends itself to the cause. Through this symbiotic network, celebrities also reposition themselves as promoters of philanthrocapitalism. These figures inevitably carry the heft of consumer capitalism into their advocacy projects while bringing greater attention to these issues.

Scott suggests that as growing populations of celebrities use technocratic approaches in advocacy, philanthrocapitalism emerges and prioritizes business models over grassroots organization.[20] Popular forms of feminism often become criticized for their legitimacy and their frequent allegiance with "corporations and non-profits alike, positioning consumerism or skill-building as panaceas for an ideological and structural issue."[21] In previous decades, civil rights movements led as market interests followed. As Edwards suggests, the celebrity model of philanthrocapitalism might not have supported any of the civil rights, feminist, or environmentalist movements because these simply did not adhere to the criteria of the business agenda.[22] Even as analytics, competition, and revenue could not be quantitatively assessed in these movements, these were social justice projects that indelibly shaped the world. Thus, as celebrity advocacy turned toward a business model of data-driven success, many feared that the qualitative aspects that carry much of cultural movements could be lost, especially as public figures increasingly support the philanthrocapitalistic model.

While many approaches to celebrity activism are successful in both reach and awareness, the specific communicative strategies employed by celebrity activists and social justice movements grow increasingly similar as media corporations channel the public discourse into promotional interests. As this pluralistic mediated capitalism reaches out through "blogging, tweeting, e-mailing and social networking lives, we believe our massively increased access to information, along with our ability to respond to and interact with and create information of our own, is the sign of a strong democracy."[23] Realistically, this volume of access diminishes our interaction with information and our individual potential for exploring and responding to intricate sociopolitical concerns. Instead, we retweet, like, or view. As Dean notes, this hinders awareness and action as "discussion, far from displaced, has itself become a barrier against acts as action is perpetually postponed."[24] We no longer debate through logical reasoning but become caught in the cycle of reflexivity that diminishes our confidence to act.

Easterly wrote of the increasing distance between celebrity protests of past and present, simplifying the issue as such: "Lennon was a rebel. Bono is not."[25] This followed the line of thought that Lennon's anti-war and social awareness activism marked a moral crusade challenging the status quo and oppressive practices of institutions and leaders. Bono resides at the other end of this spectrum insofar as he represents a technical and policy expertise in his position as a celebrity activist. Contrasting these different approaches to celebrity activism imbues the celebrity rebel—as represented by Lennon—with a sense of liberated honor elevated in contrast to the celebrity "wonk" represented by Bono. The price of Bono's public persona comes attached to these causes, linked to elitism in the example of power players who seek to spend time with a celebrity. When set into opposition with Lennon's direct antagonism against leadership, this technocratic approach resituates the expertise of a practiced communicator and liaison of the hierarchy.

Complications arise when the behavior of public figures or their corporate investments threaten the social justice causes for which they advocate. Many charities or causes undertake "due diligence on the public figures with whom they build relationships, before they get serious, to prevent any embarrassment."[26] This type of research does not necessarily equip any social justice movement if those public figures are already bound to corporate interests that run counter to the campaigns. Moreover, if the actions of public figures betray the actual cause or charity, it elevates the scandal while diminishing credibility of celebrity advocacy and inevitably, the movement itself.

> Thank you for setting precedence that just because someone was on the victim side of #MeToo that does not absolve them of responsibility if they became predators themselves. It should not discredit a movement because someone had a dark secret you did not know about.
>
> —@leOGAtheist, August 20, 2018

> When your organization demanded justice based on innuendo alone it was about crime and punishment but when one of your celebrated

finger pointers gets caught now you want to move past crime & punishment why don't I see women raging about @AsiaArgento?? We all know why . . . hypocrites!!

—@TonioJen, August 21, 2018

Did anyone ever say women couldn't be a-holes too? I don't think so.

—@KLM450, August 21, 2018

One of the greatest spikes in the Twitter discourse of #MeToo occurred when Italian director and actor Asia Argento was accused of sexually assaulting former child actor and musician Jimmy Bennett. The alleged assault occurred when Bennett was seventeen and Argento was thirty-seven, with reports detailing that Argento paid $380,000 to Bennett to secure his silence. Whereas Argento was one of the most visible and outspoken activists in the reinvigorated #MeToo movement, these allegations incited a maelstrom of criticism. Twitter exploded with accusations of hypocrisy within #MeToo, in addition to many claiming that this could be the end of the movement. As Fessler asks, "Does Argento's settling a claim of sexual-assault against her disparage the global movement to dismantle sexual harassment? Undoubtedly, critics will say yes. Ignore them."[27] As social media responses undermined the legitimacy of the movement and decried unequal responses for a female perpetrator, #MeToo opened and sustained the conversation. Argento's alleged assault and subsequent cover-up mirrored the common narrative of so many perpetrators she had originally challenged. Yet the revelation of these accusations should not shut down the discourse of sexual violence and misconduct. Instead, #MeToo can use this public discussion to consider the limitations of binaried thought surrounding men/women as perpetrators/survivors, the private toll of sexual violence and misconduct on mental and physical health, and the education and support necessary to disrupt these cycles of violence and abuse.

Reductionism

All the #MeToo that are referring to Hollywood/Harvey W. is disgusting. Most of you people in the business knew about it and let it continue

—@_BL_Gaming, October 26, 2017

The Weinstein allegations opened the floodgates of multiple allegations revealing "a politics of fear perpetrated mostly on young women Hollywood starlets."[28] Yet the fallout from Weinstein seemed a magnification, the final straw surrounding powerful alleged perpetrators such as Bill Cosby, Woody Allen, Roger Ailes, and Roman Polanski. These cases become symbolic stand-ins for the multiple unknown and common perpetrators infiltrating everyday life. One goal of this chapter is to explore the ways in which these public examples directly impacted the lives of all citizens engaged in #MeToo stories of their own. Although rape culture primarily involves representations of powerful men assaulting, exploiting, harassing, and attacking women, this perpetrates an ideology or representation of victimhood that immediately robs or silences the voices of marginalized communities outside this depiction of "Hollywood starlets."

In positioning one public face as the stand-in for multiple victims or perpetrators, celebrity advocacy suggests an illusory reductionism. Often, the most successful and far-reaching of these mediated movements are visibly supported by famous figures. A long-standing criticism of celebrity advocacy emerges in the business of fame itself: the position of a famous face often transforms the suffering of marginalized millions into spectacle. The issue of colonialism perpetrates the ongoing disparate power between (typically white, Western, wealthy) celebrity advocates and the members of marginalized, underserved, underdeveloped, and silenced communities. This remains a common trope in Western intervention around the world—public figures lend attention to the issues of those communities, yet this is often shaped in the mediated image or voice of the public figure. Celebrities will always be critiqued for inauthenticity because they exist in a privileged sphere that "glosses over the ongoing complicity of the West in a global system of injustice that reproduces the dependence of the developing world through acts of charity."[29] This places any public advocates in a precarious position, stranded between the influential power of their own privileged fame and the position of genuine activism within a neocolonialist or commercialized interest.

The inextricable bond between "the celebrity self in extra-theatrical circumstances and the character she enacts on stage, personification manages, nonetheless, to intensify rather than obliterate the distance between celebrity as persona and celebrity as performer."[30] When working as advocates and activists, public figures cannot shed their fame and in fact must often draw upon it to elevate the movement. Even as celebrity humanitarians magically retain the distance between their position of privilege and the suffering and marginalized for and with whom they speak, this becomes perceived as a performance of its own.

As social media movements extend the reach of causes, there remains a hazardous assumption that the political and cultural stratospheres of the elite will eventually impact disenfranchised or marginalized folk outside of the public eye. There are doubts surrounding the public faces and stories that may become substitutive narratives for private citizens, especially if this visibility is accepted as a solution to the systemic problem of sexual violence and misconduct. Actor Gabrielle Union noted this, discussing her own experience as a rape survivor and the long-rumored allegations against Weinstein: "It wasn't until we had, in some people's minds, the 'perfect victims.' And the pain of Hollywood white royalty was prioritized . . . unless society deems you a 'perfect victim,' your pain is quite tolerable."[31] When the mediated narrative and image of sexual harassment, exploitation, assault, and abuse features public figures, or older, powerful white men perpetrating abuse against young, powerless, but attractive white women, we obliterate the experiences of sexual violence that occurs against diverse bodies of women and men, perpetrators and victims alike.

While there remain redundant themes of powerful men who express and act on their entitlement to control, abuse, or assault women, there are systemic nuances that must be explored to strike at the core of these issues. Sexual violence and misconduct must be examined with the same lens provided other experiences dealing with nebulous networks of power. The social media platforms engaging public and private citizens illustrate how public figures perform and represent resistance in a visible microcosm of everyday citizen survival.

Social Media Is the Message

Commenting on the #MeToo Movement, rapper Cardi B stated that "video vixens have spoke about this and nobody gives a fuck. I bet if one of these women stands up and talks about it, people are going to say 'So what? You're a Ho. It don't matter.'"[32] The star also talked about her own harassment in the rap and hip-hop industry, suggesting that producers and directors voice support for #MeToo as a strategy to keep their own history of abuse covered up. After several #MeToo followers tweeted the comments and asked Burke what she thought of Cardi B's response, she offered the following:

> My thoughts on @iamcardib #MeToo comments: SHE IS RIGHT. Period. But also, when it is said that certain groups are "being left out" it means we are allowing the MEDIA to define the movement. The freedom that these words give mean that anyone can be included. (+)
>
> —@TaranaBurke, March 21, 2018

Although critics decry #MeToo for its righteous narratives featuring "rich, famous, young and beautiful women,"[33] the far-reaching impact of celebrity awareness cannot be disputed. Neither can the stories of these victims— public or private. With the collective forces of public and private citizens contributing their voices to this movement, the structural spines upholding these stories of sexual violence and misogyny may be the next to fall.

In the modern era, social media has offered a space for prominent figures to raise awareness while simultaneously encouraging private citizens to speak out on a public stage. Politicized celebrities engage in and through social media similarly to private citizens; this equanimous access may further a rhetoric of public and private identification through social justice movements. Castells posits social media platforms as spaces engendering horizontal or networked power relations, as opposed to the elitist or hegemonic structures typically imagined concerning celebrities and everyday citizens.[34] These modern media networks of horizontal power might instead give rise to the grassroots social activism of the past.

While multiple sources find that celebrity status does not necessarily guarantee public response and media coverage, social media might be the ideal vehicle for celebrity advocacy; it targets specialized audiences through the mode of narrowcasting. Forums like #MeToo as engaged through Twitter, Facebook, or Instagram strategically riff on this idea of narrowcasting. In utilizing the discrete narrative potential of a hashtag, #MeToo generated one of the largest international responses to a social media movement in modern history.

Measuring the strength and consistency of celebrity participation across social media platforms, O'Brien said of celebrities that they "have a greater potential to impact thoughts and decisions, even if that impact is only to reinforce an already held belief."[35] Whereas Western publics specifically consume entertainment news more than traditional news journalism, Twitter, Facebook, and Instagram become highly contested spaces that necessitate greater attention to celebrity advocacy.

Much as McLuhan stressed in the burgeoning era of television, the medium remains the message.[36] Twitter especially created a sociopolitical platform that brought broad focus to grassroots activism. Yet as Wheeler stresses, "celebrity activism has either been seen to be worthwhile or a shallow expression of a consumer-led culture."[37] While platforms like Twitter or Facebook might grant a forum for public figures to engage and raise recognition for grassroots movements by narrowcasting toward specific audiences, these forums have also blurred the borders between news and entertainment, public and private. In addition to the sea change of a movement like #MeToo, it also offers a scholarly contribution; it regards how celebrity advocacy and social media might positively engage grassroots activism and private citizens—often with and against the threats that it might simultaneously erode or eradicate sociopolitical culture.

Half a century past the great uprising of 1960s grassroots activism, social media has constructed a space for marginalized communities and individuals to galvanize in political agency no longer relegated to hierarchical stratospheres of economic and public power. Our digital world resituates traditional sociopolitical communication in a highly interactive, often anonymous, instantaneous forum that encourages voices that obliterate the gatekeepers of traditional media. In circumventing traditional media gatekeepers and agenda setters, social media has enabled public figures to commit to causes and disclose intimate narratives supporting these projects as never before. This widens the stage for NGOs, nonprofits, causal groups, and charitable organizations—our instantaneous digital world hastens the communicative process from celebrity tweet to altruistic validation. Yet as traditional media gates are blown open, the battleground emerges in a Wild West of social media and digital spaces where hate speech is as prevalent and accepted as progressive movements.

The mediated focus on #MeToo has amplified the voices and the scrutiny of victims everywhere. As Dubravka suggests, "standing in the public eye and speaking about an experience of assault not only takes courage; it also takes incredible strength of mind and sense of self-possession in order to remain a person, and not be reduced to, or by, the acts of violence."[38] These acts of speaking out and thereby embodying assault and exploitation involve defiance against the hegemonic controls of silencing, shaming, and security in the guise of the status quo. Davis suggests that there remain limitations for many who cannot "participate in what has now become the #MeToo movement, either because they don't have access to the (social) media or because the sanctions would be too great."[39] This is a significant consideration; it acknowledges the multiple forms of activism in correlation with the myriad strategies of oppression targeting specific communities and individuals.

A large audience of private citizens has now witnessed a moment in which social media and celebrity intervention has created identification and intimacy across the distances separating the "haves" and "have-nots." Social media has opened communication and access to the point where private citizens might see their opinions listed on equal footing as the superheroes, rock stars, and politicos once elevated by celluloid and television. Social media has also unveiled the untouchable and mysterious shroud surrounding productions of celebrity, enabling them to communicate directly with their fan bases.[40] For celebrities, social media might seem intrusive, yet it yields a great range of control for their ability to access and reveal themselves to the public. For private citizens, social media might instead elevate them to stardom. Upending the hierarchy of fame and power might prove beneficial to both groups. For celebrities, the charges of inauthenticity concerning their activism and advocacy may be diminished by daily exposure to their participation and leadership in various causes. For private citizens, the obliteration of that hierarchy and the drive toward recognition for authenticity creates a self-surveillance ensuring that public figures are diligent about their online presence and participation in causes that mean so much to so many.

Performing Activism

The commoditization of human suffering coupled with the neocolonialism robbing those victims of their own voices builds that critique of power relations in celebrity activism. There is a performative production of celebrity advocacy that often generates those critiques of inauthenticity—through spectacle, commodification, or colonialism. Yet recent social media movements and "hashtag activism" create platforms specifically for the voices of private citizens. When public figures join these movements, it sparks a fascinating dynamic in which the authenticity of celebrity activism is less important than the power of shared narratives across these public/private communities.

Increased public advocacy and engagement across social media sites have invited greater conscientious activism from celebrity populations. As Wheeler suggests, "this celebratization of politics has brought about new forms of political engagement that indicate a dialectic transformation of high politics with a populist approach to cultural citizenship."[41] While celebrity involvement raises the awareness of sociopolitical causes and the potential for private citizen engagement, this engenders a greater need for understanding these processes and practices of celebrity advocacy. In an age of digital post-democratic activism, public and private agencies carry ideological weight across eliding borders of celebrity and citizen.

Confessional discourse in the public eye "destabilizes the theatricality of personification: the performance of the voice of suffering as if it were the celebrity's own."[42] This critique explores how confessional advocacy conflates the voices of survivor, celebrity, and spectator. These positionalities assume different meanings when the public figure simultaneously takes on these roles—as in #MeToo. As previously mentioned, the intervention of celebrities within social justice projects inevitably calls up charges of inauthenticity, voyeurism, or narcissism. Yet #MeToo holds potential in utilizing Chouliaraki's "theater of pity" to reimagine these movements through confession, identifying shared narratives as strategies for committed and sustained action.

While in the past, celebrity activism and advocacy often relied on the power of one to represent the distant suffering of millions, #MeToo diminishes the alleged disconnect between public and private realms. Celebrity performativity remains embedded in a network of power that demands careful negotiations of public persona—from entertainment to politics to journalism and back again. When a privileged, powerful public figure becomes the face of an entire social movement, it works in multiple ways. While giving voice and raising awareness, it also molds that message to the previous and ongoing performances of the individual positioned as the figurehead.

When celebrities engage as active citizens raising awareness and participating in charitable works, it permits a framing of these superstars as grounded, generous, everyday people. This further collapses the otherwise vast distances between us and the faces on the screen or bodies on the stage. The narrative of celebrity advocacy may then justify the lives of luxury many assume these figures enjoy while simultaneously creating a space where that celebrity might contribute wealth and visibility to causes. This perception holds ideological functions; celebrities are proffering "ideas about personhood and individualism in a capitalist society, and illustrating both the promise and perils that the notion of individuality entails for all of us as entities upon which social forces act."[43] Our increasing knowledge of the processes and productions of celebrity as commodity might then permit and sustain our sociocultural fascination and adoration of these figures.

The debate surrounding self-interested altruism is one that celebrity advocacy calls sharply into relief. #MeToo emerged as a space for voicing the self and sharing one's story—the collective response transformed into a media moment and eventually a social movement. The inextricable egoism of altruism serves as "justification for action in the aspirational discourse of humanitarianism that constitutes an emerging property of its imaginary."[44] This leads to a post-humanitarianism or post-altruism that engenders engagement with suffering at a distance. The sharing of stories central to #MeToo marks the shift from a ceremonial personification of celebrity advocacy to a confessional style marked by intimacy and disclosure.[45] While disclosive narratives are a powerful strategy in authenticating the celebrity, these oppressions and injustices might instead become linked with the public figure, further obfuscating the domains of private victim and tragic celebrity.

The constant inquiry into concerns of narcissism or authenticity has traditionally steered public figures away from contentious issues and causes. #MeToo has upended this border of safe/risky social justice causes. At a time of widespread social activism and advocacy protesting divisive politics and advancing human rights, the once-controversial issues of sexual violence and misconduct have been realigned. The epidemic of sexual violence and misconduct is now gaining greater recognition as everyone's concern—public and private alike.

Agents of Change

Despite the disparities between public and private figures facing sexual violence and misconduct, the shared experiences across #MeToo highlight the challenges and offer support for everyone. In emphasizing intersectionality in #MeToo, it is necessary to reiterate the unique obstacles and oppressions faced by private citizens against that overwhelmingly public face propagated by the media coverage of the movement. Across public and private spheres, issues of labor and class remain integral to the discussion of #MeToo. More than one-quarter of the eighty-five thousand sexual harassment complaints filed with the U.S. Equal Employment Opportunity Commission from 2005 to 2015 occurred in service-sector industries including accommodations and food services, retail and health care, and social assistance industries.[46] This harassment is not only perpetrated by employers or managers but also by customers. Further, personal services including homecare or hairstyling note that the majority of domestic workers especially suffer abuse and harassment. The most vulnerable groups of employees are immigrant workers, who comprise nearly a quarter of the direct care workforce.[47] Caught in a network of status threats and abuse, many of these workers are further inhibited from speaking out against their abusers.

Avendaño's 2018 study on labor responses to sexual harassment reiterates the necessity of considering intersectional oppressions in worker protection. #MeToo and #TimesUp have expanded this dialogue, with some unions adopting codes of conduct in response to internal harassment scandals and allegations. Yet in the face of sweeping change, Avendaño states that these responses are limited by misogyny and sexism within labor unions. These unions are marked by the "exclusion of women from the formal labor market, and from unions, and by a distinctive form of feminism exercised by women inside the labor movement, which focuses on women's economic situation rather than on other social factors."[48] A closer focus on sexual violence and misconduct as a systemic experience could address the tradition of gendered and racial oppression or exclusion from labor unions. As the most powerful advocacy force for U.S. workers, unions hold the ability to restructure the system as one of transparency while simultaneously offering a new venue for collective and individual action against perpetrators.

When #MeToo called for private and public citizens alike to engage and respond to that hashtag, it upended the traditional constraints surrounding celebrity social justice projects. As a deep relationship between public figures and the movement already existed, #MeToo diminished concerns typical of celebrity involvement in a cause. The mobile model of Twitter eased the navigation of social media connectivity. The negotiation between private and public voices became equalized through the streamlined sharing of narratives. The inequality of the power structure separating public and private citizens was mitigated by the seemingly shared oppression of sexual violation.[49] Yet vigilance remains necessary in assessing the public and private spheres of #MeToo. While superstars such as Jennifer Lawrence and Frances McDormand use awards shows as platforms to demand equal pay in million-dollar contracts, everyday citizens and laborers continue struggling against economic and sexual exploitation in the workplace. The commodification of both celebrity and advocacy must be addressed and monitored as #MeToo continues its social media presence and growth.

Scott questioned whether the world was set to welcome a new form of celebrity activism that could rise above challenges of consumerism and reductionism, noting the success of movements where celebrities were participants rather than leaders.[50] #MeToo directly responds to this question. Celebrities embraced this movement as citizens rather than as figureheads or mouthpieces at the crossroads of capitalism and philanthropy, uniting public and private narratives of survival. As Davis notes, within #MeToo "many of the women were well-known celebrities and they situated themselves as agents, not as victims."[51] Public activism thus becomes an erasure of individual experience for the sake of framing sexual violence as a collective concern. This reasserts the importance in raising awareness, inviting participation in grassroots organization, and challenging or even dismantling the systemic supports sustaining and condoning misogynistic practices and violence.

Public figures can also open doors for stigmatized communities. Considering the many male survivors of sexual violence and abuse, public figures breaking the silencing cycles of shame often carve a path for others. When prominent men like Terry Crews make the choice to share their experiences, it creates "models for others to come forward, to tell their families, to find help . . . it becomes a less shameful thing when somebody famous says it happened to them."[52] The voices are crucial here; survivors with the greatest visibility are often as powerful as many of the perpetrators. While celebrity engagement cannot be overdetermined, "the pedagogy of the celebrity has served to articulate a public sphere different from the one constructed through the official culture, and thus heightening the affective connection of celebrities to an audience."[53]

The collective amplification of famous voices demarcates the silenced suffering of private citizens and testimonies both heard and legitimized. In situating public figures at the forefront of a movement that represents the complex experiences millions have shared regarding sexual violence and misogyny, framing emerges as a clear strategy within the hashtag identifier of #MeToo. When public figures open a shared narrative that counters their own self-interest directly (as in #MeToo), they pose both a challenge to the hegemonic power structure they have directly benefited from and a realignment with the everyday experiences of private citizens.

NOTES

1. Stephanie Zacharek, Eliana Dockterman, and Haley Sweetland Edwards, "Person of the Year 2017," *Time*, December 18, 2017, http://time.com/time-person-of-the-year-2017-silence-breakers.

2. While the selection of "The Silence Breakers" marked the revolution occurring in the wake of #MeToo, it also jarred with *Time*'s 2016 Person of the Year, Donald Trump—someone who openly bragged about sexual assault and has had several allegations of sexual misconduct made against him prior to his 2016 election as the forty-fifth U.S. president. As the *Washington Post* stressed, a history of selecting men as "Person of the Year"—sixty-six of eighty-nine times up to that point—illustrates how embedded pockets of power are, for better or worse, influencing society. Considering that a single woman has been named to the title only four times, with groups such as "American Women" or "The Silence Breakers" the only recent features of women, it is fascinating to address the choice made by *Time* in featuring not only Tarana Burke, Ashley Judd, or Rose McGowan but an entire cast of women from all walks of life.

3. Dan Brockington, "The Production and Construction of Celebrity Advocacy in International Development," *Third World Quarterly* 35, no. 1 (2014): 88–108, https://doi:10.1080/01436597.2014.868987.

4. Dan Brockington, "Celebrity Advocacy: International and Comparative Perspectives," *Celebrity Studies* 6, no. 4 (2015): 395, https://doi:10.1080/19392397.2015.1087205.

5. Brockington, "Celebrity Advocacy."

6. The fifth chapter of this text will speak directly to the international responses to the movement.

7. Kenneth Cmiel, "The Emergence of Human Rights Politics in the United States," *Journal of American History* 86, no. 3 (1999): 1231, https://doi:10.2307/2568613.

8. Dan Brockington and Spensor Henson, "Signifying the Public: Celebrity Advocacy and Post-Democratic Politics," *International Journal of Cultural Studies* 18, no. 4 (2014): 431–48, https://doi:10.1177/1367877914528532.

9. Colin Crouch, *Post-Democracy* (Cambridge: Polity Press, 2004).

10. Brockington and Henson, "Signifying the Public," 432.

11. Ilan Kapoor, *Celebrity Humanitarianism: The Ideology of Global Charity* (London: Routledge, 2012).

12. Riina Yrjölä, "The Invisible Violence of Celebrity Humanitarianism: Soft Images and Hard Words in the Making and Unmaking of Africa," *World Political Science Review* 5, no. 1 (2009).

13. Michael K. Goodman, "The Mirror of Consumption: Celebritization, Developmental Consumption and the Shifting Cultural Products of Fair Trade," *Geoforum* 41, no. 1 (2010): 104–16; Lisa Ann Richey and Stefano Ponte, "Better (Red)™ than Dead? Celebrities, Consumption and International Aid," *Third World Quarterly* 29, no. 4 (2008): 711–29.

14. Brockington, "Celebrity Advocacy."

15. James Poniewozik, "The Year of Charitainment," *Time*, December 19, 2005, http://content.time.com/time/magazine/article/0,9171,1142281,00.html.

16. Michael A. Peters and Tina Besley, "Weinstein, Sexual Predation, and 'Rape Culture': Public Pedagogies and Hashtag Internet Activism," *Educational Philosophy and Theory* (2018): 5, https://doi:10.1080/00131857.2018.1427850.

17. Brockington and Henson, "Signifying the Public," 432.

18. Lilie Chouliaraki, "The Theatricality of Humanitarianism: A Critique of Celebrity Advocacy," *Communication and Critical/Cultural Studies* 9, no. 1 (2011): 1–21.

19. Liza Tsaliki, Christos A. Frangonikolopoulos, and Asteris Huliaras, *Transnational Celebrity Activism in Global Politics: Changing the World?* (Bristol, UK: Intellect, 2011), 9.

20. James C. Scott, *Weapons of the Weak: Everyday Forms of Peasant Resistance* (New Haven: Yale University Press, 2008).

21. Sarah Banet-Weiser and Kate M. Miltner, "#MasculinitySoFragile: Culture, Structure, and Networked Misogyny," *Feminist Media Studies* 16, no. 1 (2016): 171, https//doi:10.1080/14680777.2016.1120490.

22. Michael Edwards, *Small Change: Why Business Won't Save the World* (San Francisco: Berrett-Koehler Publishers, 2010).

23. Scott, *Weapons*, 81.

24. Jodi Dean, *Blog Theory: Feedback and Capture in the Circuits of Drive* (London: Polity Press, 2010), 110.

25. William Easterly, "A Modest Proposal," review of *The End of Poverty*, by Jeffrey D. Sachs, *Washington Post*, March 13, 2005, http://www.highbeam.com/doc/1P2-20245.html?refid=easy_hf. Easterly supported this comparison with the response of the FBI, police, and immigration forces to place Lennon under constant surveillance. FBI records detailing President Nixon's four-year effort to deport Lennon were released under the Freedom of Information Act.

26. Brockington, "Production and Construction," 101.

27. Leah Fessler, "Asia Argento Has Not Wrecked the Movement She Helped Create," *Quartz*, August 20, 2018, https://qz.com/work/1363240/metoo-creator-tarana-burkes-perspective-on-asia-argentos-alleged-assault.

28. Peters and Besley, "Weinstein, Sexual Predation," 1.

29. Chouliaraki, "Theatricality of Humanitarianism," 4.

30. Chouliaraki, "Theatricality of Humanitarianism," 6.

31. Gabrielle Union, "Gabrielle Union on the #MeToo Movement: 'The Floodgates Have Opened for White Women,'" interview by Monique Judge, *Root*, December 6, 2017, https://thegrapevine.theroot.com/gabrielle-union-on-the-metoo-movement-the-floodgates-1821066542.

32. Jazmine Hughes, "Cardi B Gives Her Most Explicit Interview Yet," *Cosmopolitan*, March 19, 2018, https://www.cosmopolitan.com/entertainment/celebs/a18930050/cardi-b-cosmopolitan-cover-interview.

33. Dubravka Zarkov and Kathy Davis, "Ambiguities and Dilemmas around #MeToo: #ForHow Long and #WhereTo?" *European Journal of Women's Studies* 25, no. 1 (2018): 9, https://doi:10.1177/1350506817749436.

34. Manuel Castells, "Communication, Power and Counter-Power in the Network Society," *International Journal of Communication* 1 (2007): 238–66.

35. Peter O'Brien, "Actors and the Social Media in Politics," in *Encyclopedia of Social Media and Politics*, vol. 1, ed. Kerric Harvey (Los Angeles: Sage, 2014), 13.

36. Marshall McLuhan, *The Medium Is the Massage: An Inventory of Effects* (New York: Bantam Books/Random House, 1967).

37. Mark Wheeler, "The Mediatization of Celebrity Politics through the Social Media," *International Journal of Digital Television* 5, no. 3 (2014): 223.

38. Dubravka and Davis, "Ambiguities," 4.

39. Dubravka and Davis, "Ambiguities," 5.

40. Wheeler, "Mediatization," 225.

41. Wheeler, "Mediatization," 232.

42. Chouliaraki, "Theatricality of Humanitarianism," 15.

43. Tsaliki, Frangonikolopoulos, and Huliaras, *Transnational Celebrity*, 11.

44. Chouliaraki, "Theatricality of Humanitarianism," 14.

45. Barry King, "Articulating Stardom," in *The Celebrity Culture Reader*, ed. P. David Marshall (London: Sage, 2006), 246–47.

46. Judith Levine, "Beyond #MeToo," *New Labor Forum* 27, no. 3 (2018): 20–25.

47. Paraprofessional Healthcare Institute, 2017.

48. Ana Avendaño, "Sexual Harassment in the Workplace: Where Were the Unions?" *Labor Studies Journal*, November 12, 2018, http://journals.sagepub.com/doi/abs/10.1177/0160449X18809432.

49. However, it must be noted that shared oppression does not indicate a uniform oppression; marginalized and intersectional individuals experience multiple, diverse oppressions in vastly different ways.

50. Varihi Scott, "Is Celebrity Activism a Boom-Time Bubble that Is Facing Deflation?" *International Journal of Media & Cultural Politics* 7, no. 1 (2011): 77–84, https://doi:10.1386/mcp.7.1.77_3.

51. Dubravka and Davis, "Ambiguities," 5.

52. David Crary, "Some Male Sexual Assault Victims Feel Left Behind by #MeToo," *MSN.com*, April 19, 2018, https://www.msn.com/en-us/news/us/some-male-sexual-assault-victims-feel-left-behind-by-metoo/ar-AAw2Kpq.

53. Tsaliki, Frangonikolopoulos, and Huliaras, *Transnational Celebrity*, 12.

CHAPTER 3

Tarana Burke's Grassroots Goal and the Implications of #MeToo for Women of Color

"Sisters Still Managed to Get Diminished or Erased"

Tarana Burke leading #MeToo Survivors' March in Hollywood, California. *WENN Rights Ltd/Alamy Stock Photo*

Speaking at a Brandeis University alumni event, Dr. Anita Hill spoke about her own well-documented experience with sexual harassment in the public eye as contrasted with the viral movement of #MeToo:

> I didn't have a hashtag. . . . Some people think it's about the hashtag and it's about social media; I think that those are just platforms. I think the real goal of the MeToo movement is to build empathy and community.[1]

Anita Hill and Tarana Burke, positioned across pivotal points in U.S. his‐
tory, remain bound as two of the driving forces for recognition, change, and
support surrounding sexual violence and misconduct. Hill's 1991 testimony
against then-nominee Supreme Court Justice Clarence Thomas opened the
discourse on sexual harassment in the workplace. Hill faced myriad obsta‐
cles of gendered and racialized oppression yet stood her ground to become
a feminist icon of the twenty-first century. Hill's efforts laid the foundation
for women internationally to fight sexual violence and misconduct, eradi‐
cate victim-blaming, and expose the systemic gendered inequality support‐
ing and shrouding perpetrators. Burke's conceptualization of #MeToo built
from this foundation to reach and support underserved women of color.
Despite these two leaders being black women and survivors, "when we turn
on the TV and see debates about this brave, new heightened consciousness,
the faces and voices of black women and girls are often missing."[2]

Beyond her sudden fame as the founder of one of the most successful
social media movements, the conversation that led Burke to create Me Too
reiterated the need for survivors of color to share and support each other.
Burke explained the simple statement inciting the movement: "On one
side, it's a bold declarative statement that 'I'm not ashamed' and 'I'm not
alone.' On the other side, it's a statement from survivor to survivor that
says 'I see you, I hear you, I understand you and I'm here for you.'" The
ultimate goal was to create a network, a space for young women of color
to connect and safely share their survival stories of sexual abuse, assault,
harassment, and exploitation. Burke eventually shifted the intended
movement from youth to women of all ages, reiterating how trauma and
empathy cross demographic lines.

When journalist Britni Danielle revealed that Burke originated "Me Too"
a decade before the viral firestorm, it created a compelling new conver‐
sation reminiscent of earlier critiques of feminist movements. Poet Asha
Bandele commented: "I have my concern about the ownership of that
movement publicly being in the hands of white women. I don't know
that white women have ever led a movement that secured people outside
of their own."[3] This recalls historically specific contexts of slavery and Re‐
construction-era and pre–civil rights legislation that retains sedimentary
impact. For example, when a black woman was raped by any man it was
considered legal; yet when a white woman was raped by a black man—the
accused man was lynched.[4] These legal edicts retain punitive significance
in the current era; sexual violence in its multiple forms remains a tool of
colonization to this day.

> Love both movements b/c they're helping women. It just seems like when
> these victims came out with their painful, personal stories, you hijacked

their movement to be in the spotlight. Grandstanding is the phrase. When you tweeted the #Metoo did you know it was Tarana's?

—@Vanessa197100, January 7, 2018

Historically, feminist "whitewashing" tended to ignore or diminish the issues specific to women of color. Addressing intersectional dimensions of privilege and subordination, Wildman and Davis highlight the position of white women who occupy both categories in relation to race and gender.[5] Recognition that individuals often straddle borders of oppression and oppressed fosters a critique of the essentialist categorization of "women" when framed by the language of intersectionality. Applying intersectionality to #MeToo illustrates the vacillating possibilities for dynamic dominance and subordination for multiple citizens and communities. While the original articulations of intersectionality neither demonstrated how to explore positions of partial privilege nor how to assess the complexities of internal and external forces of oppression, it is the aim of this text to use intersectionality as a framework and tool to analyze the simultaneously expansive and specific experiences of #MeToo.

While Tarana Burke & Alicia Garza have been pushing for MeToo to focus on the conditions of domestic workers, poor women and women of color, white feminists like Margaret Atwood continually focus on the movement's potential negative impact on (mostly white) men 3/9

And in so doing, they, in typical white feministing fashion, completely ignore the leadership of BW in favor of centering themselves & their perspective—perspective woefully ill-equipped to grasp the racialized gender & class dynamics of rape culture 5/9

—@BreeNewsome, January 18, 2018

Leadership in social movements is often predicated on visibility and representation. Multidimensional factors of oppression against race, sexual orientation, gendered identity, religious affiliation, political allegiance, and continually expanding aspects of identity still pose difficulties for the intersectional individuals locked within these frameworks. This creates an entry point for essentialist thought as it promises a fight for individuals and groups denoted by singular identifiers of race, ability, class, gender, and multiple other socio-demographics. Yet the categorization of women as monolithic, homogenous, and subordinated is only possible in a self-contained gender regime. Intersectional approaches are relevant in considering not only the internal experiences and expectations of individual women but also the external oppressions of race, sexuality, class, and myriad other sociopolitical systems. As Onwuachi-Willig notes, "these examples demonstrate that the realities of white women's lives, as opposed to the distinctive harassment employed against black women and other women of color, still define the female experience."[6] Even as we've witnessed a reckoning regarding sexual violence and misconduct, changes still need to be made in understanding and valuing the different positionalities of survivors.

The impact of social influence on social media movements functions as our social identities exist and thrive regardless of the "proximity of other group members, and thereby individuals' behavior and cognitions can be highly social despite the fact that they are isolated from the direct influence of others in their group."[7] When individual identity is subsumed to the social identity or group membership, social media movements are sustained or generated from shared narratives and mutual recognition—rather than individual difference. For women of color in activism, representational visibility has often elided the lived experiences of these individuals and communities. Rather than recognize and respect the both/and of experience for women of color, social justice campaigns have often appropriated, mutated, or silenced these perspectives. Diminishing identity politics produces another form of oppression and omission against the intersectionality of experience. Using the foundational work of scholars including Kimberlé Crenshaw, Patricia Hill Collins, Maxine Baca Zinn, and Bonnie Thornton Dill, this chapter explores the legacy of activism led by women of color, the pipelines of abuse targeting women and girls of color, the online discourse for WOC survivors, and the possibilities of majority feminism in creating interventions for the 99 percent of women silenced and ignored from the conversation.

INTERSECTIONAL INTERVENTIONS

Multidimensional or intersectional oppressions are not strictly external forces but can often manifest within social justice projects. Essentialist scholarship may highlight singular identity politics, yet this is often limited; "activists and theorists challenge only the multidimensional subordination experienced by more privileged members of oppressed communities."[8] This reasserts the significance for women of color and underserved communities to seek a different form of activism specific to their experiences. In the context of #MeToo, it is necessary to revisit a history of racial oppression weighted with sexual violence and misconduct. As Hutchinson posits, "Lynching, the imposition of the death penalty in the context of interracial rape, sexual harassment, and the rape of women of color are all institutions that involve a potent intersection of racial, gender, and sexuality hierarchies."[9] Racist, white anxieties and stereotypes surrounding the heterosexual relationships of people of color buttressed these oppressive and devastating punishments.

Intersectionality staked claims that upended understanding of oppressed groups as uniform or singular, accounted for the impact of other systems of oppression before strategically resisting any one form of dominance, revealed the historical failures of movements that emerged primarily from privileged positions, and assessed intersectional forms of oppression rather than simply returning to the hierarchical struggle between privilege and subordination. This is of importance for women of color in the face of the #MeToo movement. Considering the historical oversights of feminist movements for marginalized groups and individuals, "the absence of an analysis of racial subjugation in feminist theory, for example, means that feminism will reflect the experiences and needs of white women—who do not suffer directly from racial oppression."[10] Intersectionality holds its power in moving beyond confines of feminism or racism in ways that invite conversations across various categories. This ideology permits movements to more accurately reflect the experiences of all involved rather than the privileged or visible few.

Despite the gendered aspects attending to the stereotypical representation of perpetrators and survivors, the entire discourse—the allegations and responses, and the choral jury—becomes racialized.

> I do not feel like I have a place in the #MeToo movement. Black women have been forgotten again. When I first heard about the movement people made it seem like @Alyssa_Milano created it. I wish people would credit you more. I think it would help black women feel more a part of it.
>
> —@NicoleCCarlton, February 21, 2018

@TaranaBurke responded:

> I see you sis. The work *I* do sees you and acknowledges you. Don't get caught up in what the media says this movement is—it is about ALL survivors finding resources to heal and working to interrupt sexual violence.

> I truly am thankful for the work you have put into the movement. I had to go out of my way to actually learn you founded it, but I am happy I didn't depend on just the media to teach me. Thanks for still pushing to help brown/black girls like me the media seems to have forgotten.
>
> —@NicoleCCarlton, February 22, 2018

The #MeToo movement also illustrates what Hill Collins calls the outsider-within position for black women and women of color. Group membership is often predicated in ways that maintain this positionality:

"whiteness for feminist thought, maleness for black social and political thought, and the combination for mainstream scholarship."[11] While Milano's reincarnation of Burke's "MeToo" campaign welcomed diverse voices, the media followed the pattern of an overwhelmingly celebrity, classed, and white face. As Crenshaw noted, "intervention strategies based solely on the experiences of women who do not share the same class or race backgrounds will be of limited help to women who because of race and class face different obstacles."[12] Burke's original project sought to give voice to women and girls of color in disadvantaged communities; however, many felt that they had been locked out of full group membership in a movement they helped create. This negates realities of all people of color in dealing with sexual violence and misconduct.

Suppressing knowledge production by oppressed people allows dominant groups to continue ruling. Yet this intellectual tradition makes experiential standpoint matter in assessing the contributions of scholar-activists of color such as Sojourner Truth, Gloria Anzaldúa, Young Yun Kim, and Beatrice Medicine. The outsider-within position at the crossroads of civil rights situating white women and black men at the forefront of these movements holds lasting impacts, significantly in the #MeToo discussion of sexual violence and misconduct. In addition to the loss of voice and visibility within second-wave feminism and appropriation of the work crafted by women of color, multiracially identifying feminists and activists continue to feel a sense of displacement. As activist leaders, women of color often suppress their own needs to support others in their communities. Yet this places women of color in a position of further subordination. As Burke stated, "There is a way that we embrace brothers and we've been trained and socialized to put their needs ahead of ours. And so that makes it difficult for women of color to come out and be public about being survivors."[13] This reiterates the challenging positionality and relationality that women of color navigate with and against these movements.

Despite multiple oppressions and demands, it is exactly this marginalized, outsider-within position that creates the distinct and insightful perspective of women of color. These ideas and actions in recognizing and respecting intersectionality of identity and experience offer a unique subjectivity that dominant positions (or full group membership) might not afford. Alice Walker and Angela Davis are credited as two of the earliest voices articulating arguments that recognized the intersection of race, gender, and class. Walker's "Womanism"[14] arose out of earlier feminist movements, spotlighting the multiple and intricate forms of oppression experienced by women of color. Walker scrutinized feminisms led largely by white middle-class women who advocated sociopolitical change yet negated or silenced oppressions based on classed and racial prejudices. Recuperating the black folk expression of mothers to their daughters, Walker highlighted the link of the saying "You acting womanish" with willful, bold, and audacious behavior. Moreover, Walker linked the idea of "Womanism" as love—sexually and/or nonsexually—for other women: the womanist is "committed to survival and wholeness of entire people, male and female."[15] This reasserts the intersectional approach in understanding the multiplicity of oppressions and identifiers shaping every human's understanding of the world—a critical tenet of identity politics and activism.

Following this move toward "Womanism," Davis explored the specific paradigm uniting the multiplicity of experiences for women of color, interrogating the various forces shaping these oppressions at institutional and individual levels.[16] Davis advocates for reframing historical accounts to understand the experiences of enslaved black women because "lessons can be gleaned from the slave era which will shed light upon black women's and all women's current battle for emancipation."[17] Noting how labor has always occupied a central position in the lives of women of color, Davis suggests revisiting the significance of work in these women's lives throughout history. Pointing to this legacy, Davis illustrates how slaveholders treated female slaves as genderless when it seemed more profitable to exploit them as men, but as women, they were also subjected to sexual abuse. This double-oppression endures in the intersectional oppressions against women of color today.

Baca Zinn and Thornton Dill addressed critiques that have grown out of concern with unitary theories of gender, the exclusion of women of color from feminist scholarship, and the misinterpretation of women of color and their experiences.[18] Work that links gender to other forms of domination is explored to understand how difference and diversity infuse contemporary feminist studies. This conceptual framework of multiracial feminism explores the structures of domination, most notably the importance of race in understanding the social construction of gender. The centrality of race, institutionalized racism, and struggles against racial oppression link various feminist perspectives within the overall framework.

Baca Zinn and Thornton Dill suggest that multiracial feminism offers a set of analytic premises for thinking about gender as multiracial feminism: (1) asserts that gender is constructed by a range of interlocking inequalities, or what Hill Collins calls the "matrix of domination";[19] (2) examines the intersectional nature of hierarchies at all levels of social life; (3) highlights the relational nature of dominance and subordination; (4) explores the interplay of social structure and women's agency; (5) encompasses a variety of methodological approaches and theoretical tools; and (6) unites understandings from lived experiences of diverse and continuously changing groups of women.

Crenshaw's articulation of intersectionality revealed how the legal system had long denied relief or retribution to women of color because civil rights statutes were too narrowly defined for either women or persons of color. Antidiscrimination doctrine framed the legal models accordingly, with "race plaintiffs as men of color . . . sex discrimination plaintiffs as white women."[20] Women of color filing antidiscrimination claims were subjected to a presentation as an unprotected "special class" within civil rights doctrine. Women of color and their intersectional perspectives were thus diminished and dismissed within the justice system.

Much of the groundwork being laid in the wake of #MeToo evolves from the legal community, as intrepid judicial practitioners and scholars have reassessed doctrines in the context of sexual violence and misconduct. As Onwuachi-Willig suggests, this places the discourse involving women of color in a very specific space:

> The marginalization of women of color has occurred within the #MeToo move-
> ment despite the fact that a black woman, Mechelle Vinson, was the plaintiff in
> the very first Supreme Court case to recognize a cause of action under Title VII
> for a hostile work environment created by sexual harassment; despite the fact
> that #MeToo began with a woman of color; and despite the fact that women of
> color are more vulnerable to sexual harassment than white women and are less
> likely to be believed when they report harassment, assault, and rape.[21]

In Crenshaw's analysis of antidiscrimination doctrine, she suggests that emphasizing women of color might contrast the "multidimensionality of Black women's experience with the [antidiscrimination] single-axis analysis that distorts these experiences."[22] As a critique impelling the expansion of intersectionality into multidimensional studies, scholars suggested that race and gender (among other identity constructs) do not merely intersect but structure and reify each other through dynamic mutual interaction. Kwan notably offered this critique of the original articulation of intersectionality made by Crenshaw.[23] As Kwan noted, intersectionality must also account for the co-construction, co-production, and co-synthesis of identities and oppressions. Yet as Mutua suggests, the original articulation of intersectionality (and further expansion) might already include "this insight, an insight previously made, intuited, or simply incorporated into it."[24] Scholars utilizing intersectionality have further made visible and explicit these considerations.

Intersectionality and activism for women of color interrogate the juncture of sexism, racism, and class oppression—revealing through identity politics and lived experience that these elements are inextricably bound. Addressing the strategic intersectionality in the activist practices of women of color recovers the sociopolitical significance of coalitions across multiple communities. As Crenshaw suggests, "ignoring differences within groups contributes to tension among groups, another problem of identity politics that bears on efforts to politicize violence against women."[25] Categorizing and separating identity factors in mutually exclusive contexts disregards the importance of intersectionality that informs the individual experiences and sociopolitical practices of women of color. The recognition of intersectionality illustrates how race, gender, class, sexuality, and myriad other identity factors contribute to the representational and structural aspects of violence—and specifically sexual violence.

To assess the #MeToo juggernaut, it is necessary to reiterate the principles of intersectionality within the social media campaign and throughout social activism for women of color. Despite the visibility of race, skin color "is not, and cannot be, an accurate barometer for identifying a community of diverse political, economic, sexual, and artistic interests."[26] As media covers every detail of #MeToo, issues of sexism, gender, race, ableism, culture, violence, and authenticity arise. These elements echo the perseverant voices of activists of color over centuries and around the world.

THE ACTIVISM OF EVERYDAY SURVIVAL

Cultural Guardians: Black Female Activists

Everyday survival against intersectional oppressions marks women of color and their activism differently. Often overlooked within the larger discourse, everyday group survival becomes central to black political activism. These are the equally significant strategies of "Black women's political activity within African-American communities."[27] The multiple systems of oppression necessitate similarly complex activism for women of color. In bell hooks's essential text *Feminism Is for Everybody*,[28] the author details the beginning of the feminist movement; hooks stresses that prior to academic appraisal and appropriation, feminism emerged and galvanized in small group discussions. Women from diverse backgrounds with multiple goals united to speak about their experiences of sexism and their visions for moving toward equality. These were discursive spaces of inclusion that recognized the unique contributions and experiences of intersectional knowledge sharing. Thus, even as black women's activism is recognized for its ideological content, just as important are the collective everyday moves and conversations shared by women of color.

Black women's activism across group survival consists of strategies whereby women of color exert influence within existing sociopolitical structures. When direct institutional confrontation is impossible or undesirable, these women "craft Black female spheres of influence that resist oppressive structures by undermining them."[29] These spheres build on independent and resistant identities claimed by women of color. This strategy of activism for group survival perceives black lived experiences as necessary to creating critical consciousness. As Crenshaw notes, when identity is reconceptualized, "it may be easier to understand the need for and to summon the courage to challenge groups that are after all, in one sense, 'home' to us, in the name of the parts of us that are not made at home."[30] The struggle remains in the effort this takes for everyone to recognize internal group exclusions and oppressions within activist campaigns. The discomfort of recognizing suppressive and silencing practices within social justice movements must be eradicated so that the work of hearing the multiple, diverse, and intersectional voices can truly begin.

Additionally, black women's activism directly challenges institutional forces of legal, political, and cultural rules maintaining the oppression of women of color. Struggles for institutional change often involve collaboration with other broad social justice movements. These interdependent forms of activism reiterate the power in women of color to create and perform resistant identities of their own making. However, identity politics also creates shared spaces for black women with and through each other. This highlights one significant dynamic of activism for women of color—the black woman as central to her family and community. Working as cultural guardians, black women exert "influence, authority, and power that produced a worldview markedly different from that advanced by the dominant group."[31] Internationally, women of color have resisted patriarchal, European, and white American attempts to assimilate or eradicate African-derived cultural customs. As Pala states, "the trauma of subjugation has not led to total despair. Instead it has produced an insistent interrogation and resistance by Black people all over the world."[32] Community activism for black women in the United States correlates with similar strategies across international black diasporic spaces, suggesting that attempts to dehumanize and destroy social and economic bases of black society have instead created fierce resistance.

Another key component of group survival in black women's activism springs from the lived experiences supporting "maternal politics."[33] The empowerment gained through "othermothering" and cultural resistance shapes black women's activism, resonating with Burke's activist work and her original "Me Too" mission. The strategy of "othermothering" simultaneously built on Burke's experiences while reaching young women of color in her community. The conflation of these private, public, and political spheres in black women's activism illustrates the potential of everyday experience and community resistance.

A Legacy of Silenced Voices

Even as feminists of color have long maintained the importance in recognizing how race and class structure gender identity, these ideas are often subsumed to the primary concerns of white feminist–led movements or broader social projects. There are several manifestations of these suppressive practices: disregarding the history and experience specific to women of color; paying "lip service" to inclusion while doing little to create change; and misappropriating, transforming, and depoliticizing the feminist ideas of women of color.[34] As black feminist critic Hazel Carby notes, symbolic inclusion has welcomed the work of black women into classrooms while forgetting to actually welcome black women.[35] This omission conjures the work of Burke as appropriated and celebrated in the resurgence of #MeToo while the voices of disadvantaged women of color are drowned out in the viral roar. Until the contributions of multiracial feminisms are recognized and incorporated into larger movements like #MeToo, these social justice projects remain sorely lacking.

The issue of celebrity—and inevitably, class—reenters the discussion as the celebrity voices that helped reignite the #MeToo movement often came from positions of privilege enabling them to do so. Burke acknowledged that while this strategically made a louder, more visible point, "somehow sisters still managed to get diminished or erased in these situations. A slew of people raised their voices so that that didn't happen."[36] These collective, viral protests engendered that goal of amplified voices. However, in any movement where certain voices and images are privileged over others, voices of diverse experience are often drowned out or silenced altogether.

Addressing the strategic intersectionality in the activist practices of women of color recovers the sociopolitical significance of coalitions across multiple communities. Intersectional experiences and identity politics offer a foundation for addressing numerous entry points for voices of difference to come together around complex issues. As Crenshaw notes, "in the area of rape, intersectionality provides a way of explaining why women of color have to abandon the general argument that the interests of the community require the suppression of any confrontation around interracial rape."[37] This is but one powerful example of how intersectional identity might provide a communal space for communication. Despite the treacherous nature of sexual violence and oppressive practices, time truly is up to uncover the historically concealed spaces for shared understanding across intersectional identities.

Feminist models of scholarship and activism once posited a universal or monolithic model of womanhood. That model, based primarily on white womanhood, can neither stand alone nor stand as the normative ideal. Incorporating intersectionality and multiracial feminism reveals how networks of power and subordination structure women's lives differently. Baca Zinn and Thornton Dill highlight the ways that multiracial feminism "focuses not just on differences but also on the way in which differences and domination intersect and are historically and socially constituted."[38] Understanding the intersectional and multiracial dimensions of feminist scholarship and activism revises foundational approaches shaping these disciplines and practices—most significantly, this knowledge helps reframe privilege and oppression as interrelated, fluid positions.

Throughout the various waves of feminism, the tradition of suppressing women of color was often rationalized as beneficial to the overall cause. As Burke mentioned, "when White women want our support, they use an umbrella of 'women supporting women' and forget that they didn't lend the same kind of support."[39] The intersectional oppressions of race, class, and gender positioned white women as more visible, liberated, and thus viable in advancing activist thought and practice. Against the backdrop of sexual violence, misconduct, and discrimination, this silenced the unique intersectional experiences of disadvantaged women of color. The concern of racial privilege and acceptance proved especially significant within the discourse of sexual discrimination and violence. Entrenched justification of privilege forges a legacy in which white feminists make sexual victimization visible—in their own images—while ignoring the racial privilege that enables their voices to be heard.

Ignoring the intersectional dynamic involved in the sexual abuse of women of color plays on a long legacy of sexual stereotypes. The power of representation has much to do with black women's silence regarding sexual violence and oppression. Interrogating the impact of these stereotypes, Hill Collins traces the history of the "jezebel" across distinctive systems of class, race, gender, and national oppression. The objectification and commodification of black women's bodies became a marker of class oppression. The devaluing of black women elevated the purity of white women in gendered oppression. The justification of sexual violence against black women emerged through racial oppression. And the unjust and unequal treatment in national and international laws and politics engendered global oppression.

Multiracial feminist scholarship posits similarly damaging stereotypes that limit the representational and performative possibilities for women of color. Latina/o individuals, when (infrequently) shown in mainstream culture and media, are typified as "comics/comedians, criminals, lovers/sex symbols, lower class, very religious, or unintelligent."[40] In much of Western cultural representation, colonialism and romanticism have depicted women of Arabic descent as transforming from precolonial "shrewish harassing women" to colonial and postcolonial images of the harem fantasy: "oppressed, submissive, and passive slaves to men."[41] Women of Asian descent are often framed in ways rendering them either invisible, threatening, or fetishized: "You may imagine a woman who is docile and subservient; one who is sensual or erotic ('The Geisha'); the manipulative and untrustworthy 'Dragon Lady'; or the hardworking, conscientious worker bee."[42] These are but a few of the Western-based stereotypes that generalize and categorize entire populations with little attention to the intricacies and distinctions within these populations.

Sexual exploitation, harassment, abuse, and assault often follow these historical legacies, legitimated through stereotypes like the erotic subservient Geisha or the sex-crazed, irresistible Jezebel. As Davis notes, women of color experience race-, gender-, and class-specific sexual violence differently—often with objectified stereotypes as ideological justifications.[43] This legacy holds damning consequences. Even as women of color are more likely to be sexually victimized, they are less likely to report these crimes, seek counseling, or see conviction of their attackers. The continued apathy regarding the specific viewpoints of women of color creates a border between full participation in broader social justice movements, relegating women of color to the outsider-within position yet again.

As women of color find themselves repeatedly resituated as outsiders-within, they are also reminded of how their intersectional identities and unique experiences cannot be addressed through the whitewashing of larger social movements. Crenshaw suggests that "the fact that minority women suffer from the effects of multiple subordination . . . shapes and ultimately limits the opportunities for meaningful intervention on their behalf."[44] The frustrating tradition of multiplied subordination crashes against a wall of institutional limitations in understanding intersectional contexts and positionalities. Despite the work of feminist scholars and activists such as Hill Collins, Garza, and Burke, there remains an international blind spot concerning the intersectional nature of identity politics.

Pipelines of Abuse

> We're not going to solve the problem of sexual violence by ignoring that some victims are targeted because of their race. Or that racism means they are less likely to get support. We need to address all of rape culture #MeToo
>
> —@Karnythia, November 19, 2017

For women and girls of color, legacies of stereotypes have fostered a systemic oppression and ignorance about the specific experiences these communities face. As noted by Hutchinson and Norris, "terms like 'bitch', 'ho', 'ratchet', 'thot' (that *h* over there) are frequently used to demean African American girls in ways that echo their specific history of institutionalized rape and dehumanization in the U.S. under slavery."[45] Sexual violence and misconduct encompass not only the physical abuse but these forms of oppressive and demeaning verbal assault.

Educational systems and support communities often obscure or silence the abuses suffered by girls and young women of color. Stereotypes and sexualization within these communities negate the consequences of sexual violence and misconduct. For women of color, this might lead to a tragic cycle when perceptions that they are less innocent or less deserving of protection directly contributes to elevated suspension, expulsion, or incarceration rates. Further, "in a perverse twist of justice, many girls who experience sexual abuse are routed into the juvenile justice system because of their victimization."[46] Sexual abuse has been noted as a primary predictor of these girls' and young women's entry into and experience with the juvenile justice system. These punitive actions often retrigger the trauma, expose these girls and women to increased victimization, and rob them of any possibility to seek treatment or support.

Girls and young women of color are particularly impacted by this trend. "Girls' common reactions to trauma are criminalized and exacerbated by involvement in the juvenile justice system, leading to a cycle of abuse and imprisonment,"[47] which reasserts the complexities of racialized, sexualized, and gendered violence upholding this system. In educating ourselves about the systemic criminalization of all victimized girls, it becomes apparent that this population is disproportionately comprised of girls of color. As the conversation continues surrounding the disproportionate incarceration of boys and men of color, so too must the discussion of girls' experiences with abuse across gendered and racial lines.

Within the context of the abuse and incarceration cycle, stereotypes and lack of support services are reflected in predominately black and Latino schools. Native American reservations and communities remain one of the most disproportionately criminalized populations with 3.5 percent of detained and committed girls yet only 1 percent of the general population. These statistics highlight the direct result of a pipeline system from school to prison. This directly contradicts traditional options for most white girls and young women, namely college or career. As women of color and their supporting communities grapple with these issues, the girls and young women within these populations face a new challenge—negotiating identity in the digital world.

WOC Online

Twitter released a statement pledging to support and empower multiple voices on its platform. Chief executive Jack Dorsey reiterated this, tweeting that the company intended to address allegations and stories of abuse on its site. Yet Twitter soon banned actor Rose McGowan after she accused Weinstein of rape and condemned the complicity of men in Hollywood who ignore abuse to sustain their privileged positions. While many white feminists supported McGowan and boycotted Twitter, black women like activist Ashley C. Ford instead asked these critical questions: "Where was the boycott for ESPN sports journalist Jemele Hill when her employer suspended her from her job citing a vague social media policy? Where was the boycott when actress and comedian Leslie Jones was harassed by trolls to the point of deleting her account for months?"[48] Within these digital spheres, the discourse surrounding successful, visible women of color speaks deeply to the oppressions of the millions without public platforms.

For Jemele Hill, success and prominence as a woman of color is particularly noteworthy within the male-dominated sports media world. Having negotiated multiple racial and gendered biases and oppressions during her twelve years at ESPN, Hill was one of the most visible and viable figures at the network. When Hill sent tweets criticizing Trump—and in one instance, calling him a white supremacist—ESPN issued a public statement and suspended her for two weeks. Yet Hill refused to back down from her hard-earned platform, later calling for NFL fans to boycott advertisers supporting the Dallas Cowboys and owner Jerry Jones for Jones's threat to bench players being disrespectful to the flag.[49] Three months later, Hill was reassigned to *The Undefeated*, ESPN's website covering the discourse at the intersection of race and sports. Hill's refusal to be silenced in the face of criticism engendered controversy and support; many questioned why white, male anchors in sports media frequently made public statements yet were rarely called into question. Friedman wrote that many in sports "like Hill, especially African-Americans, are cast as too stupid to step outside their area of expertise . . . [those leading] the crusade against ESPN's so-called 'liberal bias,' see the very presence of Hill—a black woman who isn't afraid to speak her mind—as an affront."[50] Despite years transcending racial and gendered biases in the sports media culture, Hill was once again reaffixed at the crux of intersectional oppression.

In an insightful reading of Leslie Jones's experience facing repetitive and invasive harassment from alt-right personality Milo Yiannopoulos, Onwuachi-Willig reiterated the significance of sexual violence and misconduct for intersectional identities. Sexual harassment imbued this online discourse, illustrating oppressions faced by women and men who deviate from dominant paradigms of appropriate gendered and racial identities. As Onwuachi-Willig suggests, this harassment "constituted intersectional race and sex harassment because it relied on both racial and gendered stereotypes of black women and involved racialized sexism against a black woman."[51] Jones is yet another woman of color abandoned in the discourse of change surrounding #MeToo because she is not so easily categorized. She is a public figure and classed accordingly. This success intersects with her marginalized position as a minority woman of color. Yet this is further tempered whereas U.S. women comprise the majority of the U.S. population. As an example, Jones reflects the intricacies of intersectional sexual violence and misconduct, especially when perpetrated on or by someone eluding the singular-identity stereotype.

Jemele Hill and Leslie Jones are two recent examples illustrating the nebulous borders of public outrage over sexual violence, misconduct, and discrimination—especially as it manifests across racial lines online. As Hill stated, "the outrage simply wasn't there for the Black women who were put in vulnerable positions by rich White men."[52] This discussion of a wall between white women and women of color is nothing new. This pattern of sexual abuse against all women is nothing new. The hope is that digital spaces can create something new: a foundational perspective on the multiple and intersectional experiences of sexism, racism, classism, colonialism, ableism, homophobia, and violence. As #MeToo gained international attention, it led to what Hill Collins called the "painstaking process of collecting the ideas and actions of 'thrown away' Black women."[53] While rescuing Burke's original cause echoes this complicated process, this is also symptomatic of a troubling ignorance or silencing of black women's activism for and by any marginalized group. When these groups are subjugated in their own campaigns, dominant forces continue to appropriate and mutate the original problems and cause. This occurs as the alleged silence from the marginalized community is used as an excuse to sustain the hegemony and pretend these oppressed voices are complicit in their victimization.[54]

Considering the stereotypes and stigmas surrounding women of color and complicity in victimization, one of the most contentious debates across Twitter regarding #MeToo emerges in Burke's continued calls for action against R&B artist R. Kelly. With multiple allegations over decades, Robert Kelly has persisted in financial and cultural success. This remains one of the driving discourses tied not only to issues of gender and sexual violence and misconduct, but to race specifically.

> R Kelly is the Harvey Weinstein of the music world & he needs to be treated as such, not least b/c there are more Weinsteins & Kellys out there
>
> —@emilylhauser, November 13, 2017

> Robert 'R' Kelly. One of the most notorious predators in entertainment. But somehow he's allowed to thrive. . . . I wonder why?
>
> —@TaranaBurke, October 25, 2017

Burke and many of the #MeToo voices also pointedly called for recognition when complicity and victim-blaming emerged in the discourse. When talk show host Wendy Williams commented that a thirteen-year-old girl had "let it go down" with R. Kelly, Burke fired back.

> It is disgraceful that as wide as your audience is and as many young girls, many Black girls watch your show that you would openly victim blame

like you did yesterday. You are the reason why we can't make headway in
our community around sexual violence

You are doing the very same thing that white folks do to our girls which
is forget that they are CHILDREN!!

—@TaranaBurke, January 26, 2018

Moving with and against this digital discourse, #MeToo opens a new
access point to understand the binaried formula of perpetrator/survivor in
cases of sexual violence and misconduct. Yet it accomplishes much more;
it opens doors to more complex discussions of victimization, complicity,
community, and power—especially against the backdrop of intersectional
oppression and identity. It also achieves results: in the wake of renewed
scrutiny galvanized by Burke's calls across #MeToo and the Lifetime docu-
mentary *Surviving R. Kelly*, Kelly was charged with ten counts of aggravated
criminal sexual abuse on February 22, 2019.

RECUPERATING THE 99 PERCENT

After actor Aurora Perrineau accused writer Murray Miller of raping her
when she was seventeen, high-profile actor and writer Lena Dunham
rushed to the defense of Miller, one of her cowriters on *Girls*. Rather than
reprint Dunham's contentious apology, Burke's Twitter feed spoke directly
to the recurrent theme of white women rejecting the experiences of all the
marginalized voices they claim to speak for and stand beside.

People wonder why I keep saying "marginalized voices need to be centered" @lenadunham is the reason why. Maybe I should be more clear: BE-
LIEVE BLACK WOMEN. Both Dunham's statement and apology are trash.

I'm (*In) this whole "me too" vital (*viral) moment there have been two
Black women who have come forward with accusations: Lupita Nyong'o
& Aurora Perrineau. Both have been publicly rebuffed or questioned.

—@TaranaBurke, November 18, 2017

Feminist scholar Nancy Fraser suggests that feminism as it stands has
served as a handmaiden to capitalism.[55] As such, a transformation of a
"majority feminism" is necessary to address neoliberal capitalism *in addition to* patriarchal subjugation and systemic sexism. Fraser's concept of
"majority feminism" would shift from modern feminist concerns for white,
professional women advocating equality in the workplace to the 99 percent

of all other women. Lauding the recognition and advancement of a few women within the same patriarchal system has historically involved the oppression and exploitation of women of color. Majority feminism uproots the very mechanisms of that system "designed to privilege the few over the majority, men over women, white over people of color, rich over poor."[56] This remains a point of contention within #MeToo. The movement has consistently (and successfully) sounded its viral roar yet this has largely served white, privileged, classed, hetero, ciswomen's voices.

In reaching the traditionally excluded and oppressed through multiple platforms, digital technology and social media help communities create spaces to speak about their experiences, organize grass-roots campaigns, and build transformative movements. For people of color, digital access has opened discourse and progress. As Fang notes, "the internet's earliest digital activities were college students of color."[57] Hashtag activism has yielded power to the oft-stifled voices of students—especially minority, underrepresented, and underserved students. This led to notable activist movements beginning with #ConcernedStudent1950, a 2015 campaign from black students at the University of Missouri detailing the contentious atmosphere of on-campus racism. Students across the United States and eventually around the world responded with stories of racial injustice, inequality, and violence. Hashtag activism gave voice to these young people of color, uniting a national community aimed toward change.

Hashtag activism also creates visibility for people of color who fight for recognition. Digital spaces disrupt the status quo that disenfranchises and silences people of color, instead encouraging shared stories and goals that recall hooks's discussion of early feminist activism. Fang suggests that for people of color, digital technology has opened a canvas for the construction of an "alternative neighborhood of classrooms, theatres, and support groups where people of color are nurtured, not ignored."[58] While it is challenging for any singular mode of technology or individual source of activism to change the world, social media and hashtag activism are expanding revolutionary possibilities for marginalized communities.

When Burke reiterates the importance of "Me Too" in letting women, "particularly young women of color know that they are not alone," there is an echo of the consistent infiltration and appropriation of black culture for the "greater good" or the "larger cause." Despite carving out safe spaces for this conversation, women of color often find themselves ignored and displaced from a dialogue they created for their specific lived experiences. Thus, "Me Too"/#MeToo works in two ways: it serves as a growing platform for multiple voices speaking out against a problem that continues despite progress, and it serves as a reminder that minority voices may find their conversation hijacked and whitewashed at the cost of that amplified communication.

As popular feminism gains ground across physical and social media spaces, engaging greater audiences and garnering more attention for girls and women across various academic, professional, and cultural spheres, the goal of equality shapes much of the discourse. Yet as Banet-Weiser and Miltner note, "only particular women have access to 'leaning in' in the first place; gendered dynamics of power intersect with racial dynamics so that women of color are structurally inhibited to an even greater degree."[59] Rape culture thrives on the stereotypes of hypersexualization embedded in cultural language and representation, especially for marginalized communities. This becomes "particularly exacerbated for women of color and indigenous women, who experience the highest rates of sexual assault, statistics that clearly outline the remnants of colonization and slavery's categorical devaluing of black and brown bodies."[60]

Like many social media movements, #MeToo has accomplished unprecedented recognition and provoked significant discourse. Arguably, this present attention is due in large part to the public faces and voices involved in the campaign. Yet the depth and impact of #MeToo was built long ago by women of color. It may be too soon to judge the long-term impact of #MeToo, especially as the movement faces backlash and criticism at all levels of the sociopolitical system. Yet in considering Fraser's aim toward "majority feminism" and Burke's goal of reaching underserved and silenced communities, #MeToo offers an opportunity to consider intersectional identities of class, race, sexuality, ethnicity, embodiment, and gender. Individual survivors must map out their own paths toward healing. For many women of color, often suffering prejudice and oppression from the justice system, there are attempts to reimagine the possibilities of justice on their own terms. #MeToo crafted an outlet beyond those designated lines of justice, driven by an activist woman of color, and reaching the girls and women of color within her community. This may offer the strongest foundation for building a far-reaching, long-lasting legacy echoing Burke's call of "Me Too."

NOTES

1. Maddie Kilgannon, "Anita Hill and Tony Goldwyn Talk Activism in Hollywood at Brandeis University," *Globe Correspondent*, June 10, 2018, https://www.bostonglobe.com/lifestyle/names/2018/06/10/anita-hill-and-tony-goldwyn-talk-activism-hollywood-brandeis-university/WcRWm45Gpr4w3tMno0ozTK/story.html.

2. Sikivu Hutchinson and Ashunda Norris, "#MeToo in Our Schools: Hearing Black Girls in the Sexual Abuse Backlash," *Huffington Post*, January 2, 2018, https://www.huffingtonpost.com/entry/metoo-in-our-schools-hearing-black-girls-in-the-sexual_us_5a4bab2de4b0d86c803c7994#.

3. Asha Bandele, interview by The Race Card, *Afropunk*, March 27, 2018, https://afropunk.com/2018/03/poet-asha-bandele-metoo-white-women-never-led-movement-secured-people-outside.

4. Michael A. Peters and Tina Besley, "Weinstein, Sexual Predation, and 'Rape Culture': Public Pedagogies and Hashtag Internet Activism," *Educational Philosophy and Theory* (2018), 1–7, https://doi:10.1080/00131857.2018.1427850.

5. Stephanie M. Wildman and Adrienne D. Davis, "Language and Silence: Making Systems of Privilege Visible," in *Critical Race Theory: The Cutting Edge*, ed. Richard Delgado (New York: New York University Press, 1995), 573–78.

6. Angela Onwuachi-Willig, "What About #UsToo? The Invisibility of Race in the #MeToo Movement," *Yale Law Journal* 128 (2018): 119.

7. Tom Postmes and Suzanne Brunsting, "Collective Action in the Age of the Internet: Mass Communication and Online Mobilization," *Social Science Computer Review* 20, no. 3 (2002): 295.

8. Darren Lenard Hutchinson, "Identity Crisis: 'Intersectionality,' 'Multidimensionality,' and the Development of an Adequate Theory of Subordination," *Michigan Journal of Race & Law* 6 (2001): 295.

9. Hutchinson, "Identity Crisis," 295.

10. Hutchinson, "Identity Crisis," 308.

11. Patricia Hill Collins, *Black Feminist Thought: Knowledge, Consciousness, and the Politics of Empowerment* (New York: Routledge, 2000), 12.

12. Kimberlé Crenshaw, "Mapping the Margins: Intersectionality, Identity Politics, and Violence Against Women of Color," *Stanford Law Review* 43, no. 6 (1991): 1246.

13. Tarana Burke, "The Real Woman Behind 'Me Too,'" *Root*, December 6, 2017, video, 3:16, https://twitter.com/theroot/status/938427427096793090?lang=en.

14. Alice Walker, *In Search of Our Mother's Gardens: Womanist Prose* (San Diego, CA: Harcourt Brace Jovanovich, 1983).

15. Walker, *In Search*, xi.

16. Angela Y. Davis, "Rape, Racism and the Capitalist Setting," *Black Scholar* 9, no. 7 (1978): 24–30, https://doi:10.1080/00064246.1978.11414005.

17. Angela Y. Davis, *Women, Race and Class* (New York: Random House, 1981), 4.

18. Maxine Baca Zinn and Bonnie Thornton Dill, "Theorizing Difference from Multiracial Feminism," *Feminist Studies* 22, no. 2 (Summer 1996): 321–31.

19. Hill Collins, *Black Feminist Thought*, 221–38.

20. Hutchinson, "Identity Crisis," 302.

21. Onwuachi-Willig, "#UsToo?" 107; Meritor Savings Bank v. Vinson, 477 U.S. 57 (1986); DeNeen L. Brown, "She Said Her Boss Raped Her in a Bank Vault. Her Sexual Harassment Case Would Make Legal History," *Washington Post*, October 13, 2017, https://www.washingtonpost.com/news/retropolis/wp/2017/10/13/she-said-her-boss-raped-her-in-a-bank-vault-her-sexual-harassment-case-would-make-legal-history/?utm_term=.338f649cf051; Katherine Giscombe, "Sexual Harassment and Women of Color," *Catalyst*, February 13, 2018, http://www.catalyst.org/blog/catalyzing/sexual-harassment-and-women-color.

22. As quoted in Athena D. Mutua, "Multidimensionality Is to Masculinities What Intersectionality Is to Feminism." *Nevada Law Journal* 13, no. 341 (2016): 349.

23. Peter Kwan, "Jeffrey Dahmer and the Cosynthesis of Categories," *Hastings Law Journal* 48 (1997): 1280–81.

24. Mutua, "Multidimensionality," 356.

25. Crenshaw, *Mapping*, 1242.

26. Peggy Phelan, *Unmarked: The Politics of Performance* (London: Routledge, 1993), 10.

27. Hill Collins, *Black Feminist Thought*, 202.

28. bell hooks, *Feminism Is for Everybody* (London: Pluto Press, 2000).

29. Hill Collins, *Black Feminist Thought*, 204.

30. Crenshaw, *Mapping*, 1298.

31. Hill Collins, *Black Feminist Thought*, 210.

32. Achola O. Pala, "Introduction," in *Connecting Across Cultures and Continents: Black Women Speak Out on Identity, Race and Development*, ed. Achola O. Pala (New York: United Nations Development Fund for Women, 1995), 9.

33. Julia Wells, "Maternal Politics in Organizing Black South African Women: The Historical Lessons," in *Sisterhood, Feminisms, and Power: From Africa to the Diaspora*, ed. Obioma Nnaemeka (Trenton, NJ: Africa World Press, 1998), 251–62.

34. Hill Collins, *Black Feminist Thought*, 6.

35. Hazel V. Carby, *Reconstructing Womanhood: The Emergence of the Afro-American Woman Novelist* (New York: Oxford University Press, 1987).

36. Zahara Hill, "A Black Woman Created the 'MeToo' Campaign against Sexual Assault 10 Years Ago," *Ebony*, October 18, 2017, https://www.ebony.com/news/black-woman-me-too-movement-tarana-burke-alyssa-milano/#axzz4wZFsGz2q.

37. Crenshaw, *Mapping*, 1298.

38. As quoted in Baca Zinn and Thornton Dill, "Theorizing Difference," 329.

39. Hill, "A Black Woman," https://www.ebony.com/news/black-woman-me-too-movement-tarana-burke-alyssa-milano/#axzz4wZFsGz2q.

40. Caroline Grell, "The Fight for Equality: The Role of Latino Stereotypes in *Jane the Virgin*," *Elon Journal of Undergraduate Research in Communications* 8, no. 1 (Spring 2017): 37.

41. Amal Al-Malki, David Kaufer, Suguru Ishizaki, and Kira Dreher, *Arab Women in Arab News: Old Stereotypes and New Media* (Doha: Bloomsbury Qatar Foundation Publishing, 2012), xiii.

42. Shruti Mukkamala and Karen Suyemoto, "Racialized Sexism/Sexualized Racism: A Multimethod Study of Intersectional Experiences of Discrimination for Asian American Women," *Asian American Journal of Psychology* 9, no. 1 (2018): 32–46.

43. Davis, *Women, Race, and Class*, 4.

44. Crenshaw, *Mapping*, 1240.

45. Hutchinson and Norris, "#MeToo in Our Schools."

46. Malika Saada Saar, Rebecca Epstein, Lindsay Rosenthal, and Yasmin Vafa, *The Sexual Abuse to Prison Pipeline: The Girls' Story*, Report, Georgetown Law Center on Poverty and Inequality; Human Rights Project for Girls; Ms. Foundation for Women, Washington, DC, 2015: 5.

47. Saar et al., *Prison Pipeline*, 13.

48. Hill, "A Black Woman."

49. Jones's policy and Hill's response occurred as part of the larger discourse on NFL Quarterback Colin Kaepernick's protests of taking a knee during the "Star-Spangled Banner."

50. Nathaniel Friedman, "What Jemele Hill's Critics Don't Realize about Them-selves," *GQ*, September 14, 2017, https://www.gq.com/story/jemele-hill-vs-the-white-house.

51. Onwuachi-Willig, "#UsToo?" 116.

52. Hill, "A Black Woman."

53. Hill Collins, *Black Feminist Thought*, 2.

54. James C. Scott, *Weapons of the Weak: Everyday Forms of Peasant Resistance* (New Haven: Yale University Press, 2008).

55. Nancy Fraser, "How Feminism Became Capitalism's Handmaiden—and How to Reclaim it," *Guardian*, October 13, 2013, https://www.theguardian.com/comment isfree/2013/oct/14/feminism-capitalist-handmaiden-neoliberal.

56. Maryam Omidi, "The Many Faces of the #MeToo Backlash," *Public Seminar*, January 18, 2018, http://www.publicseminar.org/2018/01/the-many-faces-of-the-metoo-backlash.

57. Jenn Fang, "In Defense of Hashtag Activism," *Journal of Critical Scholarship on Higher Education and Student Affairs* 2, no. 1 (2016): 139.

58. Fang, "In Defense," 141.

59. Sarah Banet-Weiser and Kate M. Miltner, "#MasculinitySoFragile: Culture, Structure, and Networked Misogyny," *Feminist Media Studies* 16, no. 1 (2016): 172, https//doi:10.1080/14680777.2016.1120490.

60. Lauren Paulk and NCLR, "Sexual Assault in the LGBT Community," National Center for Lesbian Rights, April 30, 2014, http://www.nclrights.org/sexual-assault-in-the-lgbt-community.

CHAPTER 4

The Double Bind of Silenced Sexual Victimization in the LGBTQ+ Community

"Most of Us Were Never Taught the Language with Which to Understand the Experiences of Our Youth"

Women's March, January 2018. *Elyssa Fahndrich/Unsplash*

Unfortunate that he chose this as a coming out moment instead of focusing on allegation that he, as a man, did something horrid to a child.

—@JamilahLemieux, October 30, 2017

Minimizing, deflecting, denial, fake apology all = #rapeculture. I could
care less if he's attracted to Giraffes, as long as he has consent.

—@LydiaDYork, October 30, 2017

Yeah, that was a conflation by him. Being gay had nothing to do with
trying to have sex w/a child. The latter is the issue

—@alpha1906, October 30, 2017

Sorry, Kev-O, but the "I was drunk" explanation doesn't wash, whether
you're gay or straight.

—@KellybeeHTX, October 30, 2017

When actor Anthony Rapp openly accused actor Kevin Spacey of sexual misconduct, it unraveled a thread in the conversation of #MeToo. Following his
much-maligned apologia, media coverage detailed the allegations and the
downfall of Spacey—from director Ridley Scott scrubbing the actor out of
the finished film *All the Money in the World* to Spacey's termination from his
Emmy-nominated role in the award-winning Netflix series *House of Cards.*
Yet this attention focused on the headline-grabbing scandal of the popular
and famous actor's fall from grace rather than using the opportunity to hear
Rapp as a significant voice from the LGBTQ+ community—an opportunity
missed; mediated coverage treated this example as an anomaly to the overall formula of the movement.

The LGBTQ+ community, while increasing in visibility and acceptance
over the past twenty years, remains vulnerable to sexual predators bolstered
by a historical systemic bias and discrimination. In considering the growing
public discourse surrounding gender-based sexual violence, misconduct,
and misogyny, many within the LGBTQ+ community suffer a sense of cognitive dissonance as the nonbinary and noninclusive language and images
fail to represent their experiences of sexual trauma. The frequently espoused
statement surrounding sexual violence—from rape to harassment to abuse
and exploitation—is that these acts are not about sex but power. While
power is not a gendered term, as Stephens points out, "In the context of
sexual violence dialogue . . . the conversation is still highly gendered and
heteronormative."[1]

Social media activism and the acts of retweeting and resharing stories
from marginalized communities might help ensure that LGBTQ+ folk are

heard; "the same goes for calling out and challenging homophobia, trans-phobia and biphobia."[2] Yet many within the LGBTQ+ community do not have access to support systems and spaces to share stories of abuse, trauma, and survival. Speaking out against these violations might cost them other gains made in earning equality within their public lives. Further, many may simply prefer to maintain a privacy that "coming out" narratives have already demanded they relinquish to the public. Regardless of these choices of survival and endurance for LGBTQ+ folk, #MeToo must continue working to address those most at risk in order to truly recognize all survival stories.

While #MeToo's rapid ascension, sustained cultural relevance, and com-mitment to real-world change has elevated the movement as an enduring force, the surrounding coverage and language has yet to grant similar rec-ognition to sexual violence and misconduct in the LGBTQ+ community. The rapid rise of #MeToo and its leading voices might have shaped the movement without considering larger inclusivity—specifically for voices of LGBTQ+ folk. Considering the LGBTQ+ community within the context of the #MeToo movement, it must be recognized that "as with most disparities, holders of multiple marginalized identities are even more likely to experi-ence sexual violence."[3] The disparities surrounding intersectional identity and communal marginalization bear closer examination. To hear LGBTQ+ voices and how they speak with and to #MeToo, this chapter outlines quan-titative statistics and studies accounting for sexual violence and misconduct for the LGBTQ+ population, multifaceted oppressions and abuses faced by specific communities within the larger LGBTQ+ community, internalized biases and oppressions, the impacts of binaried language, and the platform created by and for the LGBTQ+ community as a counterpoint to #MeToo.

STATISTICS AND SILENCE

In mainstream academia's relatively slow turn to acknowledge and analyze studies in the specific experiences of LGBTQ+ folk, early quantitative studies produced statistics recognizing the prevalence of sexual violence and mis-conduct within the LGBTQ+ community. In their analysis of seventy-one peer-reviewed, published articles, Rothman, Exner, and Baughman con-firmed that not only is sexual violence more prevalent within the LGBTQ+ communities, but that these individuals may be at higher risk for victimiza-tion as compared to hetero or cis populations.[4]

In 2017, the Centers for Disease Control and Prevention (CDC) released a comprehensive report covering sexual and physical violence, abuse, and harassment within the LGBTQ+ community from 2010 to 2012. It included the following statistics:

- Forty-four percent of lesbians and 61 percent of bisexual women experience rape, physical violence, and/or stalking by an intimate partner as opposed to 35 percent of heterosexual women.
- Thirty-seven percent of bisexual men report rape, physical violence, and/or stalking by an intimate partner; 29 percent of heterosexual men report these abuses.
- Forty percent of gay men and 47 percent of bisexual men experience sexual violence or abuse other than rape.[5]

In addition to the CDC survey, the National Center for Transgender Equality published a 2015 report revealing that nearly half of the respondents representing the trans community had been sexually assaulted in their lifetimes.[6]

Illustrating the impact of silencing surrounding sexual assault in general and assault perpetrated on the LGBTQ+ community specifically, the Association of American Universities (AAU) released one of the most far-reaching surveys conducted regarding college campus sexual assault.[7] The survey was published amid national attention to the issues of sexual assault and violence in collegiate settings—including the Obama administration's investigation of more than 130 postsecondary institutions accused of violating Title IX.[8] Although focused specifically on college and university campuses, the AAU survey moved beyond the 2010 CDC study; it illustrated the elevated rates of sexual assault, harassment, and exploitation in the LGBTQ+ community. While the significantly higher rates of sexual assault, harassment, and intimate partner violence (IPV) might have come as no surprise to the LGBTQ+ community, Green and Wong noted, "One aspect of the results that may be surprising, at least when considering how little the topic has figured in commentary on and coverage of the problem, is the degree to which LGBT students report being victims of sexual harassment."[9] According to the AAU survey, three out of every four LGBTQ+ collegiate students reported sexual harassment. When categorized according to gender, the respondents who do not identify as binaried (including transgendered students, genderqueer and nonconforming students, or questioning students) experienced rape at the highest rates.

Reasserting the dearth of scholarship on sexual violence and misconduct within the LGBTQ+ community, the AAU survey results were "based on student responses, [and while] still empirically limited, they do offer more information than most existing research."[10] One of the most important pieces of information is the direct contradiction with the 2015 *Inside Higher Ed* survey finding that nearly one-third of college and university presidents believe that sexual assault is prevalent on nationwide campuses (and the majority of those presidents believed it was not an issue on their *own* governed campuses).[11] Yet the AAU survey indicated that approximately 50–75 percent of students in the twenty-seven institutions did report a form of sexual violence or misconduct. Because only about a quarter of the 150,000 AAU survey respondents who'd endured forms of sexual harassment or violence reported these incidents in an official capacity, the AAU results augmented voices previously unaccounted for in official statistics taken from formal reports.

For this qualitative exploration of the discourse surrounding marginalized communities in the wake of #MeToo, the data collection reinforces the need for further scholarship regarding sexual violence and misconduct perpetrated against LGBTQ+ folk. Whereas many earlier studies grouped LGBTQ+ individuals together, Rothman, Exner, and Baughman argued for future studies to "disaggregate and present separate data for lesbians, gays and bisexuals."[12] These considerations could craft an empirical approach that might yield estimates more comparable to hetero, binaried, and cis populations. While the narratives of the LGBTQ+ communities facing sexual violence and misconduct differ widely, my aim here is not only to draw comparisons with and against hetero and cis narratives of #MeToo, but to pay attention to the varied and intersectional experiences of multiple identities within the larger LGBTQ+ community. To accomplish this, I draw upon the long-range studies capturing information for specific populations within the LGBTQ+ community—thus working toward a sense of academic rigor amid the available literature. Exploring the stories of individuals within the larger LGBTQ+ community creates a more multifaceted resistance against sexual violence and misconduct.

MULTIFACETED OPPRESSION

Questioning the silencing or shaming that emerges as a double bind for members of the LGBTQ+ community resituates the onus on those who've already carried burdens of oppression and discrimination. This, too, is a reassertion of systemic privilege that demands victims to explain or voice themselves rather than assigning blame to the perpetrators and predators of the violence and misconduct. Until a relatively recent and brief moment in human history, sexual predators, misogynists, and homophobes have rarely been asked to "come out" as such. While legislation and social justice projects like #MeToo are transforming this, for marginalized communities with less visibility and voice, it is still a situation in which the cost of speaking out marks them as targets and robs them of their dignified privacy. Multidimensional[13] and race-sexuality theoretical[14] approaches have expanded intersectional research by including and exploring the terrain of heterosexist subordination—in addition to race, gender, and class. The consideration of sexual orientation and identity reveals the particularities of experience

within the LGBTQ+ community in facing multiple oppressions and negotiating intersectional identities.

Despite participation within #MeToo, many within the LGBTQ+ community do not feel that the movement reflects their experiences or listens
to their voices. When the formulaic or stereotypical images of #MeToo are
cast into narratives and images of white, straight, cis women speaking out
against powerful, wealthy, older men, it diminishes the unique double bind
of shame and silence for the LGBTQ+ community in relation to sexual violence and misconduct. Multiple studies pointing to the LGBTQ+ community as one of the most at-risk populations and the omission of these narratives produces harmful contradictions. When #MeToo coverage elevates
one formula over the multiple intersectional experiences of marginalized
individuals and communities, it costs survivors from disadvantaged backgrounds, survivors of color, differently abled survivors, non-Western survivors, and LGBTQ+ survivors the same opportunity to share their stories.

Considering the specific LGBTQ+ concerns in the context of #MeToo, in
addition to all that could and should be done to support the community,
there remains a dire need to hold responsible the abusers, rapists, harassers, perpetrators, and bystanders alike. As Segalov states, there must be a
recognition of "the culture of sexual assault and violence that exists in our
community, as it does in others, and hold perpetrators to account. Assault
is assault, and rape is rape. That isn't the 'freedom' our community fought
for."[15] Celebrating the liberated and progressive forces that have marked the
LGBTQ+ community in the past two decades, sexual and romantic freedom
can be elevated while recognizing and calling out the necessity of consent.

Countering the stereotypical images and narratives of sexual violence
and misconduct manifests in consideration of LGBTQ+ folk. Just as victims
of abuse do not conform to narrowly defined identities, perpetrators and
bigots appear in drastically different manifestations.

> People you trusted not wanting to shake your hand anymore because
> "who knows where you put that." The German Red Cross not wanting
> your blood because apparently every trans person is a drug addicted
> prostitute.
> Lesbians labeling you as an "it"
>
> —@reddopasta, August 18, 2018[16]

As Stephens suggests, "toxic masculinity is not exclusive to cisgender, heterosexual men . . . cisgender lesbians and trans men can also be misogynistic
and/or abusive . . . we are all socialized in rape culture, regardless of our identities."[17] Incorporating LGBTQ+ communities into the conversation will not
only open the discourse but increase awareness of the multiple, varied forces
that allow, perpetrate, survive, resist, and prevent human abuses everywhere.

Fetishization

When misrepresentations and biases shape predatorial perceptions of LGBTQ+ folk, it creates a framework in which individuals are reduced to harmful stereotypes. When marginalized communities are hypersexualized and stereotyped throughout history, these same individuals become further "victimized by a rape culture that tells those assaulted they are responsible for their sexual assaults."[18] Statistically, the most commonly fetishized groups within the LGBTQ+ community include bisexual and trans folk. In addition to a fetishization of LGBTQ+ people, homophobia and bigotry amplify hateful predators seeking to dehumanize those who are differently identified. Sexual violence and misconduct might become a punitive strategy for those experiencing hatred of that which they do not understand—especially if this is an aspect that they do not understand about themselves.

The progress and shortcomings of #MeToo in addressing the LGBTQ+ community stress the need to further interrogate the rape culture silencing all survivors. For example, "corrective rape," a particularly heinous form of sexual violence, emerges as a manifestation of sociopsychological predatorial impulses of a heterosexual who punitively rapes an LGBTQ+ person or uses rape as an attempt to alter someone's sexual orientation.

> TW: rape I made a new friend last October. We played truth or dare once and ended up kissing, so I again clarified how I was not attracted to him or any men. He decided to prove me wrong by repeatedly raping me from 2 a.m.-7 a.m. after getting me blackout drunk.
>
> —@trinchillaa[19]

This remains a specific form of sexual violence perpetrated on the LGBTQ+ community by bigoted, homo-, bi-, and transphobic predators. Yet this is not necessarily articulated or addressed within the domain of #MeToo. Nor are the multiplicity of specific predatory sexual and physically violent and harassing practices experienced by the individuals within the LGBTQ+ community.

> The phenomenon of "corrective rape," where—usually—men rape people who self-identify as queer, continues to this day . . . meanwhile, bisexual women are at increased risk of intimate partner violence in much of the developed world, with far higher rates of sexual assault, rape and physical assault. Male-dominated media tends to fetishize bisexual women, which can reinforce an association between bisexuality and sexual promiscuity. This often manifests in storylines that tacitly contribute to victim blaming when sexual and physical assault does occur. On top of this, the very act of bi-erasure does incredible violence to bisexual people.[20]

As Kaletsky states, "I'm already feeling vulnerable whenever I talk about sexual assault and rape culture—I can't feel liberated from the weight of misogyny if I'm simultaneously dealing with language that invalidates my gender identity."[21] Movements like #MeToo attempt to recuperate power and provide safe spaces away from damaging hegemonic oppressions and violence. However, without further efforts to destabilize and deconstruct the binaried nature of these conversations, hegemonic oppression and violence remains.

Bisexuality

> Coming out as bi:
> Most Dudes: Great, so, threesome?
> Most Chicks: Cool! So how hot do you think I am?
> Assorted lesbians: Sorry, I can't date you.
> Everyone else: Sooooo you're just a slut who can't decide?
>
> —ElizSchumacher, August 19, 2018

> Just remembered: Talking to then-best friend: "Well I can tolerate trans people, they're just born like that, but people who can't decide what gender they are are sick and just want to trick people." Couldn't stay friends after that.
>
> —@pandaer1k, August 17, 2018

Biphobia and objectification have turned bisexuality into a curiosity or fetish. Taking cues from pornography, popular culture has depicted bisexuality as a trope of willingness and display for the male gaze. These portrayals hold real-life implications when men internalize a sense of entitlement to the bisexual female figure.[22] Turning bisexuality into entertainment or pornography creates a fetishization justifying predatorial and entitled behaviors. This perception casts doubt on the sexual violence and misconduct against the bisexual community, while the claims made by these individuals become stifled against a context that refuses to take orientation seriously.

Despite claims that lesbians and bisexual women find greater acceptance than the rest of the LGBTQ+ community,[23] this is often the product of fetishization, specifically when femme lesbians and bisexuals are positioned as commodities or objects for consumption. As Paul wrote, "I find it crucial that we first separate acceptance from fetishization . . . fetishization reduces these women to things that are only wanted for consumption by a privileged group."[24] Because femme lesbians and bisexual women are often criticized by both their own communities and objectified by privileged groups, there remains a dire threat to their security; they are perceived as targets in need of "conversion" by men. This reiterates the prejudiced position that these women are not making choices based on their own desires and truths but as subordinated or confused women who simply need the guidance of a man.

When man irl and online tell me, that it's wrong to be queer. And, if I really wouldn't like to try it again with a man.

—@Marierriot, August 18, 2018[25]

Trans Community

[The Bathroom Debate™] "You should be glad you're not getting killed here for being that way, no need for extra privilege."

—@fanpersoningfox, August 18, 2018[26]

Because two-thirds of the trans population experiences sexual assault, LGBTQ+ activists have advocated for gender-neutral restrooms and facilities on academic campuses from elementary through postgraduate school. Thus, when fundamentalists argue against these safe spaces designated as gender-neutral—based on archaic stereotypes of transgendered or nonbinaried folk and their alleged predatory behaviors—it undermines and disparages the original motivation for these individuals to seek these spaces.

Correlating with the majority of hate crimes and violence, "transgender individuals are the most likely to be affected in the LGBT community. A staggering 64% of transgender people have experienced sexual assault" in their lifetimes.[27]

we [must] dedicate ourselves 2 centering intersectionality in our activism & holding many ideas in our minds at once, as hard as that can be . . . #s or political power shouldn't matter, our priority should b 2 center the experience of the most vulnerable ppl in relation to an issue. <3

—@QueerDSA, March 2, 2018

Trans women and men continue speaking up about sexual violence and misconduct, building the magnitude of #MeToo. Despite their contributions, the trans community often finds themselves displaced or alienated from the platform. Considering how survivors of sexual assault already face issues of victim-blaming and baseline disbelief, transgender survivors often encounter further barriers in disclosing their traumas. While white, hetero, cis, able-bodied women continue amassing mediated attention in the #MeToo movement, trans women and men are often marginalized from experiences that they have suffered through for everyday survival. Additionally, trans women and femmes face dual-oppression and internalization: they are either discounted as so undesirable that they could not be targeted for sexual violence or misconduct, or they are targeted directly as fetishized objects. In neither case does mainstream society speak to the reality of the trans community. When cis survivors fail to include trans women and femmes or educate themselves about the oppressions of binaried thought, it further alienates and oppresses marginalized communities—but it also stifles the growth of any activist movement. As Raquel Willis, activist with the Transgender Law Center, stated, "being able to claim womanhood on your own terms is powerful . . . as someone who moves through the world as a binary trans woman, I have an obligation and a duty to lift up folks who don't fit that script and who don't want to fit that script."[28] Much as Willis reasserts this for her own work as an activist and advocate, cis women too have a responsibility to lift others up, regardless of the script before them.

LGBTQ+ Youth

Despite #MeToo's viral reincarnation and sustained relevance, the mediated coverage of the movement remains inadequate in considering "the disproportionate impact of sexual harassment, assault, and relationship abuse on LGBTQ youth, who may not feel safe coming forward to say #MeToo because of social stigma and discrimination."[29] In considering the educational support systems in place for the LGBTQ+ community, several mention the challenges of growing up with few, if any, positive queer role models or guiding language and images surrounding healthy sexual and love partnerships. Lack of comprehensive and inclusive sex, health, and relationship education for all youth inevitably leads to confusion in recognizing sexual or intimate partner violence and harassment. Without education and guidance in navigating these already complicated dynamics, young LGBTQ+ individuals are further ostracized and silenced based on the multiple oppressions of homophobia, biphobia, transphobia, and coercive threats of identity disclosure or corrective rape.

A void in education and comprehensive language creates further obstacles for LGBTQ+ folk in #MeToo. Heteronormative vocabulary and representation plagues anti-harassment policies in education—despite the rampant sexual violence and harassment young LGBTQ+ individuals face in schools.[30] As a 2015 National School Climate Survey noted, approximately one in ten students reported an anti-harassment policy inclusive of sexual orientation, gender identity, and gender expression. Without the language to grapple with healthy or abusive sexual experiences, LGBTQ+ youth face difficulties educating themselves and learning from others. This is problematized further as "inclusive same-sex education in schools isn't mandatory, being LGBTQ+ doesn't often run in the family, and there are fewer role models to learn from . . . we navigate sex blindly."[31] The omission of comprehensive and inclusive sexual and relational education resonates in the following #MeQueer tweets:

Being years behind most of your peers in matters of sex and love. Having to constantly lie to those who are closest to you. Feeling your life would be over if your "secret" got out. Loneliness. These are things you learn being a child/adolescent and gay.

—@hivan76, August 25, 2018

When I grew up the word queer didn't exist in my vocabulary, ppl were either lesbian/gay or hetero. I felt I was "different," but I didn't know the words nonbinary + pan. Even gay was hardly ever subject of conversations except when it was about those dying in the 80s.

My whole teenage years I didn't know who else was not just hetero. Everyone in my surroundings was in the closet. So we have been so fucking lonely, bc we just didn't know this of each other.

—@MikaMurstein, August 18, 2018

Not having words when I was a kid for how I felt. Living in suburbia with conservative parents, Republicans, conservative family. Playing a role all the time, especially at home, knowing I wouldn't be accepted. Being called gay by kids as I walked home from school.

—@lo_down_woman, August 18, 2018

Another silencing mechanism emerges in the social stigma of LGBTQ+ partnerships and sex. Speaking out about sexual practices and abuses is thus already burdened with prejudice and risk; it reaffirms bigoted misunderstandings and stereotypes surrounding the LGBTQ+ community, often legitimizing further stigmatization. Questioning sexual assault and misconduct becomes problematic within gay culture, especially for coming-of-age gay men. In detailing "dark rooms"—spaces where anonymous men can meet within a club and engage in sexual activities—Segalov asks whether taking a step into these rooms automatically signifies consent: "There aren't necessarily right or wrong answers to all of these questions, but in the context of #MeToo these are conversations that need to be had."[32] Despite the progress made in recent years, the long reach of history proves how centuries of taboo, stereotyping, and criminalization have embedded biases against the sexual and romantic partnerships of the LGBTQ+ community.

Despite these challenges, LGBTQ+ youth continue striving for recognition and representation. Many have shared their #MeToo stories and expressed gratitude for the movement's platform connecting people of all intersectional identities and marginalized community memberships. As LGBTQ+ folk contribute their own unique perspectives, narratives, and experiences to #MeToo, increased visibility of intersectional oppressions and misrepresentations emerges in the conversation.

INTERNALIZATION

The overwhelming force of systemic prejudice and discrimination against the LGBTQ+ community also prevents many from seeking help and protection from the institutions of law enforcement, hospitals, or crisis centers and shelters. For every public face of #MeToo, multiple citizens choose anonymity in survival. These individuals seek to protect their identities within small communities, save their livelihood, stave off threats of deportation or imprisonment, or save their lives. Similarly, many LGBTQ+ survivors do not seek help because they fear being "outed" or facing further discrimination or punitive violence—they are often looking for lifelines to survive.

Based on external oppression and internalized doubt, many LGBTQ+ folk fear sharing stories of sexual violence and misconduct. For communities already pathologized and stereotyped as sexually uncontrollable or sinful, there are increased feelings of anxiety in sharing these details. Intersectional pressures shape the silenced voices of marginalized communities within the #MeToo movement. Greater awareness of these issues is necessary—not only from the movement and its leaders, but from legislation, education, and all other institutions that have turned their backs for far too long on the unique problems of the LGBTQ+ community.

The further silencing of the LGBTQ+ community emerges as many believe (and have been taught) that their experiences or traumas will be invalidated, mocked, or shamed. When LGBTQ+ sexual violence and misconduct is misrepresented, underrepresented, or not represented, it becomes even more challenging for survivors to come forward. In addition to fearing that their claims will not be recognized, many LGBTQ+ individuals are inhibited from speaking out as "they felt defined solely by their identity—to the extent that any sort of abuse they experienced must somehow be connected to their gender or sexuality rather than an issue of general relationship violence."[33] When the institutions intended to protect and educate are perceived as ineffectual or biased against marginalized communities, they fail everyone in this fight.

When assaults are perpetrated by LGBTQ+ community members, this further constricts the voices of survivors. Because many LGBTQ+ populations within the larger sociopolitical umbrella are quite close-knit, "survivors of assault may not know where to turn, either because they fear they will not be believed or supported, or because they do not want to malign another member of the community or reinforce negative stereotypes."[34] Additionally, seeking traditional institutional services again requires a "coming out"—whether the individual already has or has yet to process this life-changing and life-affirming moment.

Considering the pipelines of abuse for the LGBTQ+ community, the impact of hegemonic masculine oppression has far-reaching effects. Homosexual male survivors of sexual violence and misconduct are often subjected to a double victimization. When hegemonic institutions affix deviant labels to homosexual, bisexual, and nonbinaried men, it is an indictment of their alleged failure within the heteronormative structure. Despite LGBTQ+ youth representing 5 to 7 percent of the general population, they comprise 13 to 15 percent of young people who encounter the juvenile justice system.[35] This marginalization further alienates male rape survivors—especially as institutional police, judicial, and counseling systems may not understand or offer the appropriate services to these boys and men based on sexual orientation or gendered identity.

As Lu suggests, "more attention needs to be paid to people of marginalized or underrepresented groups in order to truly reduce stigma and create an open dialogue about consent as it pertains to all different types of relationships."[36] The culture of silence and shame surrounding sexual violence and misconduct often mirrors and magnifies the experiences of oppression faced by those within the LGBTQ+ community. #MeToo offers an ideal moment to rupture this double bind and encourage greater legislation, education, and cultural awareness surrounding LGBTQ+-inclusive sexual and relationship violence and misconduct.

While much of the discourse surrounding #MeToo speaks directly to the spectrum of possible abusive, misogynist, and inappropriate behaviors and attitudes, the #MeToo movement must take the next step in inclusivity by scrutinizing all abuses and forms of misconduct across the intersectional spectrum of survivors and perpetrators.

BINARIED LANGUAGE

Writing shortly after Milano's first tweet on October 15, 2017, Rodriguez-Cayro detailed how many members of the LGBTQ+ community felt excluded from the viral wave and mediated coverage of #MeToo. Despite the active response and participation of LGBTQ+ folk in #MeToo, "some members of LGBTQ community feel that the campaign focuses too strongly on the gender binary, and seems to erase nonbinary or genderqueer people from the conversation."[37] This emerged not through any explicit rejection of these voices, but from the use of the language involved in the movement and the ensuing media coverage.

> As we see all the #MeToo statuses, let's remember that #trans and #nonbinary folks are often those most impacted by #rapeculture.
>
> —@therapistnicole, October 16, 2017

> Really disappointed at the lack of LGBTQ+ inclusion in #metoo [emoji]. It's not just men and women [emoji] check your language
>
> —@YogicAmnesiac, October 18, 2017

Considering the inherent bias within language, many shift the movement to address how common narratives about sexual assault, abuse, and exploitation remain binaried. These confines of language remain, despite the high rates of sexual violence and misconduct directly impacting the LGBTQ+ community. Transforming our use and understanding of language offers a powerful step in inclusivity for nonbinary and trans people.

Even as institutions strive for inclusivity, the legacy of heteronormative and binaried language informs progressive legislation. For example, the U.S. Violence Against Women Act of 2013 extended nondiscrimination protections to the LGBTQ+ community in providing domestic and sexual violence resources. Yet the fact that this "progressive" act used the binaried term of "women" and simultaneously applied the legislation to the LGBTQ+ community illustrates the void of communicative sensitivity and cultural competency undermining service and support for all survivors of sexual violence and misconduct.

Rather than sweep over the voices of intersectionality, #MeToo must now use its platform to assess and address how we use communication within the discourse of sexual violence and misconduct. Activist movements must consider inclusivity in language and representation. When there is a void of voices and language for nonbinaried individuals, it inhibits their participation in the conversation. This creates a barrier; entering safe spaces designated for "women" might cause discomfort and disruption. Yet it also blocks nonbinaried folk from adding their voices when they must relinquish nonbinary aspects of identity to enter those spaces. If sharing narratives automatically assigns a gender or identity to nonbinary individuals, this becomes a moment of misidentification or misrepresentation. Faced with these multiple oppressions and negotiations, many opt not to share stories at all. Rather than participate in a conversation seemingly ambivalent or ignorant of nonbinary and inclusive language, many refuse to dedicate themselves to causes and organizers that cannot reciprocate and respect this commitment. This creates a void for LGBTQ+ survivors. Where is that safe space of inclusivity?

#MEQUEER

Rather than accept the shame or blame for failing within dominant or heteronormative models, queer and marginalized figures might take up alternative routes that critique oppressive structures. As Halberstam suggests, exploring this terrain demands a detour from "the confines of conventional knowledge and into the unregulated territories of failure, loss, and unbecoming."[38] When mainstream discourse or media coverage disregard the experiences of the LGBTQ+ community as inauthentic and dictate the terms of sexual violence and misconduct through heteronormative images and voices, marginalized individuals might still actively create and pursue new goals apart from the chains of hegemonic and heteronormative language.

#MeToo may have led the movement in awareness against sexual violence and misconduct, yet within that overwhelming sea of voices, many marginalized groups have been drowned out. As such, multiple communities have found their own safe spaces through hashtags that use inclusive language to address sexual and physical misconduct directly in the unique context of intersectional identity and marginalization.

One fascinating response or evolution of #MeToo emerged in #MeQueer. Originating in London as a platform to share narratives of sexual, physical, and emotional abuse, sexism, homophobia, violence, and misconduct, writer Hartmut Schrewe was inspired to create #MeQueer after hearing his husband mention him as a "buddy" to a work colleague. Schrewe's hashtag incited a global firestorm with LGBTQ+ individuals and allies contributing to the viral movement. Some #MeQueer responses detailed confiding in and coming out to family and friends—the support or rejection faced in these moments:

> @LenaTwittOrt: Secretly watching Brokeback Mountain at night together with my grandfather. Grandma mustn't know. Asking him why he's crying. "It's horrible that people don't understand that you don't choose who you love."

> @hivan76: Seeing your partner attacked and covered in blood. Feeling friends and family's love is conditional. Having your partner referred to as a friend. Not having your relationships taken seriously. Realising 25 years later problems stem from living in constant fear growing up

> @finebiene: When I came out to my grandma, I told her I didn't know how to tell my grandpa and uncle since they said some homophobic things in the past. She told me not to worry about it, she'll take care of it. I never faced any negativity from them after that.

Others tweeted the discriminatory, ignorant, and vile quotes indelibly etched into their minds.

> @greenwhitebobo: "I've got nothing against homosexuals. I'm a music teacher, there are lots of gays & lesbians I work with for theater." "What about bisexuals?" "Oh heck no. They freak me out—choose one side already!" My host mom during my 2nd stay in the US. I left shortly after.

> @Alex_Basti_: "You're gay? You're a piece of shit! Go and kill yourself!" [Next tweet]: My former best friend said this to me after my coming out.

@EternalEien: "So you're gay, hey it's your life. I like some gays: nothing wrong with 2 women getting it on, it's nice to look at and gets me hard for when sex ACTUALLY starts! Now, 2 men rubbing their dicks together or whatever, that's just disgusting tho!"

In a flashy intro exploring the boon of #MeQueer, Smith writes, "Move over women and #MeToo movement, the LGBT community wants a piece of the action and their share of the limelight with their very own #MeQueer hashtag to condemn their own experiences of verbal abuse, sexual attack and physical violence."[39] While the attention to #MeQueer is well deserved, the reductionist language employed operates on the assumption that these social media movements are mere grabs at the public spotlight. A critique linked to the public/private issues raised in the second chapter, this misrepresents these causes. Raising awareness and voicing experience on a social media platform often leads to increased coverage and representation; this is rarely a reward for that "piece of the action" but a reiteration of the cost for so many survivors of sexual violence and misconduct. These are not typically people seeking the "limelight" but rather those who've suffered the oppressive force of silencing and shaming practices in the aftermath of these traumas.

As social movements like #MeToo grow, limitations become evident in the centralized positioning of hetero, cisgender women. This excludes and "erases the lived realities of those whose gender identity and expression leave them at their most vulnerable—trans and gender-nonbinary people."[40] #MeToo and #MeQueer are not intended to grab "a piece of the action" but to create shelters where victims of sexual violence and misconduct can unite in the telling of their narratives. The international, viral responses might generate intense media coverage for these movements; however, this magnitude is not intended for that coverage but is representative of the sheer volume of individuals who have experienced and suffered these sexual traumas. The following #MeQueer tweets indicate the depth and difference of these experiences, while illustrating their significance for all involved in these conversations.

My ex best friend texted me over Instagram "You're lesbian cuz you are depressed." Gal, I'm even more gay when I'm fucking happy.

—@v_shinodasquad, August 20, 2018

My wife after the Pulse shooting in Orlando: "I'd rather get shot for holding your hand than not holding it at all." We live in Texas.

—@MarleneNovalis, August 20, 2018

Subjectivities that refuse to conform to normalization or universalization perform disidentification for survival and creation, resistance and innovation.[41] Rather than conform to hegemonic and heteronormative ideologies driving the larger #MeToo movement and media coverage, many members of the international LGBTQ+ community have instead created a new space of narratives reflecting marginalized and intersectional experiences and oppressions. Cultivating a forum like #MeQueer simultaneously pays tribute and culturally critiques the heteronormative, binaried approach to sexual violence and misconduct. In resisting further allegiance to a movement that fails to address intersectional and marginalized experiences of the LGBTQ+ community, #MeQueer also rejects dominant modes of power that offer only one representation of sexual violence and misconduct.

These spaces beyond heteronormative visibility resonate with the repressed. As Edelman suggests, queerness assumes this "figural status as resistance to the viability of the social while insisting on the inextricability of such resistance from every social structure."[42] Bound to the dominant social structure, queerness still counters the forces propelling that structure. This underscores the active critique of #MeToo—a commanding movement that the LGBTQ+ community is bound to even as its marginalization demands active resistance and alternate spaces. Springing from the margins, queerness creates an absent presence challenging prevailing paradigms. Similarly, the LGBTQ+ community and social media movements like #MeQueer possess an ephemerality that erases as it traces. This erasure of memory is key to the appeal and identity of #MeQueer, illuminating the power in the temporary, fleeting, and of-the-moment.

Queering the stereotypical representations of sexual violence and misconduct rejects sociopolitical ideologies of visibility. Through marginalized representational strategies and language, LGBTQ+ individuals can instead reveal the power of disappearance and absence beyond mainstream attention and heteronormative representation. When the framework of heteronormative privilege fails or ignores queer resistance, the spaces beyond those mainstream activisms open up to a compelling and progressive resistance of marginalized narratives, vocabularies, and identities.

A WORTHY GOAL

The heteronormative gendered framing of sexual violence and intimate partner violence holds a negative impact not only on the LGBTQ+ community but on any movement against human rights violations. Throughout the research of this chapter, I became increasingly unnerved by the wide body of literature criticizing the lack of scholarship studying sexual violence and misconduct on the LGBTQ+ community.[43] As Stephens notes, "I thought that if *The Huffington Post*, *National Geographic*, and *Vice News* were reporting on LGBTQ issues, I should not have any problems finding articles in mainstream sociology journals. I was wrong."[44] Much of the scholarship relating to issues of IPV, sexual assault, harassment, or abuse can be found in LGBTQ+-specific academic journals. While the work being done in this field of academia is largely progressive, rigorous, and often engaged directly with the voices of the community, this overlooks the continuing tradition of silence and omission. Silence within the academic community signifies that LGBTQ+ folk are not a population worthy of study and that their voices and experiences cannot contribute to the discourse. When historically progressive forces such as liberal arts scholarship or grassroots movements fail to recognize and explore the unique circumstances and experiences of marginalized communities like the LGBTQ+ population, greater understanding and activism also fails.

Rothman, Exner, and Baughman stress that summary findings in their comprehensive research are limited by the accuracy of the aggregated studies upon which their work is based. Yet this remains only "a starting point for assessing the nature and quality of the available literature . . . improving the rigor of sexual violence research in general, and studies of GLB sexual violence victimization specifically, is a worthy goal."[45] The #MeToo movement has increased cultural and critical scholarship engaging with the impact of sexual violence and misconduct. Now it is time for a similar surge in academic attention paid to intersectional oppressions and abuses faced by the LGBTQ+ community.

Returns to biological determinism have emerged to support anti-transgender arguments such as the Trump administration's proposal limiting the definition of gender as an immutable and biological condition determined by one's genitalia at birth in the United States. This would impact multiple federal programs, including the Trump administration's Health and Human Services proposal of a Title IX revision defining sex as male or female and determined by biological sex at birth. As Williams notes, "at a time when the Trump administration appears to be pressuring federal agencies to not even say the word 'transgender,' it's critical that #MeToo helps to ensure that voices are not silenced."[46] While the #MeToo movement works to provide a safe space of shared narratives, media coverage tends to prioritize certain voices and images. This reasserts binaried representation and language that largely dismisses and omits the voices outside of these dichotomous spaces. Through the inclusion of LGBTQ+ voices and images, the #MeToo movement could create new possibilities for deconstructing gendered and binaried language in the context of sexual violence and misconduct.

To tackle the unique issues facing the LGBTQ+ community, activists must consider a multi-pronged approach, starting with comprehensive sex, health, and relational education. Counseling, shelter, and guidance from community centers and leaders continue this support and education. To bolster either of these instrumental interventions, government funding and legislation is necessary. When inclusive sex and relationship education is not available to young members of the LGBTQ+ community and entrenched biases constrain the experiences of all members of this population, speaking out in mainstream society is challenging enough. Yet if #MeToo truly intends to disrupt and dismantle the hegemonic oppressions supporting and encouraging acts of sexual violence and misconduct, it must strive to provide the inclusive vocabulary and comprehensive education for members of the LGBTQ+ community.

Despite the growing vocabulary of inclusion surrounding multiple and intersectional identities, social media platforms—which as of this moment have given rise to a renaissance in activism—create limitations as well as opportunities. As Kaletsky notes, "sure, nonbinary-inclusive language is difficult to fit into a 140-character tweet, but without it, trans and nonbinary folks are subtly receiving the message that their voice might not be welcome."[47] Embodiment and identity are then lost to the hegemonic language structure—and rendered vulnerable to that systemic exploitation and oppression yet again.

> I'm so sick and tired about being told I'm only allowed to exist if I do so quietly and don't disturb heteronormative society invalidating anyone who doesn't fit the straight and narrow idea of what a human being should be! For fuck's sake!
>
> —@ConnieWiegand, August 18, 2018[48]

Language matters. Representation is real. Openly inviting—rather than assuming the cause is welcoming enough—survivors from all marginalized communities like the LGBTQ+ communities in which the language of the past ignores or diminishes identity becomes necessary for creating a space welcoming all. In raising awareness to eradicate sexual violence and misconduct, the #MeToo movement has been wildly successful. The goal originated in destroying hegemonic institutions that have marginalized and silenced women throughout history. This reckoning cannot be accomplished if the same marginalized and silenced women are subsequently marginalizing and silencing all survivors and supporters.

Considering the networks of power surrounding acts of sexual violence and misconduct, LGBTQ+ folk face multiple layers of victimization in addition to the trauma of abuse. While hetero, cis, and LGBTQ+ communities all experience forms of sexual and violent abuse ranging from stalking to rape to emotional threat, it is necessary to explore the additional tiers of victimization specific to the LGBTQ+ community. IPV often becomes perceived as a fair fight between same-sex couples when addressed in the institutions of law enforcement, social work, and counseling.[49] While hetero and cis-gendered populations might experience coercive control or threats based on existent power dynamics of gender relations, for the LGBTQ+ community, there are again deeper levels of control. As Stephens notes, "coercive control may include the threat of being outed, which may result in the loss of employment, housing or child custody."[50] Additionally, when sexual predators target LGBTQ+ and transgendered youth, this is a critical concern that resonates; these groups are often forced out of their homes, rejected from any familial support systems, and comprise growing homeless populations.[51] While many cast these as LGBTQ+-specific issues, these are necessary concerns for us all—especially for everyone interested in addressing the hegemonic systems maintaining unequal power relations that support the spread of sexual violence and misconduct.

Prism of Reckoning

Stigma, stereotypes, misrepresentation, and myths create a prism around the LGBTQ+ community in which truth is reflected and refracted by the biases, bigotry, ignorance, and fear of the privileged. These are the privileged who have too long controlled the narrative of normative and deviant. Willis reports: "I actually am a little aggravated with that conversation because I think there's still this idea that trans women are other from women's rights and women's issues."[52] This leads to the significance of conversations with cis women, feminists, and activists who have often overlooked or even generated damage to the trans community generally and trans women specifically. This remains but one dynamic of the much larger conversations surrounding the necessity of inclusion for the LGBTQ+ community in the discourse of #MeToo.

For LGBTQ+ folk, those prism walls have opened in recent years—slightly, but ever more so—unleashing the brilliance of diversity and intersectionality within a dynamic activist community. Yet even in a time of growing acceptance and celebration of LGBTQ+ individuals, sexual assault and abuse against this community continues rising.

> The LGBT+ community saved my life and I'm more than ready to fight like hell for those who did the same for me. We're family & a family looks out for one another 5/
>
> —@MadieRaybin, September 6, 2018[53]

> MeQueer:
> So . . . In Austria and Germany #MeQueer has been getting quite a bit of attention . . .
> But it's not for me to share my story here . . .
> It hurts too much, the wounds have not healed yet (and maybe they never will)

I have shared a bit on here, but the rest is for my friends 1/2
without who—I am quite sure—I wouldn't be here any more . . . Please,
listen to our stories, listen, even if it hurts, because we have to live with
this every day . . .

—@MeerderWorter, October 2, 2018[54]

Considering suggestions that mainstream advocacy and academia has at
best not recognized the experiences of the LGBTQ+ community and at worst
ignored these experiences completely, the impact of #MeToo has been felt
across all populations. The day prior to the historical mid-term U.S. elections of 2018, Leung wrote of #MeToo's massive impact on socio-politics:
"one response to the movement is the mobilization of LGBTQ individuals
to run for political office to fight sexual harassment and assault."[55] Among
the record-breaking number of political challengers from the LGBTQ+
community was Allison Dahle, who won the general election of the North
Carolina House seat in the 11th District after soundly defeating incumbent
Democratic Duane Hall in the primary. Hall had faced allegations of sexual
misconduct from five women. In Montana, candidate Amelia D. Marquez
won the Democratic primary with 65 percent of the vote and challenged Re-
publican candidate Rodney Garcia—convicted of domestic violence by his
ex-wife. Marquez hoped to become the first openly trans woman of color
seated in a state legislature in U.S. history. LGBTQ+ candidates emerged in
record numbers to run for office, with an unprecedented 240 of these candidates winning primaries. Following the 2018 mid-term elections, for the
first time in U.S. history, Jared Polis of Colorado became the first openly gay
man elected governor and Kate Brown became the first bisexual governor;
Sharice Davids became the first Native American and LGBTQ+ person to
represent Kansas in Congress; Angie Craig and Chris Pappas became the
first openly gay congresspeople representing Minnesota and New Hampshire, respectively. Additionally, New Hampshire elected two transgender
women—Gerri Cannon and Lisa Bunker—to the House of Representatives.

As members of the LGBTQ+ community continue carving paths toward
representation—through politics, culture, activism, academia, and multiple
arenas—a mainstay of their platforms and causes is the impetus to enact
legislation and raise awareness of sexual harassment and assault. In many
cases, "this fights the narrative that LGBTQ people are sexual predators, as
was perpetuated with the Briggs Initiative and continues to be argued today,
especially in bathroom bills that discriminate against transgender individuals."[56] While LGBTQ+ figures rise to fight on behalf of larger populations in
the face of multiple oppressions, it bears repeating that for many benefiting
from their hard-fought battles, it is crucial to include these voices within all
civil rights narratives.

Beyond actively queering the #MeToo movement in a critique of heteronormativity, #MeQueer further implodes binaries and expands vocabularies surrounding sexual violence and misconduct. The inclusion of
#MeQueer and LGBTQ+ narratives within #MeToo might help accomplish
a comprehensive interrogation of the heteronormative, hegemonic modes
of regulation, surveillance, oppression, and violence against marginalized
populations. A binaried representation of sexual violence and misconduct
of the male perpetrator violating the female victim limits our knowledge of
this pervasive problem. Further, it fails to offer the same strategic responses
that might recognize and provide safety for survivors of nonbinaried gender identities or sexual orientations. This informs individual psychological
responses to sexual assault, exploitation, rape, harassment, homophobia,
stalking, coercive control, biphobia, fetishization, misogyny, transphobia,
corrective rape, and the many, many other forms of sexual and physical
oppression and abuse. When individuals are never validated for their own
identity, educated with inclusive language of sexual and physical abuse, or
represented within the conversation of sexual violence and misconduct,
they question their own experiences through internalized blame, self-
doubt, and silence—the opposite ends of all that #MeToo seeks to accomplish for its survivors.

As one of the most visible movements seeking to dismantle these institutions and addressing sociopolitical imbalances that engender violence
against marginalized communities, #MeToo presents an opportunity
to intervene and include the LGBTQ+ community. In addressing the
heteronormative framing of sexual and intimate partner violence that
misrepresents these experiences as perpetrated solely on young, white,
cis, hetero women, the #MeToo movement can engage directly with the
LGBTQ+ community to hear their narratives of abuse as equal in weight
and unique in oppression. The LGBTQ+ community has gained visibility
and acceptance in multiple ways over recent years; this has helped ease the
trauma of invalidation, silence, and shame. Yet even as LGBTQ+ individuals find their voices on an international stage, #MeToo must also work to
grant representation to the specific and intersectional experiences of these
survivors—to validate, amplify, and proudly recognize a community that
can teach us all about survival.

NOTES

1. Sarah A. Stephens, "Research on Sexual and Intimate Partner Violence Should
Go Beyond Studying Only Cisgender, Heterosexual Men," *Inside Higher Ed*, October
20, 2017, https://www.insidehighered.com.

2. Steve Williams, "The #MeToo Movement Must Be LGBT-Inclusive to Succeed," *Care2Causes*, December 25, 2017, https://www.care2.com/causes/the-metoo-move ment-must-be-lgbt-inclusive-to-succeed.html.

3. Lauren Paulk and NCLR, "Sexual Assault in the LGBT Community," National Center for Lesbian Rights, April 30, 2014, http://www.nclrights.org/sexual-as sault-in-the-lgbt-community.

4. Emily F. Rothman, Deinera Exner, and Allyson L. Baughman, "The Prevalence of Sexual Assault Against People Who Identify as Gay, Lesbian, or Bisexual in the United States: A Systematic Review," *Trauma, Violence, & Abuse* 12, no. 2 (2011): 55–66, https://doi:10.1177/1524838010390707.

5. Michele C. Black, Kathleen C. Basile, Matthew J. Breiding, Sharon G. Smith, Mikel L. Walters, Melissa T. Merrick, Jieru Chen, and Mark R. Stevens, "NISVS: An Overview of 2010 Findings on Victimization by Sexual Orientation," National Intimate Partner and Sexual Violence Survey (NISVS), https://www.cdc.gov/violence prevention/pdf/cdc_nisvs_victimization_final-a.pdf.

6. National Center for Transgender Equality, "NCTE Annual Report 2015," http:// www.transequality.org/sites/default/files/docs/NCTE%20Annual%20Report%20 2015%20final.pdf.

7. David Cantor, Bonnie Fisher, Susan Chibnall, Reanne Townsend, Hyunshik Lee, Carol Bruce, and Gail Thomas, "Report of the AAU Campus Climate Survey on Sexual Assault and Sexual Misconduct," *Westat*, October 20, 2017 (revised), https:// www.aau.edu/sites/default/files/AAU-Files/Key-Issues/Campus-Safety/AAU-Cam pus-Climate-Survey-FINAL-10-20-17.pdf.

8. Jennifer Steinhauer and David S. Joachim, "55 Colleges Named in Federal Inquiry into Handling of Sexual Assault Cases," *New York Times*, May 1, 2014, https:// www.nytimes.com/2014/05/02/us/politics/us-lists-colleges-under-inquiry-over-sex -assault-cases.html.

9. Adrienne Green and Alia Wong, "LGBT Students and Campus Sexual Assault," *Atlantic*, September 22, 2015, https://www.theatlantic.com/education/archive/ 2015/09/campus-sexual-assault-lgbt-students/406684.

10. Green and Wong, "LGBT Students."

11. Scott Jaschik and Doug Lederman, "The 2015 *Inside Higher Ed* Survey of College & University Presidents," *Inside Higher Ed*, http://big.assets.huffingtonpost .com/2015IHE_PresidentsSurvey.pdf.

12. Rothman, Exner, and Baughman, "Prevalence of Sexual Assault," 60.

13. Darren Lenard Hutchinson, "Identity Crisis: 'Intersectionality,' 'Multidimensionality,' and the Development of an Adequate Theory of Subordination," *Michigan Journal of Race & Law* 6 (2001): 285–317; Athena D. Mutua, "Multidimensionality Is to Masculinities What Intersectionality Is to Feminism," *Nevada Law Journal* 13, no. 341 (2016): 341–67.

14. Francisco Valdes, "Beyond Sexual Orientation in Queer Legal Theory: Majoritarianism, Multidimensionality, and Responsibility in Social Justice Scholarship or Legal Scholars as Cultural Warriors," *Denver University Law Review* 75 (1998): 1409–15.

15. Michael Segalov, "Why Hasn't the Gay Community Had a #MeToo Moment?" *Guardian*, March 7, 2018, https://www.theguardian.com/commentisfree/2018/ mar/07/gay-community-metoo-moment-conversation-consent-sexual-assault.

16. #MeQueer, *Twitter*. Developed as an LGBTQ+ specific forum, #MeQueer is detailed fully in this chapter. As many of the tweets incorporated in this chapter are pulled from #MeQueer, these tweets will be denoted distinctly from the #MeToo tweets across the majority of the text.

17. Stephens, "Research."

18. Paulk and NCLR, "Sexual Assault."

19. #MeQueer, *Twitter*.

20. Williams, "#MeToo Movement."

21. Kim Kaletsky, "The Dangerous Exclusivity of Spaces for 'Women' Sexual Assault Survivors," *Establishment*, October 20, 2016, https://medium.com/the-es tablishment/the-dangerous-exclusivity-of-spaces-for-women-sexual-assault-survi vors-9a1c82381b17.

22. Alia E. Dastagir, "She Was Sexually Assaulted within Months of Coming Out. She Isn't Alone," *USA Today*, June 13, 2018, https://www.usatoday.com/story/ news/2018/06/13/sarah-mcbride-gay-survivors-helped-launch-me-too-but-rates -lgbt-abuse-largely-overlooked/692094002.

23. Gregory M. Herek, "Hate Crimes and Stigma-Related Experiences among Sexual Minority Adults in the United States: Prevalence Estimates from a National Probability Sample," *Journal of Interpersonal Violence* 24, no. 1 (2009): 54–74.

24. Morgan Paul, "The Fetishization of Lesbians and Bisexual Women," UMKC Women's Center, April 18, 2014, https://info.umkc.edu/womenc/2014/04/18/ the-fetishization-of-lesbians-and-bisexual-women.

25. #MeQueer, *Twitter*.

26. #MeQueer, *Twitter*.

27. Paulk and NCLR, "Sexual Assault."

28. Raquel Willis, "The Women's Movement Must Be More Inclusive of Trans Women," interview by Hannah Smothers, *Cosmopolitan*, October 29, 2017, https://www.cosmopolitan.com/politics/a13114228/raquel-willis-womens-conven tion-transgender-inclusivity.

29. Wendy Lu, "For LGBTQ Youth, #MeToo Is Not a Heteronormative Issue," *Rewire.News*, October 9, 2018, https://rewire.news/article/2018/10/09/for-lgbtq-youth -metoo-is-not-a-heteronormative-issue.

30. Joseph G. Kosciw, Emily A. Greytak, Noreen M. Giga, Christian Villenas, and David J. Danischewski, *The 2015 National School Climate Survey: The Experiences of Lesbian, Gay, Bisexual, Transgender, and Queer Youth in Our Nation's Schools* (New York: GLSEN, 2016).

31. Segalov, "Gay Community."

32. Segalov, "Gay Community."

33. Lu, "LGBTQ Youth."

34. Paulk and NCLR, "Sexual Assault."

35. Malika Saada Saar, Rebecca Epstein, Lindsay Rosenthal, and Yasmin Vafa, *The Sexual Abuse to Prison Pipeline: The Girls' Story*. Report, Georgetown Law Center on Poverty and Inequality; Human Rights Project for Girls; Ms. Foundation for Women, Washington, DC, 2015: 1–48.

36. Lu, "LGBTQ Youth."

37. Kyli Rodriguez-Cayro, "Some Members of the LGBTQ Community Feel Excluded by the Me Too Hashtag, & It's a Reminder of How Important Inclusive

Language Is," *Bustle*, October 19, 2017, https://www.bustle.com/p/some-members
-of-the-lgbtq-community-feel-excluded-by-the-me-too-hashtag-its-a-reminder-of
-how-important-inclusive-language-is-2953162.

38. Judith Halberstam, *The Queer Art of Failure* (Durham: Duke University Press, 2011).

39. Savannah Smith, "Move Over, #MeToo, LGBT Takes the Twitter Limelight With #MeQueer." *The Goldwater US*, October 22, 2018, https://thegoldwater.com/news/34812-Move-Over-MeToo-LGBT-Takes-the-Twitter-Limelight-With-MeQueer.

40. Meredith Talusan, "Trans Women and Femmes Are Shouting #MeToo—But Are You Listening?" *them*, March 2, 2018, https://www.them.us/story/trans-women -me-too.

41. José Esteban Muñoz, *Disidentifications: Queers of Color and the Performance of Politics* (Minneapolis: University of Minnesota Press, 1999).

42. Lee Edelman, *No Future Queer Theory and the Death Drive* (Durham: Duke University Press, 2007), 3.

43. Green and Wong, "LGBT Students."

44. Stephens, "Research."

45. Rothman, Exner, and Baughman, "Prevalence of Sexual Assault," 61.

46. Williams, "#MeToo Movement."

47. Kaletsky, "Dangerous Exclusivity."

48. #MeQueer, *Twitter*.

49. Taylor N. T. Brown and Jody L. Herman, "Intimate Partner Violence and Sexual Abuse Among LGBT People: A Review of Existing Research," *Williams Institute*, November 2015, https://williamsinstitute.law.ucla.edu/wp-content/uploads/Intimate-Partner-Violence-and-Sexual-Abuse-among-LGBT-People.pdf.

50. Stephens, "Research."

51. Green and Wong, "LGBT Students."

52. Willis, interview.

53. #MeQueer, *Twitter*.

54. #MeQueer, *Twitter*.

55. Rowel Leung, "LGBTQ Candidates & the #MeToo Movement—LGBTQ Victory Fund," LGBTQ Victory Fund, November 5, 2018, https://victoryfund.org/me -too-lgbtq-responses.

56. Leung, "LGBTQ Candidates."

CHAPTER 5

Global Responses to #MeToo

"The Fastest Way to Discredit Any Women's Rights Struggle Is to Say It Comes from Somewhere Else"

"Nous Voulons L'égalité" (We Too). Equal Rights March against Sexual and Physical Violence and Discrimination in Paris, France. *Claude Szmulewicz/Alamy Stock Photo*

The #MeToo movement sparked an international conversation about sexual violence and misconduct as accusations and protests emerged around the world. The far-reaching effects manifested in hashtags capturing the energy and essence of the movement within the following sampling of countries:

#IBelieveHere—Northern Ireland
#YoTambien—Spanish-speaking nations

#QuellaVoltaChe—Italy
#AnaKaman—Arabic-speaking nations
#BalanceTonPorc—France

Within the first twenty-four hours of the #MeToo call to action, similar movements erupted in multiple languages and cultures. Survivors and supporters spoke up in Arabic, Farsi, German, French, Hindi, and Spanish across eighty-five nations to bring attention to sexual violence and misconduct.[1] The response created a cultural flashpoint for international populations to demand and enact change.

The impact of #MeToo on a global scale may not have had such far-reaching impact without the decades of work in gender equality in multiple nations, many of which held firmly entrenched patriarchal oppressions and traditional values of gender roles. As Mahdavi states, "by mobilizing communities, establishing strategies of resistance, raising awareness, and breaking down the taboos that have traditionally silenced conversations about women's rights, these earlier movements allowed #MeToo to become a global phenomenon."[2] Much like the work done over decades by women of color and LGBTQ+ folk, international communities have also laid groundwork that welcomes and sustains the growth of #MeToo abroad.

#MeToo and its encouragement to speak and share stories has eroded a huge obstacle in the recognition and prosecution of sexual violence and misconduct—the historical doubt and diminishment of victims' voices. A cyclical system emerged as initially, a few women spoke out, then these voices were united in a collective, ultimately leading to a demand that these stories be not only heard but believed.[3] This incited and united movements around the world; subsequently, a wave of alleged predators toppled from their positions of power. The ongoing conversation continues to strive toward institutional change, especially as consequences do not equate to protection and prevention of sexual violence and misconduct.

The universality of these experiences resonates as a critical commentary on the impunity allowing predators to continue their behavior and abuse. The digital capabilities of a social media movement enable survivors to educate themselves, which is particularly significant in cultures where education on gender equality and sexual violence and misconduct remains scarce. Further, learning about progressive movements through social media platforms encourages survivors around the world to connect and share, creating a contagious network of support as people seek change at the local, regional, and global levels.

Kantor and Twohey refer to the "machinery" of sexual violence, misconduct, and complicity in their award-winning work exposing Weinstein's multiple abuses. This machine has protected predators and silenced survivors of sexual violence and misconduct through "hefty payoffs and inept human-resources departments; complicit bystanders who include women and men; as well as a culture that, for a long time, simply did not accept that a woman coming forward to accuse a man could be telling the truth."[4] #MeToo has thrown a wrench in the machine, succeeding where legal, governmental, educational, and corporate institutions failed.

Considering oppression not as a monolithic or top-down subordination, intersectionality shifts our understanding of hegemony as constructed from mutually reinforcing, entrenched, and intertwined networks.[5] This becomes especially relevant in the discussion of global social movements. Intersectional approaches offer strategies for women to share their unique experiences "as women from an ethnic minority, Muslim women, or women in polygamous relationships . . . the traditional unidimensional approach just assumes that all women share the same experiences because of their gender."[6] When a platform pays careful attention to these individual experiences of intersectional identity, it reveals the mechanisms of oppression often overlooked.

Movements like #MeToo face intricate negotiations in trying to comprehend the multiple differences among communities while advocating for gender equality as a universal standard. The challenge remains in navigating the disparity between imposing similar standards of women's rights without reflecting the expectations of change dependent on actual lived experiences across different cultures and nations. This is not addressed by simply marking different "starting lines" for progress across these countries or offering different expectations of the institutions and individuals of those cultures. The tension between cultural relativism and universal rights demands closer analysis of the governmental, corporate, educational, and justice systems of each country. Yet this also requires greater consideration for cultural traditions, customs, and narratives. Rather than drown these culturally specific aspects in the larger viral roar, #MeToo can effect global change by studying the particular institutions and norms that shape responses to universal rights and equality. To grasp the rise, response, and reaction to #MeToo internationally, this chapter analyzes activist foundations as precursors for #MeToo, systemic and collective measures addressing sexual violence and misconduct, statistical evidence of abuses surrounding the contested notion of consent, and a sample of direct #MeToo responses and protests from various cultures and countries. These multiple, diverse, and intersectional global conversations help shape the shared language of #MeToo worldwide.

ME TOO RISING WORLDWIDE

What would happen if one woman told the truth about her life? The world would split open.

—Muriel Rukeyser, "Käthe Kollwitz," 1968

These words emerge against a matte black background, opening the "Me Too Rising" project. Through "Me Too Rising," Google Trends created a visualization of the growth and spread of the movement around the world. As our revolving planet emerges in the background, the words "Me Too Rising" materialize on the screen.[7] Soundscapes play as the planet continues turning; upon hitting the explore button, the globe lights up with multicolored flares across different countries; these sparks light as the timeline spins to "TODAY." In real time, the viewer watches the world respond and contribute to #MeToo as top searching cities from Brewongle, Australia to Chicalim, India to Mississippi Mills, Canada appear to the right of the screen. The top search results relating to #MeToo in those cities then appear as links that take the viewer directly to the stories. Arrows to the left or right transport the viewer around the globe to "drop in" on #MeToo conversations in each location. The home screen also takes the viewer to a list of sexual assault resources with further links to Facebook, Twitter, and an information button about the project itself.

Data aggregates like "Me Too Rising" reveal how #MeToo has resonated in certain regions or nations more than others; this is often shaped by social media access or free press within each country or diaspora. Yet in countries where lack of access, threats of censorship, or a sense of anti-Western sentiment prevails, #MeToo has still gained traction; it adds to conversations surrounding protection and legislation for gender equality. Many of these regions have witnessed increased support and advocacy for victims of sexual violence and misconduct; survivor stories are being perceived as credible in ways not seen before.[8] #MeToo thus offers an international signal to communities of every culture to push for systemic change and individual support—especially in countries and diasporas with less access, education, and opportunity.

For many nations and cultures, women's rights or feminist movements serve as larger umbrellas under which #MeToo is one campaign shifting cultural awareness to an urgent discourse integral to the overall cause. To gauge the success of this campaign and impact on the larger movement, one needs to focus on real-world change at the local, regional, and global levels. Blanchard notes that many feminist scholars have "emphasized a conversational approach of feminist perspectives."[9] Within global engagement discourse, prejudiced assumptions create obstacles in opening those shared spaces of discourse. International safety and security issues evolve in the age of #MeToo, yet it remains to be seen how much further these legislative acts might progress if gender is voiced equally in these decisions.

The #MeToo movement underscores ongoing cultural dialogues surrounding women's rights, gender equality, and sexual violence and misconduct. Considering Iran, which has focused on women's movements and human rights following the constitutional revolution of 1905–1911, it is notable that prior to #MeToo's global sweep, activism across social media platforms had galvanized in response to gendered oppression. Following the violent death of Neda Agha-Soltan during the Green Movement protests, women across the Middle East were motivated to challenge and subvert the "moral rule" through which then-President Mahmoud Ahmadinejad reigned. Created by exiled Iranian-born activist Masih Alinejad, the 2014 movement "My Stealthy Freedom" featured Iranian women snapping photographs in public without wearing their hijabs.[10] This movement created a foundation for later antigovernment protests and the appreciation of the Western-born #MeToo movement. Multiple Iranians responded directly to the hashtag, sharing their stories and photographs of themselves wearing white hijabs (signifying peace).

Egyptian women similarly found ways to participate in #MeToo, despite the multiple forms of physical and sexual oppression surrounding their roles in the Arab Spring. The potential for #MeToo to gain acceptance in Egypt occurred in conjunction with the ongoing cultural protests of #NudePhotoRevolutionary, another social media project that called for Egyptian women to post photographs of themselves as a collective statement regarding "agency, morality, and autonomy."[11] Egyptian Aliaa Elmahdy began this project, featuring censored and controversial nude posts of herself: "The yellow rectangles on my eyes, mouth and sex organ resemble the censoring of our knowledge, expression and sexuality."[12]

Despite facing some of the highest rates of violence against women internationally,[13] Latin American countries had begun laying legislative and activist foundations for change before #MeToo. In February 2016, a Guatemalan court convicted two former military soldiers for committing widespread acts of sexual violence throughout the civil war from 1960 to 1996. After being tried for the sexual abuse of fifteen indigenous women, the court found these men guilty of crimes against humanity and sentenced them to a combined 360 years in prison. After decades calling for reproductive and abortion rights in Chile, August of 2017 witnessed the Mujeres En Marcha Chile, a sweeping women's movement calling for legislation that legalizes abortion under certain circumstances. In addition to seeking common human rights including peace and demilitarization, the World March of Women highlights issues specific to national legislation and education as noted in the Chilean protests "Aborto Libre, Seguro Y Gratuito."[14]

Following the horrific gang rape and murder of a young woman on a Delhi bus in 2012, multiple protests emerged in India as groups organized and demanded legislative reforms against sexual violence. Although these protests gained massive attention and enacted legislative change, #MeToo provided an even larger platform that Indian protestors embraced. Indian activists speak to how the hashtag's prevalence has exposed the historical extent of sexual violence and misconduct in their culture.[15] The model of

#MeToo has ensured that Indian protestors legitimize the widespread accusations against politicians, celebrities, and other powerful public figures with extensive histories of abuse.

Pakistani laws have followed deeply ingrained cultural beliefs surrounding gender roles. Sexual harassment laws are not merely ineffective but threatening; in many cases complainants have been imprisoned on charges of adultery. Honor killings in Pakistan still abound. Sheema Kermani, a renowned Pakistani dancer, organized a women's march on March 8, 2018 to bridge the large class division in the country for the cause of gender equality. Kermani notes that her position permits a spotlight and that because of class division, #MeToo only permeates in certain class spaces.

Khoja-Mooliji's study of hashtag feminism in the global south[16] addressed the aftermath of the kidnapping of approximately three hundred female students in Chibok, Nigeria in April 2014. As global attention turned to the plight of these young students, a surge of tweets urged #BringBackOurGirls. The campaign exemplified the power of social media to rally international support and motivate global governments to intervene on behalf of human rights injustices. Many countries like Nigeria face systemic rape and trafficking as strategies of war; patriarchal cultures also support genital mutilation, child marriage, and polygamy as culturally accepted traditions. Thus, #MeToo might seem an impossible Western call stifled by deep, historical layers of hegemonic oppression. Yet #BringBackOurGirls, "My Stealthy Freedom," and #NudePhotoRevolutionary—among the multiple instances listed here—were all forms of activism and advocacy that began long before the #MeToo hashtag emerged internationally.

These examples of activism and #MeToo participation directly implode Western assumptions and prejudices surrounding the gender inequality of Middle Eastern, African, and Latin American countries as generalized groups facing monolithic gendered oppressions. This serves as a reminder that every nation, jurisdiction, diaspora, and culture deserves greater attention for the grassroots work of everyday citizens—often at the threat of greater punishment or even death.

Collective Understanding

Despite the watershed moment and profound impact of #MeToo, the movement seemed a nonstarter in many nations and diasporas. Academic and political acknowledgment of gender inclusivity often meets a stalwart in global or international relations. NYU professor of global affairs Anne Marie Goetz lamented of #MeToo: "I wish it hadn't started in the U.S. . . . The fastest way to discredit any women's rights struggle is to say it comes from somewhere else. That's been a longstanding putdown of feminist movements all around the world."[17] Much research has revealed the possibility that in addition to other challenges, resistance to U.S. or Westernized cultural movements and trends might be blocking participation in regions and nations to #MeToo.[18] Yet as Blanchard articulates: "Academic feminism and IR [International Relations] are contemporaries, each developing through the war-torn twentieth century and motivated by some of the same international events."[19] When women are misrepresented, underrepresented, or completely erased from roles in the dialogue of international relations, progress, and equality, hegemonic thought prevails.

The international impact of #MeToo is further complicated because sexual violence and misconduct often go underreported in multiple countries. Many survivors of these traumas have not been educated or equipped with the language to identify as victims of these acts. #MeToo cannot apply equally across all nations when there is no common global standard of sexual violence and misconduct. Yet some experts and activists suggest that #MeToo might offer the opportunity to align our perceptions and represent these experiences for other survivors to recognize and identify. Czech women's rights activist Andrea Molocea states: "it's for the first time in our history as women that we can speak the same language of sorrow and despair and of subordination."[20] MacKinnon states that "constitutionalism is too restrictive a cabin for the legal issues raised by taking the substance of sex inequality seriously."[21] Women's rights movements born of U.S. and Westernized cultures often revert to this paradigm without considering the import of opening the discourse to the intricacies of individual cultures.

Traditional borders of the legal system, governmental institutions, and academic disciplines must fall in order to comprehend the greater vistas of gender equality. This holds true in discussions of gender equality and women's rights movements across international borders. #MeToo can engender a moment of opening discourse and experience rather than confining narratives to specific nations or cultures. The greater challenge might remain in assuring that the movement does not simply push a Western ideology forward but instead invites culturally specific responses from around the world.

As the initial wave of #MeToo empowerment subsided, many began asking questions to assess the current and future goals of the movement. Exploring complicated issues about the scope of #MeToo included debates about space (exclusively workplace or across all areas), aims (sexual violence and misconduct or gender inequality in all its manifestations), and perpetrators (the spectrum of abuses, legitimization of claims, and punitive impact). Attempts to address these issues engendered a multiplicity of opinions, which some suggest created division or "exposed rifts and differences of opinion between women."[22] However, the open discourse surrounding sexual violence and misconduct, or gender equality, must also be welcoming of multiple, diverse, and even oppositional opinions.

Just as collective movements might promise greater awareness and change, collectivity can become problematic. Assumptions about shared, monolithic goals are unrealistic considering the multiplicity and intersectionality of those involved. International movements, including #MeToo, often emerge in response to specific forms of suffering, abuse, and violence. However, these forms of activism might take a broader view of events and experiences in favor of familiar tropes that disregard entire cultural histories—the positive and negative aspects alike. Cultural studies scholarship has long provided much more incisive weapons to dismantle these generalizations: "a deep engagement with history, understanding the entanglements of the local with the global, and exploring the unequal gendered relations of power that produce violence against women and girls" must be acknowledged prior to rising in collective action.[23] The call for hashtag or social media activism must then strive to engage more directly with fields of feminist, gender, sexuality, race, ethnicity, embodiment, class, and myriad other principles and politics in order to challenge and vanquish the intersectional oppressions faced at the local, regional, and global levels of experience.

The reiteration of rifts within #MeToo and various feminist and women's movements is a common trope in social justice campaigns. In her discussion of "her-meneutics," Barak-Erez suggests that Supreme Court decisions in Israel, South Africa, and the United States reveal the continued tension surrounding multiple feminist viewpoints.[24] As Barak-Erez distinguishes between the forms of feminisms, she reasserts the importance of "asking the woman question" against the context of disparity and difference—across not only the manifestations of feminisms but the specificities of women's experiences around the world.

Many sexual violence and misconduct survivors suggest that #MeToo is not a safe space for shared narratives and support, but another stressor pressuring them to relive their traumas. Others still have spoken of the movement in positive ways; it has created a space for them to find solidarity and share their narratives. These acts of sustained sharing through talking (or tweeting) have subsequently encouraged survivors to address their abuses and abusers—perhaps the most necessary component of real-world change. While this is a qualitative project grounded in content analysis, it is also necessary to address these basic concerns with quantitative statistics from the international community. An exploration of the statistics of sexual violence and misconduct provides a foundation leading into the narrative construction of #MeToo and its global responses.

Statistical Consent

The United Nations Entity for Gender Equality and the Empowerment of Women reported that 35 percent of women around the world experienced physical or sexual violence in their lifetimes.[25] World Health Organization studies and surveys estimate that internationally, approximately 120 million girls and women have experienced a form of "forced intercourse" or other nonconsensual sexual acts. Additionally, 35 percent of women have experienced sexual or physical partner or nonpartner violence.[26] Regardless of these shocking statistics and the mass mobilization brought on in large part because of the #MeToo movement, legislation continues to fail the survivors and victims of sexual violence and misconduct around much of the world.

Statistics also support the sustained patterns of violence and misconduct in countries traditionally ascribing to patriarchal values and subordination of women. The United Nations surveyed 10,000 men in Asia and the Pacific, with half of the men interviewed reporting that they had perpetrated physical/sexual violence against a woman.[27] Additionally, among the nine sites studied in six countries—Bangladesh, Cambodia, China, Indonesia, Sri Lanka, and Papua New Guinea—nearly a quarter of the interviewed men also reported raping a woman or a girl.

In 2017, *Equality Now* compiled a report on sexual violence legislation in eighty-two international jurisdictions, including seventy-three UN member states. In providing a general picture of various laws on sexual violence, the findings suggest that rape specifically continues to be defined and constrained by the patriarchal systems and ideologies of specific cultures and countries. These reports illustrate how many governments must address the laws, policies, and practices barring survivors of sexual violence to seek justice.

The report offered the following findings:[28]

At least fifteen jurisdictions—including Afghanistan, Belgium, and China—used terminology of humiliation, outrage, honor, modesty, chastity, or morality in the language—situating sexual assault as a moral crime against society rather than a violation of bodily integrity. This also places the focus on the survivor as much as the perpetrator, positing the woman or girl as "repository of the so-called honour of her community rather than putting the opprobrium squarely where it should lie—on the perpetrator."[29]

At least ten jurisdictions do not criminalize marital rape, including India, Indonesia, and Jordan. Additionally, multiple jurisdictions allow rapists to be exempt from punishment if they marry the survivors. This is articulated through "marriage as settlement" legislation in Greece, Iraq, Jordan, Kuwait, Tunisia, Thailand, Serbia, and Russia. In many of these jurisdictions, these laws are provisional for statutory rape—or in Greece, marriage as settlement is encoded for the "seduction of a child." In four jurisdictions, marital rape is not classified as a crime even when the marriage violates a minimum age law.

Multiple jurisdictions—including Lebanon, Malawi, Pakistan, Panama, Peru, and Yemen—require medical examiners' reports prior to discharging the burden of proof in rape cases. These evidence and witness corroboration laws often construct obstacles so insurmountable that survivors never proceed to trial. Additionally, judicial discretion in countries such as Bolivia, Luxembourg, Morocco, and Spain permits reduction of charges or redefinition of evidence. This opens possibilities for biases, stereotypes, and prejudices to heavily influence the judicial decisions.

In addition to these startling findings, systemic and individual oppressions often fail to address educational and legislative voids surrounding sexual violence and misconduct. These intersecting oppressions remain problematic across all cultures—specifically in addressing the nature of consent. Rape legislation and misrepresentation of rape become further complicated by "myths and stereotypes surrounding what amounts to 'real rape,' often perceived as the young virginal women attacked and overpowered by a stranger."[30] This perpetuates a limited representation of rape that ignores and invalidates the innumerable variations and cases that do not fall neatly into this frequently perpetuated construct of rape. When legal or educational definitions of rape require or define the act as taking place by force, it reiterates the burden of proof as chained to violence. This disregards cases in which mentally incapacitated survivors are not able to offer consent verbally or otherwise. This discounts cases in which underaged survivors are targeted specifically because their knowledge of consent has not been fully informed. As German justice minister Heiko Maas criticized this definition in 2016: "Does a woman need to be killed or severely beaten to prove she did not consent to rape?" Defining rape in terms of consent rather than force or coercion follows recent shifts in many jurisdictions that use an equality approach in interpreting consent. This belatedly enlightened approach asks not whether plaintiffs or complainants say "no" but if they ever said "yes."

Considering international human rights laws, all nonconsensual sexual acts must be prosecuted in domestic states. After the release of the Equality Now results specifying the stifling language of consent in international rape laws, there emerged a "universal trend towards regarding lack of consent as the essential element of rape and sexual abuse."[31] For example, the European Court of Human Rights critiqued rigid judicial demands for proof of force or resistance. This position was further buttressed by the 2010 Committee on the Elimination of Discrimination Against Women articulating rape as defined by either the absence of "unequivocal and voluntary agreement" or an act that occurred under coercive circumstances.

The results of these international and national surveys, while dire, have garnered significant attention and concrete actions from legislative, cultural, and political forces. This sociohistorical framework seemed ready, even eager to welcome the viral force of #MeToo. Yet responses have varied drastically throughout the international community—in some cases, generating outright rejection and in others, wholesale acceptance. It is also considerable that in many cultures, silence echoed despite the viral roar. Even as individual access, systemic oppressions, threats of silencing, and shaming through censorship or violence continued, the swath of varied international responses to #MeToo reasserts the significance of a platform for shared experiences and diverse voices.

Global Responses

By early November of 2017, social media analytics tool Talkwalker, Google Trends' "Me Too Rising" project, and Twitter aggregated data to record the heaviest use of the #MeToo hashtag in the United States, United Kingdom, India, France, and Canada. This can be compared with the regions where #MeToo faced its greatest obstacles in acceptance: China, Russia, and sub-Saharan Africa.[32] To highlight the multiplicity of intersectional oppressions and experiences throughout the international community, I turn to the evolving discourse generating specific national and cultural responses to #MeToo.

These global conversations surrounding sexual violence and misconduct become informed by educational outreach and legislative commitments. Even as the language of consent over force or coercion has begun shifting international responses to rape and abuse, there must be continued connection across international borders and cultures. This might challenge stereotypes of sexual violence and misconduct like "real rape" and the ingrained and patriarchally informed attitudes surrounding what does or does not constitute abuses, violations, and misconduct. Movements like #MeToo can accomplish these goals through the shared narrative experiences connecting survivors around the world. While by no means comprehensive of all cultural and national experiences, these collective responses weave into the narrative fabric of #MeToo.

Australia

Allegations amassed over two decades against Australian television personality Don Burke came to the national forefront when journalist Tracey Spicer asked women who had been assaulted, abused, or harassed in Australian media to share their experiences on social media. Inspired by the #MeToo movement, Spicer called the immediate and massive response across Australia a "tsunami of justice." To navigate this tsunami, Spicer joined with Australia's media union to direct the hundreds of people who shared their stories to legal, police, and counseling support. As Spicer told the *Telegraph*, "globalisation, connectivity and the women's rights movement have created the perfect storm. . . . Suddenly, we realise we're not alone. And our experiences are being believed."[33] Following Spicer's call for responses, more than thirty women from Australian media and entertainment forged the Now Australia movement.

> Drumroll, please! We are proud to unveil @NOW_aust—our version of Time's Up. Join our movement at now.org.au to help anyone who has been sexually harassed, intimidated or assaulted in the workplace, NOW and for the next generation #thetimeisNOW #NOWAustralia
>
> —@TraceySpicer, March 24, 2018

Spicer and public figures such as Tina Arena, Sarah Blasko, Danielle Cormack, and Deborah Mailman are spearheading the Now Australia campaign to combat rampant sexual violence and misconduct across Australian workplaces. This embodies the strategic power of social media movements. Individuals gather in safe spaces to share their experiences and information, creating a connection that becomes a united force to confront perpetrators of sexual violence and assault—especially those repeat offenders who populate the shared narratives of survivors online.

Brazil

#MeToo has met obstacles in nations that claim the U.S.-born movement does not fit or could erode much of what makes their cultures unique. Critics in Brazil have charged #MeToo and its supporters with eradicating its "affectionate, warm, and physical" social customs and interactions. Despite this hesitation surrounding cultural norms and traditional communication, "Brazilians draw clear lines between what they consider immoral, offensive, unjust, or a violation."[34] This illustrates how consent does not need be dictated by cultural customs, nor does speaking out against violations of that consent indicate an attack on culture. Instead, #Nao-Me-Toque, the Brazilian version of #MeToo, may simply offer survivors a safe space to share their stories, find support, and reassert the line of consent across all cultures.

In Brazil, Carnival has long been a space for open groping, harassment, and assault. Following the international attention to #MeToo, many Brazilian women chose instead to celebrate the holiday with block parties of all-female musicians while donning garb that read empowering anti-harassment messages.[35] In a presidential election year for Brazil, the annual festivities incorporated sociopolitical themes. Many of the participants waved fans that read "não é não" or "No Means No." While the debauchery of Carnival might have remained, the women of Brazil articulated a strong stance for potential perpetrators to keep their hands to themselves. Despite these visible and vibrant protests, #MeToo has made only modest gains in

Brazil and several Latin American countries—many populations with the highest rates of violence against women.

China

China's discussion of #MeToo is entangled with both censorship issues surrounding social media and cultural suspicion of U.S.-born movements. Against the tide of #MeToo, the Chinese government continued its reputation of suppression and censorship against social media. Yet Chinese women continue coming forward with their stories and accusations of sexual violence and misconduct, even against prominent public figures. Following the initial attention of #MeToo in the United States, the movement reached China on college campuses where multiple female academics alleged sexual misconduct against university officials. The response from the Chinese government was swift: quashing not the careers of the alleged predators but the voices of the accusers. The *South China Morning Post* reported that in the second half of January alone, government censors deleted hundreds of social media posts supporting the general #MeToo movement and the primary hashtag #MeTooInChina. The Chinese government is known for blocking language to effectively "reroute" internet and social media searches; censors focus on topic forums including phrases such as "sexual harassment," "sexual assault," or "rape."

Many have argued that China's Communist Party positions gender equality as a prominent concern of the party; this rhetoric counters the rejections of #MeToo. Yet as women's rights activist Ye Haiyan suggests, this might be due to traditional Chinese culture: "There is still a belief in China . . . that it is a virtue of women to be submissive to the wishes of others."[36] The continued dominance of men in positions of power further sustains this dynamic. Despite the rapid-firewalls of censorship, when new accusations opened with a letter on WeChat in July 2018, China witnessed a reawakening of #MeTooInChina. An anonymous woman accused Lei Chuang, a prominent anti-discrimination activist, of raping her on a charity trip in 2015 when she was twenty years old. Within a day, the open letter sent a viral message ending with Lei resigning from his leadership position at the charity. And when Chinese academic Luo Xixi—now based in the United States—accused a well-respected professor in Beijing of sexual misconduct, multiple women followed suit and the professor was fired. Attention focused on this case in large part because social media users in China found creative new ways to build hashtags like #RiceBunny—which translates to the Chinese pronunciation of "me too." The swift public process of justice had a domino effect when hundreds of other women began writing their own open letters about nonconsensual encounters with multiple public figures.

Denmark

Nordic countries have long ranked high for gender equality; however, #MeToo still exposed multiple scandals across these nations. Often, more progressive or open-minded cultures were associated with dismissive attitudes surrounding sexual misconduct. When people are offended, it is labeled puritanical or prudish. Yet language and behaviors that are treated as the norm can also grow into more harsh or violent transgressions when unchecked, tolerated, or even appreciated. Functioning as an exclusionary and oppressive machine, sexual violence and misconduct permeate all cultures regardless of the progressive or puritanical ideologies informing the collective conscious.

Danish film producer Peter Aalbæk was known for his provocative behaviors—including spanking employees and inviting his staff members to skinny dip. In the open-minded Danish culture, none of these behaviors were perceived as abusive; a history of protection for visionary, creative artists within Denmark had often trivialized these behaviors. As #MeToo spread to Denmark, Aalbæk was criticized for the behaviors he'd exhibited for years and placed on sabbatical by his superiors. He soon returned, with little impact on his overall career. "Several voices critical of #MeToo have referred to Danish liberalism and humor as values we need to protect . . . it is a sad attempt to derail the discussion and cling on to a nostalgic and outdated masculinity."[37] This seems to embody the #MeToo movement in more progressive countries like Denmark—even as the discourse surrounding sexual misconduct and abuse has opened, there remains a need for concrete action.

England

Public allegations in England also demonstrated the force of #MeToo awareness, motivating many political leaders to form new grievance procedures for Parliament. After many British political and public figures were accused of getting intoxicated and "handsy" at social gatherings, undercover reports and allegations against Parliament ignited national scandals.

> Yes, & now it's bringing down Government ministers in UK. Brilliant job Alyssa. Let's destroy the patriarchy.
>
> —@chemosh933, October 29, 2017

> More than 30 women say they were sexually harassed or raped by men in the European Parliament #MeToo
>
> —@nowthisnews, October 30, 2017

Although many questioned the commitment to enact permanent legislative, cultural, and systemic change in the wake of #MeToo, the fallout proved that sexual violence and misconduct in the upper echelon of British society would be swiftly addressed. After the *Financial Times* sent an undercover reporter to the annual all-male Presidents Club Charity Dinner, the reporter documented multiple guests harassing and groping female hostesses at the event. For England, the most visible reverberation of #MeToo and the Weinstein fallout emerged in the allegations against the Palace of Westminster. When claims were levied against British defense secretary Michael Fallon and deputy first prime minister Damian Green, the "Pestminster" scandal garnered major media coverage and international attention.

France

France holds one of the most divisive discourses surrounding #MeToo. The corresponding French hashtag launched by journalist Sandra Muller called on people to #Balancetonporc—"Denounce your pig." In addition to survivors sharing their experiences of sexual violence and misconduct, many participants began detailing and depicting their attackers and abusers to warn other potential victims. Yet much of the most vocal backlash against #MeToo has come from France.

Citing the strides made by #MeToo, French minister for gender equality Marlène Schiappa successfully introduced legislation against catcalling and verbal harassment in public. As Schiappa announced, "women have come together across the world at the same time to share similar experiences. #MeToo is an act—and tangible evidence—of solidarity between women."[38] In one of the most notable critical responses to Schiappa's legislation and the #MeToo movement, one hundred French women penned and signed an open letter to *Le Monde* denouncing the movement as puritanical American groupthink: "like in the good old witch-hunt days . . . claiming to promote the liberation and protection of women, only to enslave them to a status of eternal victim."[39] The letter continued to say that "we don't recognize ourselves in this feminism that, beyond the denunciation of abuses of power, takes the face of a hatred of men and sexuality." While this offered an international counterpoint to the overwhelming wave of #MeToo voices and support, it engendered greater division in France specifically; a multitude of French women soon denounced the open letter and voiced their support for #MeToo.

Kenya

Aside from South Africa, considered a liberal outlier, there have not been explicit responses and public accusations inspired by #MeToo in sub-Saharan Africa. While this is in large part due to the distinct oppressions faced in African nations and diasporas (as contrasted with the West), there remain multiple constraints of surveillance, control, and violence that are deeply embedded within these cultures. When Kenyan regional governor Okoth Obado was accused of murdering twenty-six-year-old student Sharon Otieno in September 2018, the Kenyan media largely overlooked the fact that Otieno was seven months pregnant and intimately involved with Obado.[40] Instead, media coverage framed Otieno as promiscuous and Obado as pitiable (for his sparse prison diet). On a continent where sexual violence is more often perpetrated by intimate partners and sustained by local communities, "Kenyan women are not waiting for #MeToo to bring them liberation, because we are responding to a totally different context."[41]

In January 2018, several mothers were allegedly sexually assaulted while breastfeeding at Kenyatta National Hospital. Kenyatta, the largest hospital in Kenya, refuted these claims and accused the women of lying. Futility in the face of this strain of sexual violence and victim-shaming may have occurred in the past. However, #MeToo had already made its way around the world, offering a powerful model for survivors to speak up and encourage others to advocate. Hundreds marched on the streets of Nairobi to protest the Kenyatta National Hospital and voice their support for the women. Following these protests, the Kenyan health minister initiated a full investigation of Kenyatta and the allegations.

India

As one of the most recognizable film industries in the world, Bollywood had an opportunity to take a stand against sexual harassment when actress Tanushree Dutta made allegations against the iconic Nana Patekar. Dutta claimed that costar Patekar orchestrated a dance sequence that would involve him touching her inappropriately (and repeatedly throughout rehearsals and filming). Patekar denied the accusations, supported by a system: "In India's multibillion-dollar movie industry, accusations of sexual abuse, harassment and even rape are often viewed as a concoction by attention-hungry actresses or, if true, as the price of fame."[42] Dutta was met with such fierce backlash and skepticism, it reinscribed an internationally recognizable model of silencing. Aashna Sharma asks, "is it surprising then, that the #MeToo movement hasn't quite taken off in India? Ours is a culture where victim-blaming is so deeply embedded that concern has become a tool of oppression."[43] Dutta quit the industry and moved to the United States. Yet when #MeToo emerged, it refocused the spotlight on allegations long ignored within multiple industries—especially within the cinematic world following the Weinstein fallout.

When sexual misconduct allegations against more than sixty academics in India was crowdsourced and posted on Facebook by U.S.-based law student Raya Sarkar (with contributions from students in India), many criticized the list for its sparse details beyond naming the accused. While due process has become a major contention in the wake of #MeToo, there remains a tradition across many countries and cultures in which silence is privileged and advocated as a strategy for survivors by institutions like companies and universities or even by friends and family. As Sharma states, "Saying #MeToo comes with the silent admittance that you were right, and I was wrong. . . . It paves the way for even more policing, for further loss of autonomy."[44] In cultures where the victim is blamed for stepping outside the safety of the home, the family, and patriarchal expectations, any sexual violence or misconduct they experience becomes relegated to a consequence of the victim's behavior.

Ireland

Four men in Belfast—Ulster rugby team members Paddy Jackson and Stuart Olding and their friends Blane McIlroy and Rory Harrison—were acquitted on all charges after being accused of rape by a young woman. In court, the admission of Whatsapp messages shared by these men with language about "Belfast sluts" and "spit roasts" was dismissed as swagger—"lads being lads." Meanwhile, the woman endured eight days of antagonistic cross-examination designed to shame and discredit her. This demonstrated the double standard in which systemic structures presume the innocence of men—or at the very least, diminish behavior and language as "lads being lads" while questioning the motives of a woman who speaks up.

> Everything about the Belfast rape case was vile. The entitlement, the privilege, the utterly misogynist whatsapp messages, the classist statements from defence barristers, the bloody knickers on display.
>
> —@VoteHollandSF, March 28, 2018

While the ensuing protests emerging across Ireland directly responded to the verdict in the Belfast rape trial, #IBelieveHer became a tipping point, similar to the galvanization of #MeToo. O'Connor states: "While this trial, those texts, and that cross examination may have inspired it, it's about so much more and has sparked long overdue conversations on consent, misogyny, and how the justice system works for victims of sexual crime."[45] #IBelieveHer is a movement responding to historical and systemic oppressions that victim-blame while excusing misogynist language and behavior.

Japan

Fearing victim-blaming, many survivors of sexual violence and misconduct do not speak out in Japan. Yet Japanese journalist Shiori Ito appeared on television in May 2017 to publicly accuse Noriyuki Yamaguchi, former Washington, D.C. bureau chief for the Tokyo Broadcasting System, of rape. After suffering multiple injustices and humiliations in pursuing her allegations, Ito found her only recourse in detailing the harrowing event and subsequent miscarriage of justice to a televised audience. The initial broadcast only offered her first name. Following the viral explosion of #MeToo less than six months later, Ito published a book detailing her trauma and revealing her full identity. Ito's article in *Politico* addressed the shaming and silencing practices in Japanese society, reiterating the significance of language surrounding sexual violence and misconduct: "It is taboo to even use the word 'rape,' which is often replaced by 'violated' or 'tricked' if the victim was underage. This contributes to public ignorance."[46] As Ito noted, Japan has much ground to cover and has therefore yet to see its #MeToo movement; Japanese society continues silencing survivors—even when those brave survivors attempt to come forward with allegations. Ito called for systemic change to a system that retains a 110-year-old rape law.

Philippines

#MeToo has generated interest in the Philippines; many have chosen the moment to speak out against many misogynist men in positions of power—most notably Philippine president Rodrigo Duterte. Known internationally for boasting about his affairs, alternately objectifying then attacking female journalists, kissing women publicly and uninvited, and making jokes about rape, Duterte has presided over a simmering population refusing to allow this behavior to continue. After Duterte announced that he did not want a vacant, top governmental post occupied by a woman, Filipinas (and many men) galvanized around hashtags #LalabanAko ("I will fight back") and #BabaeAko ("I am a woman"). The solidarity of the mass responses to Duterte's objectification and abuse eventually hit the ground on Philippine Independence Day in 2018.[47]

Many in the Philippines remain fearful to share their survivor stories or make accusations in a country where the highest elected official has regularly mocked and openly harassed women. The Filipino culture has sustained this cycle of discrediting girls and women, placing the burden on survivors to raise their voices rather than overhaul a sociopolitical system that permits, supports, and even encourages misogyny, abuse, and violence. Yet #MeToo has provided a new call to action and resistance resounding in cultures marred by systemic oppression: "If you are looking for the right time to speak up, then the time is now. Let's do it together because if there's anything we learned from previous movements, it's that working together makes us powerful."[48] While Filipino customs and traditions are deeply entrenched in this unique culture, so too are the bonds that seek to protect the lives of daughters, granddaughters, sons, and grandsons in boldly declaring #LalabanAko and #BabaeAko.

Russia

In Russia, systemic rejection of feminism decried all movements as liberal Western propaganda attacking traditional Russian gender roles. As a highly visible example of this discursive response, a throng of women stripped in front of the U.S. Embassy in Moscow while bearing a sign that read "Harvey Weinstein Welcome to Russia." When five female journalists and a spokeswoman from the foreign ministry accused Russian lawmaker Leonid Slutsky of sexual harassment, the parliamentary ethics committee dismissed the multiple claims. After treating the initial claims as jokes, Slutsky later boasted that he had prevented the Western conspiracy of #MeToo from entering Russia.[49]

As Adam and Booth suggest, advocating for women's rights in Russia has been perceived as "superfluous in a country where women gained many freedoms during the Communist era—including the right to vote and access to legal abortion—decades ahead of their Western counterparts."[50] This has engendered a sustained response of victim-blaming, which has endured and was possibly amplified in the era of #MeToo. Yet there have been prominent public campaigns against sexual assault and domestic violence in Russia. The largest was #Янебоюсьсказать, or #IAmNotAfraidToSay, a campaign popularized by a Ukrainian activist named Anastasia Melnichenko. The movement encouraged thousands of women in the Ukraine and Russia to share stories of assault widely viewed as shameful or taboo in the public eye.

South Korea

In one of the highest-profile cases emerging in the #MeToo era, South Korean governor of South Chungcheong province and presidential hopeful Ahn Hee-jung was accused of rape and assault by his secretary, Kim Ji-eun. Despite being charged with multiple counts of sexual harassment and five counts of sexual coercion by an employer, Ahn was acquitted of all charges. While the Seoul Western District public prosecutor's office swore to appeal and the global outcry highlighted the sense of injustice, this particular case reasserted the intricate negotiation between entrenched patriarchal values and the awakening of #MeToo around the world.

For many women in South Korea, there is an expectation to remain "silent and accepting in the face of unfair treatment or even sexual assault. . . .

Female sexual assault victims are often themselves criticized for not behaving 'properly' or not having requisite 'shame' about revealing sexual behavior, even if it was not consensual."[51] Yet #MeToo's global reach as a digital platform encouraged millions to share their narratives to raise awareness and create solidarity. In response, South Korea has revisited sexual violence legislation—raising the maximum punishment and extending the statute of limitations. And South Korean citizens continue pushing because there is much ground left to cover. On June 9, 2018, the most populated women's rally in Seoul's history protested misogynist practices including "molka"— hidden cameras used to film primarily unsuspecting female victims. This awareness and activism helped the case of a university art class male model who spoke up when he realized he had been unknowingly photographed by a South Korean woman.

Spain

When a court in Navarre found five men guilty of sexual abuse yet cleared them of raping an eighteen-year-old woman at the 2016 San Fermín (Running of the Bulls) festival, tens of thousands gathered in spontaneous protests across Spain. After the five perpetrators used a chat app to share footage of the gang rape on their cellphones, the case became known as "La Manada"—which translates to "The Pack." The footage itself was used by the defense as evidence; in their verdict, judges stated that as it appeared that neither violence nor intimidation was used, it failed to meet two requirements for "sexual assault under Spanish law."[52] Spain responded directly to the ruling with #Cuéntalo (#Tell it).

While #MeToo emerged prior to "La Manada," it offered a model for resistance. In addition to #Cuéntalo, the Spanish population responded with #YoTambien and diverse grassroots protests reflecting the momentum of the movement. Led primarily by women, this activism surged to combat sexual and physical violence, abuse, and discrimination—in addition to a system supporting it.

> Tengo 42 palos, he visto y sufrido todo tipo de situaciones y aún no he conocido una sola mujer que no haya sufrido algún tipo de abuso o agresión. Ni una de nosotras ha llegado a la edad adulta sin algún percance o trauma. Sois conscientes de la magnitud? #Cuentalo

> —@ilargiblue, April 28, 2018

> I'm forty-two years old, I've seen and been through all kinds of situations and I am still yet to meet a single woman who hasn't suffered some kind of abuse or assault. None of us have reached adulthood without some kind of mishap or trauma. Are you aware of the scale of this? #Cuéntalo

Sweden

As mentioned in #MeToo responses from Denmark and France, many cultures and countries consider the movement a puritanical or groupthink Western reaction. This perspective has not hindered the impact of #MeToo on enacting real change in many of these progressive populations. #MeToo has incited "dialogue about power dynamics and gender inequality, and the following phrase is often repeated: 'It's easier to address these issues in the wake of #MeToo.'"[53]

In Sweden, the renowned Swedish Academy was rocked by scandal evocative of the fallout surrounding Weinstein and others in the wake of #MeToo. When allegations from eighteen women were made against Jean-Claude Arnault, a French ally of the cultural institution, the Academy saw massive resignations demonstrating the scope of these accusations. As the members of the Academy struggled over how to handle the allegations, former head of the Academy Horace Engdahl publicly likened #MeToo with the Reign of Terror in eighteenth-century France. As Engdahl stated, "We live in this period that is very much defined in Sweden by the onset of the #MeToo movement and the atmosphere that has created."[54] Although Arnault was sentenced to only two years in prison—the minimum sentence for rape—this verdict marked a turning point for a nation with a historical allegiance to gender equality. Exposing the historical abuses and cronyism embedded in the institution responsible for selecting Nobel Prize winners, Sweden's #MeToo movement ensured that a man who used his access to power could no longer be afforded a pass based on alliances and prestige.

#MeToo and the international attention to the Academy scandal has encouraged and enacted political and cultural change. This includes reassessing mediated and cultural responses to survivors of sexual violence and misconduct, starting with legislation surrounding consent. The Swedish government issued a proposal to stipulate that explicit consent prior to sexual contact is required in its rape laws. These transformations have been made possible not only in Sweden but as it reaches across its borders to allied countries with similar perspectives on gender equality. Women across Sweden and Iceland have joined and created their own social media campaigns to spread awareness surrounding systemic sexual misconduct in multiple professional sectors.[55] Sweden has also created distinct #MeToo hashtags for every industry, thus recognizing the widespread urgency of sexual violence and misconduct and that each workplace and all laborers must be considered equal in terms of their traumas. If the movement has enabled cultures to shift the dialogue to greater recognition of abuses of power and sexually offensive, demeaning, and violent behavior, this will ensure that the conversation is no longer dismissed as puritanical or prudish but relevant and necessary.

These global responses to #MeToo create a dynamic framework illustrating the greater need for culturally specific attention to gender equality and intersectional oppressions. Noting the diverse discourse surrounding #MeToo—this is only possible if the social media clarion call transforms into an international platform inclusive of all cultural and national voices. Studying the impacts of #MeToo and the myriad global movements and responses that have followed, it is possible to enact large-scale public projects that also create those currents of change for everyday individuals.

THE SHARED LANGUAGE OF CHANGE

#MeToo has been critiqued for its potentially Western imperialist nature, reaching globally yet without equal attention to the marginalized and intersectional voices and oppressions involved in this narrative. When Western attention lands on developing or underdeveloped, non-Western or traditional cultures, it often creates a division entrenched in historical colonialism and imperialism. If women and girls from nonprivileged, non-Western spaces are foregrounded in the #MeToo movement, does this serve as an empowering move? Or does it simply target these women and girls as "symbolic sites of western liberal projects"?[56]

Past the anniversary of the #MeToo hashtag, many media sources examined the impact and efficacy of the movement. Despite the myriad obstacles in global adoption of #MeToo—from access to censorship to systemic gender violence and oppression—there was international recognition of those now famous two words. This attention might be perceived as a "testament to the prevalence of sexual violence against women and speaks to the sheer magnitude of the problem, which continues to transcend international borders."[57] In places where massive marches took to the street, there was visibility. In places where awareness of support emerged, there was alliance. Through everyday conversation and global protests, #MeToo has amplified voices already speaking and offered platforms for those long silenced.

Digital platforms have drastically changed the potential for activism and advocacy, especially in creating safe spaces to share traumatic experiences. As Spicer told the *Telegraph*, "our personal devices are such an intimate part of our lives, these women feel comfortable using social mediums—at any time of the day or night—to share details about these experiences. And it's easy to connect with other alleged victims."[58] Social media movements and hashtag activism provoke debates surrounding issues of credibility and privacy, due process or "trial by media." Yet considering the prevailing forces of silencing and shaming across international spaces, the connectivity and anonymity afforded by social media may be the only means of protest or support for many marginalized activists and cultures.

The global responses to #MeToo have varied drastically based on multiple factors highlighted across this chapter. Yet through shared narratives of survivors and media coverage, the overall response to #MeToo suggests that the movement has provided a platform and paved the way for citizens everywhere to articulate their experiences and garner strength and support from other survivors. "As women raise their voices together, their harrowing stories, drowned out for so long, are becoming a coherent and determined voice of change."[59] #MeToo has also signaled a call to challenge sexual predators and the systemic forces of impunity protecting them. Further, the movement offers a model for education and language that addresses issues of consent, power, sex, and solidarity.

In #MeToo's birthplace the drastic impact of the movement could be seen in the multitude of shared narratives signifying an era of culpability over impunity. Yet as Kristof says, "we need a global effort—by rich and poor nations alike—to make the #MeToo principles truly universal."[60] This globalization can happen through a sense of collective awareness and understanding. Considering the language surrounding international sociopolitical human rights concerns, #MeToo might also offer the opportunity to transform the language surrounding sexual violence and misconduct. Human rights violations including genocide, torture, or censorship often awaken the global community to intervene and contribute to the cause. Yet as Kristof suggests, "gender violence is not only far more common but also sometimes institutionalized and shaped by legal codes and government policy."[61] The voices of #MeToo can speak to this, recognizing the multiple survivors while reasserting that sexual violence and misconduct impacts not only women but entire communities, cultures, and nations. #MeToo must be about unity "across all kinds of boundaries—rich or poor, black or white, North or South . . . if you get an explosion of #MeToo, you start getting the protection of numbers, and a growing mass of evidence that there's a real problem—not just one individual making this up."[62] Much as LGBTQ+ rights or civil rights were not exclusive issues to those communities, #MeToo and gender equality movements illustrate how these are human-rights violations that demand our attention, response, and action.

#MeToo has offered a stage, microphone, and megaphone with international reach. Activists, advocates, and allies around the world have been "doing the work" for decades; #MeToo is simply helping to shine a brighter light on these remarkable efforts and sacrifices. Regardless of its global influence, acceptance, or rejection, #MeToo illustrates the potential for women's and civil rights groups to unite and build upon shared experiences, goals, and successes. Despite the multiplicities of cultural differences, individual and systemic oppressions are now being challenged by a collective, global force of change. Increasing aid and training about sexual violence and misconduct for global jurisdictions across police forces, courts, hospitals, clinics, and governmental agencies can help address systemic oppressions. While education for girls and young women will help them become agents of change in their countries and communities, international goals for education centered on consent will instill knowledge and respect for human rights everywhere.

NOTES

1. Andrea Park, "#MeToo Reaches 85 Countries with 1.7M Tweets," *CBS News*, October 24, 2017, https://www.cbsnews.com/news/metoo-reaches-85-countries -with-1-7-million-tweets.

2. Pardis Mahdavi, "How #MeToo Became a Global Movement," *Foreign Affairs*, March 16, 2018, https://www.foreignaffairs.com/articles/2018-03-06/how-me too-became-global-movement.

3. John T. Jost, Julia Becker, Danny Osborne, and Vivienne Badaan, "Missing in (Collective) Action," *Current Directions in Psychological Science* 26, no. 2 (2017): 99–108, https://doi:10.1177/0963721417690633.

4. Jodi Kantor and Megan Twohey, "Harvey Weinstein Paid Off Sexual Harassment Accusers for Decades," *New York Times*, October 5, 2017, https://www.nytimes .com/2017/10/05/us/harvey-weinstein-harassmnt-allegations.html.

5. Beverley Baines, Daphne Barak-Erez, and Tsvi Kahana, eds., *Feminist Constitutionalism: Global Perspectives* (Cambridge, UK: Cambridge University Press, 2012), 91.

6. Anna Katherina Mangold, review of *Feminist Constitutionalism: Global Perspectives*, by Beverley Baines, Daphne Barak-Erez, and Tsvi Kahana, *International Journal of Constitutional Law*, December 18, 2013.

7. See https://metoorising.withgoogle.com.

8. Rebecca Seales, "What Has #MeToo Actually Changed?" *BBC News*, May 12, 2018, https://www.bbc.com/news/world-44045291.

9. Eric M. Blanchard, "Gender, International Relations, and the Development of Feminist Security Theory," *Signs: Journal of Women in Culture and Society* 28, no. 4 (2003): 1290.

10. WITW Staff, "Exiled My Stealthy Freedom Founder Receives Death Threats for Campaign against Compulsory Hijab," *Women in the World*, June 29, 2017, https:// womenintheworld.com/2017/06/29/exiled-my-stealthy-freedom-founder-receives -death-threats-for-campaign-against-compulsory-hijab.

11. Mahdavi, "Global Movement."

12. As told to and translated by Egyptian news source Almasry Alyoum.

13. Leonie Rauls and Tamar Ziff, "High Rates of Violence Against Women in Latin America Despite Femicide Legislation: Possible Steps Forward," *Dialogue*, November 6, 2018, https://www.thedialogue.org/blogs/2018/10/high-rates-of-violence -against-women-in-latin-america-despite-femicide-legislation-possible-steps-forward.

14. Angie Mendoza Araneda, "Persistence of the Dictatorship of the Body in Chile: Abortion a Pending Right," *Mujeres En Marcha*, October 8, 2018, https://www .marchamujereschile.cl/2018/10/persistencia-de-la-dictadura-del-cuerpo.html.

15. Mahdavi, "Global Movement."

16. Shenila Khoja-Moolji, "Becoming an 'Intimate Publics': Exploring the Affective Intensities of Hashtag Feminism," *Feminist Media Studies* 15, no. 2 (2015): 347–50.

17. Associated Press, "Not Every Country Is Down with the #MeToo Movement," *New York Post*, March 7, 2018, https://nypost.com/2018/03/06/not-every-country-is-down-with-the-metoo-movement.

18. Kaitlynn Mendes, Jessica Ringrose, and Jessalynn Keller, "#MeToo and the Promise and Pitfalls of Challenging Rape Culture through Digital Feminist Activism," *European Journal of Women's Studies* 25, no. 2 (2018): 236–46; Michael A. Peters and Tina Besley, "Weinstein, Sexual Predation, and 'Rape Culture': Public Pedagogies and Hashtag Internet Activism," *Educational Philosophy and Theory* (2018): 1–7, https://doi:10.1080/00131857.2018.1427850; Seales, "#MeToo Actually Changed?"

19. Blanchard, "Gender, International Relations," 1289.

20. Sintia Radu, "How #MeToo Has Awoken Women Around the World," *U.S. News*, October 25, 2017, https://www.usnews.com/news/best-countries/articles/2017-10-25/how-metoo-has-awoken-women-around-the-world.

21. Catherine A. MacKinnon, "Foreword," in *Feminist Constitutionalism: Global Perspectives*, ed. Beverley Baines, Daphne Barak-Erez, and Tsvi Kahana (Cambridge, UK: Cambridge University Press, 2012), xi.

22. Anisa Subedar, "Has #MeToo Divided Women?" *BBC News*, August 17, 2018, https://www.bbc.com/news/blogs-trending-44958160.

23. Khoja-Moolji, "Affective Intensities," 349.

24. Daphne Barak-Erez, "Her-meneutics: Feminism and Interpretation," in *Feminist Constitutionalism: Global Perspectives*, ed. Beverley Baines, Daphne Barak-Erez, and Tsvi Kahana (Cambridge, UK: Cambridge University Press, 2012), 85–97.

25. Emma Fulu, Xian Warner, Stephanie Miedema, Rachel Jewkes, Tim Roselli, and James Lang, *Why Do Some Men Use Violence Against Women and How Can We Prevent It? Quantitative Findings from the United Nations Multi-Country Study on Men and Violence in Asia and the Pacific* (Bangkok: UNDP, UNFPA, UN Women and UNV, 2013).

26. "Global and Regional Estimates of Violence against Women," World Health Organization, November 28, 2014, https://www.who.int/reproductivehealth/publications/violence/9789241564625/en.

27. Fulu et al., *Quantitative Findings*.

28. Equality Now, "The Global Rape Epidemic," February 2017, https://www.equalitynow.org/the_global_rape_epidemic_campaign?locale=en.

29. Equality Now, "Global Rape Epidemic," 21.

30. Eithne Dowds, "An International Legal Response to #MeToo, Rape and Sexual Abuse Is Needed," *Theconversation.com*, November 5, 2018, https://theconversation.com/an-international-legal-response-to-metoo-rape-and-sexual-abuse-is-needed-95617.

31. Dowds, "International Legal Response."

32. Karla Adam and William Booth, "A Year after It Began, Has #MeToo Become a Global Movement?" *Washington Post*, October 5, 2018, https://www.washingtonpost.com/world/a-year-after-it-began-has-metoo-become-a-global-movement/2018/10/05/1fc0929e-c71a-11e8-9c0f-2ffaf6d422aa_story.html?utm_term=.8e442085822d.

33. Louise Burke, "The #MeToo Shockwave: How the Movement Has Reverberated Around the World," *Telegraph*, March 9, 2018, https://www.telegraph.co.uk/news/world/metoo-shockwave.

34. "Brazilian Version of MeToo Faces Its Critics," Ataraxik, June 8, 2018, https://www.atarxik.com/2018/05/29/brazilian-version-of-metoo.

35. Ernesto Londoño, "Rio Carnival Kicks Off with Samba, Blocos and Nod to #MeToo," *New York Times*, February 10, 2018, https://www.nytimes.com/2018/02/10/world/americas/rio-carnival-me-too.html.

36. Simon Denyer and Amber Ziye Wang, "Chinese Women Reveal Sexual Harassment, but #MeToo Movement Struggles for Air," *Washington Post*, January 9, 2018, https://www.washingtonpost.com/world/asia_pacific/chinese-women-reveal-sexual-harassment-but-metoo-movement-struggles-for-air/2018/01/08/ac591c26-cc0d-4d5a-b2ca-d14a7f763fe0_story.html?utm_term=.e4d47c697098.

37. Ane Larsen, "#MeToo vs. Denmark," *Humanity in Action*, 2018, https://www.humanityinaction.org/knowledgebase/788-metoo-vs-denmark.

38. "Marlène Schiappa: Gender Equality, a Priority for the French Chairmanship of the Council of Europe in 2019," November 20, 2018, https://www.coe.int/en/web/portal/-/marlene-schiappa-gender-equality-a-priority-for-the-french-chairmanship-of-the-council-of-europe-in-2019.

39. "Full Translation of French Anti-#MeToo Manifesto Signed by Catherine Deneuve," *Le Monde*, January 10, 2018, https://www.worldcrunch.com/opinion-analysis/full-translation-of-french-anti-metoo-manifesto-signed-by-catherine-deneuve.

40. Damilola Odufuwa, "Kenyan Governor Charged in Murder of Pregnant Student," *CNN*, September 25, 2018, https://www.cnn.com/2018/09/24/africa/kenyan-governor-charged-otieno-murder-intl/index.html.

41. Nanjala Nyabola, "A Year After It Began, Has #MeToo Become a Global Movement?" interview by Karla Adam and William Booth, *Washington Post*, October 5, 2018.

42. Adam and Booth, "A Year After."

43. *Broadly* Staff, "#MeToo Anniversary: Women Around the World Speak on Its Impact," *Vice*, October 22, 2018, https://www.vice.com/en_asia/article/3km77w/me-too-anniversary-global-impact.

44. *Broadly* Staff, "#MeToo Anniversary."

45. Amy O'Connor, "'The #IBelieveHer Moment Has Been a Long Time Coming,'" *Daily Edge*, March 30, 2018, https://www.dailyedge.ie/i-believe-her-ireland-3932731-Mar2018.

46. Shiori Ito, "Saying #MeToo in Japan," *Politico*, January 4, 2018, https://www.politico.eu/article/metoo-sexual-assault-women-rights-japan.

47. *Broadly* Staff, "#MeToo Anniversary."

48. Aubrey Alejo, "#MeToo Movement Is Not Working in the Philippines and Here's Why," *Meg*, November 8, 2018, https://meg.onemega.com/metoo-movement-philippines.

49. Andrew Roth, "Putin Suggests #MeToo Movement Is a Media Conspiracy," *Guardian*, June 7, 2018, https://www.theguardian.com/world/2018/jun/07/putin-criticises-metoo-for-delays-in-alleged-attack-reports.

50. Adam and Booth, "A Year After."

51. Joshua Berlinger, Jake Kwon, and Yoonjung Seo, "Former Political Rising Star in South Korea Acquitted of Sexual Assault," *CNN*, August 14, 2018, https://www .cnn.com/2018/08/14/asia/ahn-hee-jung-south-korea-intl/index.html.

52. Emilio Sánchez Hidalgo, "#Cuéntalo: The Hashtag Women Are Using to Tell Their Stories of Abuse," *El País*, April 30, 2018, https://elpais.com/elpais/ 2018/04/30/inenglish/1525091693_227611.html.

53. Seales, "#MeToo Actually Changed?"

54. Richard Orange, "Nobel Prize: The Continuing Crisis Inside the Swedish Academy," *TheTLS*, October 19, 2018, https://www.the-tls.co.uk/articles/public/ nobel-prize-crisis-swedish-academy.

55. MÄN, *Men, Masculinity and #MeToo: Nordic Experiences That Shattered the Culture of Silence.* Report, MÄN, 2018, 1–27.

56. Khoja-Moolji, "Affective Intensities," 348.

57. *Broadly* Staff, "#MeToo Anniversary."

58. Louise Burke, "The #MeToo Shockwave: How the Movement has Reverberated Around the World," *Telegraph*, March 9, 2018, https://www.telegraph.co.uk/ news/world/metoo-shockwave.

59. Mahdavi, "Global Movement."

60. Nicholas D. Kristof, "#MeToo Movement Goes Global," *Seattle Times*, May 4, 2018, https://www.seattletimes.com/opinion/metoo-movement-goes-global.

61. Kristof, "#MeToo Movement."

62. Associated Press, "Not Every Country."

CHAPTER 6

The Omission of People with Disabilities from #MeToo

"Disability Is the One Minority Group We Can All Join"

"For the Full Inclusion of Women and Girls with Disabilities." International Women's Day March in New York City. *Ethel Wolvovitz/Alamy Stock Photo*

In partnership with the Disability Visibility Project, the Call for Stories from advocacy group Rooted in Rights requested participation from the disabled and differently abled community. Inviting people with disabilities to submit their own narratives in response to the "omission of disability from larger conversations taking place within the #MeToo movement," the project strategically expands the dialogue of experiences through blog posts, tweets, and links to previously published stories.[1]

> Heartened by how many disabled people have spoken out/continue to speak out about #MeToo, and yet my fury is two-fold: fury that we have to have these conversations at all, and fury that we are so often excluded from them.
>
>   —@emily_ladau, February 21, 2018

> A6: People can be dismissed and retraumatized altogether when they try to report incidences. This is why many refuse to come forward—who will believe us?
>
>   —@VilissaThompson, February 21, 2018[2]

In the watershed moment of #MeToo, people with disabilities have largely been ignored within the conversation. As Neal suggests, "this might partly have to do with the way our society views people with disabilities as asexual; after all, how can you consent to sex if nobody finds you sexy?"[3] The tragedy of this statement is bound in the mainstream cultural dismissal of disabled folk. In the specific context of sexual violence and misconduct or the larger discourse surrounding the sexuality of disabled folk, #MeToo provides a platform and call for greater awareness, justice, and education.

With mainstream media coverage focusing on the familiar images of straight, white, cis, privileged, and nondisabled women, it reiterates a stereotypical idea of perpetrator/survivor. Even as #MeToo continues expanding its discourse and reach, enlightening a global community about the prevalence and persistence of sexual violence and misconduct, marginalized groups are still being excluded or overlooked in the conversation or in the scope of representation. The invisibility of entire populations obstructs progress in combating sexual violence and misconduct. #MeToo must place emphasis in the "power when people with disabilities—and their allies without disabilities—use their common shared experience to create systemic change."[4] Expanding the narrative of sexual violence and misconduct addresses the frequent omission of voices from these intersections of disabled and nondisabled communities.

Mainstream attention surrounding #MeToo has largely ignored the experiences of disabled survivors. This is especially important because this community is significantly more likely to be victimized by sexual violence and misconduct. Even as social justice projects like #MeToo strive to reframe the discourse of rape culture around power rather than sex, "disabled people's desexualization still means that they're often discounted in conversations like these about sexual violence."[5] To forge inclusivity in the #MeToo movement, issues like accessibility in rape crisis centers or representation focusing on disabled individuals as sexual citizens could revise the mainstream myths and stigmas surrounding survivors with disabilities.

People with disabilities are familiar with the dearth of education and access, making their narratives even more significant to the larger discourse of #MeToo. Education for disabled folk is only one side of a coin. Law enforcement, crisis support and shelters, and agencies for advocacy and activism typically have little or no training regarding disabled survivors.[6] Further, the testimony of these survivors is often discounted either at the level of direct interaction—medical, caretakers, or kinship networks—or at the level of judicial interaction in law enforcement or courts. Education must operate not only at the community level for folks with disabilities, but also in informing and equipping attorneys and judges, law enforcement, first responders, crisis professionals and therapists, and all other supporting professions with these integral tools.

Elevated rates of sexual violence and misconduct for people with disabilities reifies the urgency for #MeToo inclusion. Further, the knowledge and experiences of this community could serve as a guiding force within the movement. This chapter explores the identity politics of people with disabilities through rights and responsibilities of sexual citizenship; stigmatization and fetishization of people with disabilities; the need for systemic progress in ensuring protection, education, and justice for disabled folk; and the validation of intersectional experiences for the disability community.

SEXUAL CITIZENSHIP

Over a month before the #MeToo hashtag erupted, Shah wrote an article detailing the need to support sexual identity, well-being, and safety for young people with disabilities. In explaining the obstacles for disabled youth in accessing equal rights and representation regarding sexuality, sexual expression, and healthy relationships, Shah stressed the necessity of these rights to autonomy, choice, and access as fundamental to physical and emotional well-being:

> However, societal misconceptions of disabled bodies being non-normative, other, or deviant has somewhat shaped how the sexuality of disabled people has been constructed as problematic under the public gaze. The pervasive belief that disabled people are asexual creates barriers to sexual citizenship for disabled

young people, thereby causing them to have lower levels of sexual knowledge and inadequate sex education compared to their non-disabled peers.[7]

One primary consequence of this is the exposure to exploitative, marginalizing, and abusive sexual relationships. Foregrounding a discussion of sexuality in all its manifestations poses challenges in relation to folk with disabilities. The word *disabled* is frequently constructed as the binaried opposite of *abled,* and in the medical community disabilities are often constructed in opposition to *healthy* or *whole*—despite occupying multiple positions across a continuum of health and illness. These preconceptions thus problematize the notion of able or healthy sexuality, desire, and physicality within disability communities. Yet as Kuppers suggests, this binary might actually forge a structural similarity: "like sex, disabled bodies are disavowed, shut away from the mainstream, locked into bedrooms."[8] Sex and disability—and often, even the mere discussion of either—often threatens "bodily boundaries that are essential to categorical certainty and, as such, they provoke widespread anxiety."[9] Taboos, silencing practices, and invisibility in representation are woven into both the discourse surrounding sexualities (which are imagined as Other) and these communities.

The cultural conversation surrounding consent, especially in relation to the #MeToo movement, must become inclusive and expansive. This moment balances on a greater understanding that marginalized, differently abled people matter as much as all the other voices calling "Me Too." Neal states that those with "disabilities are the world's largest minority, and as such, conversations about our bodies should be met with the utmost respect instead of suspicion, derision, and condescension."[10] Many members of this community face a world in which their disabilities—often visible—present to others before any other opportunity to interact. Thus, the human and that human's body and mind become secondary in communication, with the disability always presented first as an identification.

While conversations surrounding sexual violence and misconduct touch on the significance of consent—from stronger legislation to mediated attention, there are few communities that deal with issues of consent and the body daily like people with disabilities. This conversational void necessitates specific discussions of consent for folk with disabilities, especially whereas "we don't talk about the fact that physically disabled people may not be able to 'fight back' or flee, that we may not be able to kick, scream, or run, that we may be easy to physically overpower."[11] When social justice movements overlook the nuances of intersectional experience in the face of sexual violence and misconduct, it reifies the formulaic images of perpetrators and survivors, creating a limited space of inclusion in the conversation.

Disability culture emerges in a shift from medical diagnoses defining the individual toward an understanding of disabilities as a marginalized cultural phenomenon. This provides context for understanding how and why people with disabilities continue to find themselves displaced from conversations about sexuality, desire, sexual violence and misconduct, and #MeToo. As Karolyn Gehrig, queer disabled writer, activist, and artist states, "I understand why #TimesUp initially forgot about Disabled people, I do. We are not there. We are not visible on the carpet, in movies, in the workplace. Our bodies are not sexualized, or understood as rapeable."[12] Excluding folk with disabilities from the #MeToo discussion follows a cultural narrative; the presence of anyone with a disability "threatens a shift in the status quo, a momentary visibility of one's own body or self as potentially different, as one is faced by that which is 'disruptive.'"[13] This psychic trauma necessitates the supporting ideology of abled/disabled binaries that might eradicate the threat of Otherness.

Although often articulated as a matter of privacy, equal rights to sexual activity, expression, choice, access, and education remain regulated by systemic and social norms and values. As Shah notes, "it can be argued that as disabled bodies are constructed as non-normative, the sexuality of disabled people is not accepted but seen as problematic under the public gaze."[14] When people with disabilities are omitted from any normative representation or conversation surrounding sexuality, they are further isolated, marginalized, and rendered vulnerable to exploitation, abuse, assault, and harassment.[15] For sexually healthy relationships, the dynamics of attraction are also impacted because many assume that folk with disabilities are neither capable of nor interested in sexual acts, or that if they are attracted to someone with a disability it could be perceived as abusive or wrong.[16] Stigma, silence, and oppression create confusion and shame, reducing disabled folk's experiences of sexuality and diminishing their voices in conversations that might enlighten and empower them as sexual citizens.

Additionally, the fact that people with disabilities share the commonality of depending on others for assistance and care often places them at further risk for abuse. Considering the community of people with intellectual disabilities, Shapiro noted that these individuals especially "can be easy to manipulate, because they've been taught to be trusting . . . they need to rely upon other adults, the parents, teachers, staff who help them."[17] Often, survivors are unable to communicate entirely and the abuse is only exposed when a female victim ends up pregnant, or a victim is diagnosed with a sexually transmitted disease. This is especially prevalent within institutionalized settings. More than 80 percent of rapes perpetrated against intellectually disabled women are committed by people whom they know. Further, when people with intellectual, physical, or mental disabilities are faced with the trauma of sexual violence and misconduct, they are often robbed of the same strategies to deal with these experiences in therapeutic and healthy ways. Predators target people with intellectual disabilities because they have access to manipulate them; additionally, these perpetrators are aware of the challenges people with disabilities face in conveying their experiences and testifying in formal settings.

People with disabilities remain largely absent in cultural representations at the local, regional, and global levels. Despite the love, affiliation, and sexual needs that all humans experience, many citizens with disabilities engage in the world with the knowledge "that in the eyes of the rest of the world, they're not seen as people who are going to find love, or romance or sex. They're considered childlike, or incapable, or just uninterested."[18] As for all marginalized communities, when stereotypes and stigmas misrepresent, the reality of identity is skewed; for disabled folk, these misrepresentations hold deleterious effects. This deepens the sense of alienation, silence, and invisibility—all factors that stifle the discourse of sexuality and elide the sexual identities of people with disabilities.

> People don't believe that disabled people are sexual beings with equal human rights, so our sexuality can easily be taken from us. I experienced harassment in the streets of Brooklyn while hearing cis men correct themselves because I was disabled. It was So strange.
>
> —@powernotpity, February 21, 2018

The ongoing conversation surrounding #MeToo and consent must reiterate that "while The Future is Female, it is *also* #inclusive, and #accessible. That's *real* progress. Anything else just isn't."[19] While sexual violence and misconduct is rooted in power, rather than sexuality or desire, as Imani notes: "consent is inherent to every human being's sexuality and personhood, and when society segregates us from discourse around sexuality— whether that be in sexual education classes or hashtag conversations— society fails to allow us to represent ourselves as people able to consent."[20] There remains a void in conversations not only about healthy sexual relationships, representation, and language speaking with and to the disability community, but in the glaring omission within the discourse surrounding sexual violence and misconduct. Stereotypes and stigmas silencing or obscuring the sexuality of disabled folk not only diminishes their embodiment and desires, but further marginalizes a community often overlooked and ignored.

A Personhood Up for Grabs

The fact that individuals with disabilities may not be perceived as sexual, sensual, and desiring does not mean that others do not view them as potential victims of sexual violence and misconduct. As Flores writes: "Not only does ignoring sexuality dehumanize disabled people, but it can lead to us being targeted by violence. Being infantilized and finding myself in a situation where my disability doesn't allow me to defend myself is scary."[21] This is particularly alarming in spaces where able-bodied people occupy positions as carers—therapists, doctors, nurses, etc. For people of advanced age in nursing home care, individuals with varying degrees of mental disabilities, and folk with diverse physical disabilities, a hierarchy already exists because those from the able-bodied community are positioned as trustworthy caretakers or authority figures. This contributes to the statistics offered by the Bureau of Justice Statistics report on Crimes Against People with Disabilities: "Persons with a disability had an age-adjusted rate of rape or sexual assault that was more than twice the rate for persons without a disability."[22] Focusing on the victimization of individuals with disabilities, the report defined disability as a long-term condition of one or multiple categories: ambulatory, cognitive, hearing, independent living, self-care, and vision. Rape and sexual assault were reported at a rate of 2.1 for persons with disabilities as opposed to 0.6 of those without disabilities (in the comparison group). Women with disabilities and people with multiple disabilities are estimated to experience even higher rates of sexual violence and/or misconduct.

The discourse of sexuality, desire, and abuse provokes significations of disability, especially whereas stigma surrounds the deployment of sexuality and physicality for differently abled bodies. Discussions of sexuality thus become intersectional in traversing the planes of invisibility and taboo, visibility and fetishization. Disability as a discursive concept demands "a thorough and careful analysis of reading practices, the investigation of different blind spots, different ways of making meaning, and an analysis and awareness of the power structures inherent in any acts of performativity, performance and mediation."[23] Cultural assumptions and emotional responses in the representation (or underrepresentation) of disability further inform the reading of these experiences in the context of #MeToo.

People with disabilities are often relegated to extremes in the context of sexuality—either absence of sexuality or fetishized objectification. In neither extreme does this account for the actual lived experience and desire of individuals with disabilities. In considering the amount of uninvited and nonconsensual touching that folk with disabilities must endure, Imani writes: "Because our bodies are considered oddities by everyone else, our personhood is often up for grabs—literally."[24] While power remains centered in the #MeToo discourse, embodiment must also be considered—in all its diverse manifestations.

> i was groped rolling down the street in my scooter and told that "i liked it" i was at a new years party and kissed a man who took that to be an invitation to attempt to force intercourse. a year later he ask me to perform at his party bc disabled burlesque was funny to him.

> —@YoYoYates, February 23, 2018

There is also the challenge of sexual fetishization. The historical and cultural legacy of "freak shows" continues to structure the simultaneous forces in desiring to look and feeling compelled to turn away, especially as "the freak . . . represents a realm in which the contradictions of conflicting cultural norms are played out—the bodily reminder of that which society expels."[25] Throughout history, individuals with disabilities have thus been situated as alternately spectacle and invisible, engendering fascination yet never rupturing the structuring processes of marginalization. The fetishization of disabled bodies reaffixes that individual within a binary of difference, negating and omitting the whole person in elevation of physical Otherness. The attendant power of visibility in fetishization can destabilize the dominant/subordinate relations, yet this is ultimately fleeting; outside of sexual engagement the disabled body becomes invisible once again.

> I was sexually assaulted while having a seizure. I then talked to the perpetrator and he asked why I didn't say anything . . . because I was having a seizure . . . when I tried to bring that up I was told my story was too nuanced and wasn't really a #metoo story.
>
> —@Somesaylezzels, February 21, 2018

The disabled body generates a sociopolitical discourse on the person, suggesting that "the disabled body created an impaired, childlike, dependent self that lacked elements of sexuality and was deprived of its previous functions, such as in the area of gender."[26] This is of significance to a study of this marginalized community in the discussion of sexual violence and misconduct. Despite the dominance of sexuality and gender in constructing identity, the invisibility or desexualization of disabled folk creates subsequent silence around the possibilities that predators and perpetrators may target this community. This is due in large part to the infantilization of individuals with disabilities, often in their communities of caretakers and support. When nondisabled people perceive disabled folk as childlike, their language and behavior might evoke condescension or even sexually harassing or demeaning communication.

Locked within the assumed vulnerability of the disabled community lies a knot of misunderstanding: the desexualizing of these individuals forgoes entire and important aspects of their identities; the desexualizing of these individuals creates a shield of ignorance and silence that distracts from the predators targeting this community. It is unimaginable because of the utter cruelty of that predatory targeting, but it is also unfathomable because of a mainstream culture that infantilizes, silences, and dismisses our disability communities. This exposes these folk as more vulnerable and more silenced—if only because we never see or hear them in discussions relating to the spectrum of sexuality. In reiterating the holistic concept of disabled folk focusing on the whole person rather than their specific disabilities and challenges, it is possible to transform thought from the culturally bound assumptions and subsequent invisibilities surrounding these communities.

Educational Justice

Engaging with the world and themselves as sexual citizens requires negotiating multiple challenges—from specific limitations surrounding individual disabilities to the larger factors constructing an intersectional sexual identity. When able-bodied ideologies situate disabled folk at extremes of hypersexuality or asexuality, it becomes challenging for people with disabilities to constitute their own sexual identities. There are stark differences between the expectation that disabled and differently abled folk hold equal rights to sexual and reproductive rights and the overwhelming omission regarding their sexual and reproductive needs, desires, and rights within society. Cultural edicts shape perceptions that "people with disabilities are infantilized and held to be asexual (or in some cases, hypersexual), incapable of reproduction and unfit sexual/marriage partners or parents."[27] Thus, disabilities scholarship and activism continues to advocate for the sexual and reproductive health and rights of disabled and differently abled folk as sexual citizens.

Sex education for disabled and differently abled folk is severely lacking. While sexual health and sexual relationship education is still desperately wanting across the United States—let alone internationally—even this basic, formulaic information is not afforded to the disabled and differently abled population. As the majority of special education programs do not offer sexual education curricula, disabled and differently abled students may not recognize either healthy or abusive sexual behaviors.[28] Implementing age-appropriate sex education and training is especially important in providing the necessary language for disabled and differently abled folk to understand when and how to discuss what might be happening to them. Already saddled with a sense of alienation, that lack of information supplied to their peers furthers the sense of isolation and subsequent vulnerability.

> A2 TW I've been sexually harassed and assaulted and targeted because of my disability. Some people seem surprised it happens to us, ironically, while we're at greater risk.
>
> —@glapointewriter, February 21, 2018

Education that is specific to the unique experiences of disabled and differently abled folk can enlighten and empower them, illustrating the importance of sexual identity, expression, and safety. Considering the elevated risk for the disabled and differently abled communities, sex education—through lessons or workshops—must also attend to the specific needs of these folk.[29] Information is general and vague, often forgoing key elements of subtitles or audio-narrated videos that might help the hearing-impaired community, for example. The visual images used across sex education literature is also key—rarely, if ever, are there images featuring disabled and differently abled individuals. Representation and identification are integral to inclusivity in educational and support outreach concerning sexuality, sexual health, and sexual violence and misconduct.

Continuing debates over sexual education across the United States illustrate the uphill battle in enriching this education for nondisabled students, much less using it as an opportunity to speak directly to the experiences of marginalized youth. Stereotypes and stigma are wound about this aspect, reminding us that while no child should be "left behind," these efforts differ vastly from child to child. Children of color are frequently presumed to be adults, in need of little protection from sexual violence and misconduct. Conversely, disabled and differently abled children are stereotyped as eternally asexual, distanced from any discourse of sexuality. And these communities remain the most at risk for abuse or institutionalization.

Statistics on institutionalization surrounding the disabled and differently abled communities is especially daunting. Disabled and differently abled folk are often under surveillance and threatened with the possibility of institutionalization, especially as universal health care and support services are cut in the United States and globally. Stigmatization, ignorance, and prejudice surrounding disabilities further silence their narratives and subsequently increase their vulnerability. In response to the National Public Radio (NPR) series "Abused and Betrayed," Stafford notes that the statistics used from the Department of Justice (DOJ) neglected those living in group homes or institutionalized facilities: "If you add in other names from institutional and group homes, you are really looking at 70 percent of people with developmental disabilities having been abused, and out of those, about 50 percent have had ten or more occurrences."[30] These staggering numbers, atop those released from the DOJ and in the NPR series, illustrate how the disabled and differently abled are targeted by predators and further silenced by systemic abuses.

The disabled and differently abled communities face further obstacles in seeking justice for survivors of rape, abuse, exploitation, and harassment. For those with intellectual disabilities, there has been a legacy of silence and disbelief; rape cases are one of the hardest crimes for police to investigate or for prosecutors to win. Small groups of advocates within the prosecution community are working to change the system and the ways in which these cases are brought to justice. This population is often the most victimized and underreported because they often do not identify what has happened to them as abuse, cannot find the language to share their stories, or find that when they do report, they are not believed. Shapiro reports of the efforts of advocates within the justice system and law enforcement to communicate in different ways with these survivors: "People with intellectual disabilities often do have trouble speaking or describing things in detail or in proper time sequence . . . our investigation found that makes it harder for police to investigate and for prosecutors to win these cases in court."[31] Perpetrators often rely on these inequities and challenges in the justice system. This perpetuates a cycle of abuse and victimization that reaches epidemic levels with little recourse or intervention in sight.

> A2. I have problems with my memory and that was used against me in a calculated way by a rapist. It was then used by police to dismiss me despite evidence.
>
> —@shalyndra42, February 21, 2018

> A2: I've experienced sexual harassment & coercion by another PWD which led to my exclusion from local disability groups. I experienced shaming from both PWDs and those at a state agency that is supposed to serve PWD.
>
> —@blinkbutterfly, February 21, 2018

Education and recognition of disabled and differently abled folk as sexual beings must also be addressed through health care systems, social support professions, and family and kinship circles. Frequently excluded from the dominant discourse and representation of love, sex, and reproduction—all subjects quite resonant in language and visibility of their nondisabled peers—disabled youth are limited in access to viable education and honest conversation. Despite the constant discussion of respecting self and others for youth populations, "if you are disabled, it is likely that many of the adults in your life might never consider you as a sexual being, meaning that the usual safety advice and strategies are rarely discussed. You are doubly vulnerable if you can't physically remove yourself easily from an awkward situation."[32] When family and friends, educational, health, and social professionals feel unequipped or uncomfortable discussing sexuality—from expression to enjoyment, abuse to access—it reifies cultural assumptions surrounding disabled folk as desexualized, infantilized, Other. Additional forces of surveillance and segregation limit the potential for youth with disabilities to socialize and to develop and explore their sexuality and physicality in the same way as their nondisabled peers. While this education must be equal to that of their nondisabled peers, it must also address the intersectional experiences of each individual.

Issues of sexual citizenship and equality also raise challenging questions. Already facing intersectional oppressions, disabled folk often find their sexualities obscured, unrecognizable and misunderstood by others and subsequently by themselves. Thus, projects advocating for sexual citizenship may necessitate foregrounding that "Otherness" to secure such rights. As Shildrick suggests, "if freedom of sexual expression is at least one goal of contemporary disability activism, then reliance on the attribution of sexual citizenship to deliver such a potential cannot be taken for granted."[33] The involvement of governance creates another level of surveillance and regulation for citizens, yet it can also work to protect the rights of individuals as sexual citizens.

The construction and representation of people with disabilities often emerges in a narrative elevating individuals who work to overcome their challenges and gain greater autonomy. This therapeutic narrative constructs an idealized social identity of disability yet disregards the multiple, intersectional oppressions beyond the physical, intellectual, or mental disability. This construction of the successful, self-reliant citizen runs counter to the arguments for specific and necessary disability rights. In the discourse of sexual citizenship, the constructs of intersectional identity further impede policies directed toward embodiment in the discussion of rights. A person with disabilities "encouraged by authoritative voices to avail herself of the plentiful range of sexual self-help manuals for example, is trapped into developing her own coping mechanisms which operate at the level of individual inadequacy, rather than challenging the inherent ableism that marks her sexual otherness as problematic."[34] The inclusion of multiple marginalized individuals in sexual citizenship issues and policy thus crafts a double bind. This occurs as governmental intervention might secure important rights, yet these policies may deploy from a dominant ideology into the private lives of Others.

Considering the disabled community, many of these individuals were never offered the language to express inappropriate and violent behaviors— further, many have been deprived of the abilities to access the language necessary to report such violations. The language engaged to explore sexual violence and misconduct also presents quite differently in various situations and for different communities—especially for disabled folk. It remains oppressive, dehumanizing, exploitative, and silencing. Yet nondisabled individuals might not be aware of the language and behaviors used to violate, abuse, harass, exploit, and silence the disabled population. #MeToo must use not only language but action to support their activists, advocates, and allies with disabilities. Because disabled folk are at greater risk of sexual violence and misconduct, their contributions to the conversation strengthen the momentum and visibility of the movement. While this is a common theme throughout this text, it bears repeating that tailoring our literature to marginalized communities remains essential in educational efforts. The increase of literature and imagery educating and advocating within the

#MeToo movement must include "providing content in multiple formats, such as print, video, audio, captioned, transcribed, and other measures to ensure everyone can engage with that content."[35] Most significantly, there must be attention paid to the issues of access and visibility in educating the nondisabled community. If the experiences and lessons from disabled people are not included within this education and activism, any movement emphasizing intersectionality has failed.

BLANK BOXES AND INTERSECTIONALITY

Even as survivors, activists, and advocates with disabilities continue lauding the #MeToo movement (in addition to other social justice projects), there is a common refrain that hopes "the public listens to and believes victims that didn't fit the narrative of what a believable victim looks like."[36] #MeToo has expanded the conversation surrounding sexual violence and misconduct globally and systemically, shining its spotlights around the world and in every industry and workspace. Yet it may now be time for the movement to move the dialogue to the margins, or better yet, upend the binary of mainstream/margin entirely.

Activism and advocacy surrounding sexual violence and misconduct has continued focusing on representations and visibility of able-bodied individuals. This happens even as the abuse of disabled folk continues to proliferate internationally—this occurs from care centers for mentally challenged youth to elder care centers and hospice. Wafula Strike states that "as disabled women, we are constantly having to validate our existence, which is frustrating and exhausting. It often feels as though every box is ticked while we, disabled women, are left blank."[37] Revisiting the notion of inclusion within activist and advocacy projects becomes more necessary in the wake of movements like #BlackLivesMatter and #MeToo—these movements have emphasized the significance of racial and gendered inclusivity. Yet there remains a need within those larger projects to continue the work of opening doors for greater inclusivity. When dedicated to amplifying the voices of every individual, attention to the oft-silenced community of disabled folk must be paid.

Intersectionality and alliances might shift the discourse surrounding sexuality in disability communities into a positive framework. Understanding that a specific disability is not the sole obstacle or contributing factor in that individual's sexuality and sexual experience remains central to this discussion. Disabled folk share lessons about the nature of embodiment, illustrating how "social knowledge, internalized beliefs, identities and bodily practices are objectified into size, shape and appearance, then made subjective again through practice."[38] Cultural knowledge itself thus becomes incorporated, stored, and reproduced through the body. In an argument for intersectionality, one of the most significant steps forward is in recognizing and engaging the whole person—not just sexual orientation, gender, class, age, race, ethnicity, or disability.

Disability studies and scholarship has already contributed a wealth of literature regarding sociopolitical relationships between and among disabled and nondisabled communities. These relations further inform cultural constructions and productions of identity.

> We all know about #MeToo. What we don't talk about is the epidemic of sexual assault against PWDs. Rooted in Rights and @DisVisibility collaborated to lift up the voices of disabled survivors so that their stories could be heard.
>
> —@rootedinrights, May 24, 2018[39]

One policy concern is that rather than simply accessing equal rights within heteronormative society, marginalized activists, advocates, and allies might instead seek to challenge the confines of that dominant structure. Recognition and inclusivity of sexual citizenship for people with disabilities could be problematized in a similar way. When policies are enacted to secure equal rights, there remain aspects of sexuality disavowed by heteronormative structures and governance. Political and legal institutions and policies remain insufficient; the dominant ideology supporting these structures continuously reduces the intersectionality of marginalized citizens generally and disabled bodies specifically. The discourse of sexuality might instead illustrate "new forms of embodied connection that take account equally of the intersectionality of the socio-political, the meaning of the erotic and the significance of the cultural imaginary,"[40] providing a path forward in embracing recognition, inclusion, and intersectionality.

In a discourse that is largely focused on the nature of consent, there perhaps is no better opportunity to learn about permission than from disability communities. Neal states that "for most disabled people, consent factors into our daily lives in ways that it doesn't for the able-bodied . . . the experiences of the disabled teach that it actually serves as a mutual platform of respect, regardless of situation and circumstance."[41] This largely involves the power dynamics that are not only integral to discussions on sexual violence and misconduct but also in daily communicative interactions. Disabled folk consistently experience verbal and nonverbal moments in which nondisabled individuals exhibit condescension or appropriation of the Other in the name of kindness, curiosity, or helpfulness. While there are genuinely kind, curious, and helpful individuals in the world, the general lack of awareness and education surrounding the experiences of those with disabilities creates a distance in which their efforts present as clumsy at best and offensive at worst. Encroaching on any other human's physical space or presuming a diminishment of any other human's autonomy occurs more often as an infringement on disabled folk. These experiences surrounding consent and the body signal a call for the inclusion and wisdom of these communities within the discourse of #MeToo.

Arguing for citizenship rights to protect people with disabilities as a sexual minority, Siebers articulates that the status of sexual citizenship for this community would further "advance the cause of other sexually oppressed groups."[42] While considering the underlying respect that no one is obligated to share or teach others in this movement, disabled activists and advocates have often used narrative in their own healing: "struggling to find and place pain allowed many disabled performers to develop a complex relation to language and bodily fantasy."[43] In working to develop and share a vocabulary of pain and healing, disabled folk are uniquely equipped to contribute language to a still-evolving discourse of #MeToo survival and identity. People with disabilities "take these powers of story-telling, space-making, truth-saying, time-shaping, and make the frames of everyday experiences, private experiences and public knowledge visible."[44] Sharing the stories of one's life creates a powerful and resistant strategy for intervention that reasserts specificity of identity while building narrative bridges through similar experiences.

As disabled folk are becoming increasingly recognized in debates and scholarship surrounding their rights as sexual citizens, they are forging greater alliances with other movements like the LGBTQ+ community and feminist activism. This inter-movement conversation and collaboration elevates the visibility and volume of these marginalized groups in obtaining greater rights and freedoms in their pursuits of love, sex, pleasure, relationships, health, and reproduction.

> I think one key question in this movement is: how do we create therapeutic social spaces? Disability politics gives us many ways to imagine what these might look & feel like.
>
> —@lldiedrich, February 21, 2018

With the momentum of the #MeToo movement, it is time to cast the gaze beyond the mainstream and provide support, platforms, and tools for those silenced at the margins. Stories of survival from disability communities must be included in the dialogue—"including and especially as members of survivor groups, advocate groups, and vocal members of the #MeToo movement."[45] The international conversation surrounding #MeToo must take steps forward to address sexual violence and misconduct through policies and legislation. This is especially pertinent to those with disabilities; they have often been excluded in representation and conversation.

Flores states that "for the disability community, saying 'me too' means becoming rid of stigmas, rid of sexual assault, and rid of ableist ideals. For me, saying 'me too' is a form of solidarity, and in a way, becoming liberated of the sexual taboo that's been placed on my disabled body."[46] When disabled folk feel further excluded from mainstream movements, even those that speak directly to activism and advocacy, it shuts down the possibilities of conversations that halt these repeated violations. Sexual violence and misconduct may appear "different for the disability community than they can for nondisabled people."[47] Further, disabled folk often face doubt and mockery from those they trust to report to, thus making conversations far more difficult and deepening that sense of alienation. True inclusion would ensure that disabled folk are invited to the conversation and encouraged to share their experiences—moreover, a recognition of all aspects of sexuality for the disabled and differently abled communities might encourage greater visibility.

As Stafford states: "Disability is the one minority group we can all join."[48] This reiterates the significance of including these voices within all social justice conversations, especially whereas we may learn more about strength, compassion, and resilience. Much like other marginalized groups structured by singular identifiers such as race, gender, sexual orientation, or class, disabled folk have continued asserting the intersectionality of their identities and oppressions, questioning and subverting the meanings assigned to them. Further, these communities have had to overcome physical and social loss, trauma, and dependency in ways that elevate them as specifically informed not only to participate but to lead discussions about aspects of embodiment and autonomy within #MeToo.

NOTES

1. Emily Ladau and Alice Wong, "Call for Stories: #MeToo and the Disability Community," *Rooted in Rights*, February 6, 2018, https://www.rootedinrights.org/call-for-stories-metoo-and-the-disability-community.

2. #DisVisibility, *Twitter*. Developed from the "Call for Stories" conversation in partnership with the Disability Visibility Project, the majority of tweets incorporated in this chapter are pulled from #DisVisibility. These tweets took place in an online forum in February 2018 and unless otherwise noted, all included tweets are from this feed.

3. D'Arcee Neal, "The #MeToo Movement Has Ignored Disabled People, but We Need It More Than Ever," *them*, April 16, 2018, https://www.them.us/story/me-too-movement-must-include-disabled-people.

4. James Meadours and Leigh Ann Davis, "#MeToo Survivors with Disabilities: We Will Not be Forgotten," *Medium*, National Sexual Violence Resource Center, and

NSVRC, April 18, 2018, https://medium.com/sexual-assault-awareness-month-2018/metoo-survivors-with-disabilities-we-will-not-be-forgotten-2e075e7098a8.

5. s.e. smith, "Disability Should Be Integral to the #MeToo Conversation," *Rewire.News*, November 1, 2017, https://rewire.news/article/2017/11/01/disability-integral-metoo-conversation.

6. Meadours and Davis, "#MeToo Survivors with Disabilities."

7. Sonali Shah, "'Disabled People Are Sexual Citizens Too': Supporting Sexual Identity, Well-Being, and Safety for Disabled Young People," *Frontiers*, September 4, 2017, https://www.frontiersin.org/articles/10.3389/feduc.2017.00046/full#B20.

8. Petra Kuppers, *Disability and Contemporary Perspectives: Bodies on Edge* (New York: Routledge, 2003), 44.

9. Margrit Shildrick, "Sexual Citizenship, Governance and Disability: From Foucault to Deleuze," in *Beyond Citizenship: Feminism and the Transformation of Belonging*, ed. Sasha Roseneil (New York: Palgrave Macmillan, 2013), 138–59.

10. Neal, "Ignored Disabled People."

11. Alaina Leary, "We Need to Remember Disability When We Talk about Sexual Assault," *Ravishly*, April 18, 2017, https://ravishly.com/we-need-remember-disability-when-we-talk-about-sexual-assault.

12. Karolyn Gehrig, "Time's Up for Me, Too," *Guernica*, March 1, 2018, https://www.guernicamag.com/times-up-for-me-too.

13. Kuppers, *Disability and Contemporary Perspective*, 6.

14. Shah, "'Sexual Citizens Too.'"

15. Deborah Ann Payne, Huhana Hickey, Anna Nelson, Katherine Rees, Henrietta Bollinger, and Stephanie Hartley, "Physically Disabled Women and Sexual Identity: A PhotoVoice Study," *Disability & Society* 31, no. 8 (2016): 1030–49.

16. Emily Yates, "Disability and Sex Are Not Mutually Exclusive," interview by Joan McFadden, *Guardian*, October 15, 2016, https://www.theguardian.com/lifeandstyle/2016/oct/15/disability-and-sex-are-not-mutually-exclusive.

17. Joseph Shapiro, "Abused and Betrayed," aired January 16, 2018 on NPR.com, audio, 8:15, https://www.npr.org/series/575502633/abused-and-betrayed.

18. Shapiro, "Abused and Betrayed."

19. Neal, "Ignored Disabled People."

20. Imani, "#MeToo? To Address Sexual Assault Among Disabled, People Need to Stop Desexualizing & Segregating Us," *Crutches & Spice*, November 21, 2017, https://crutchesandspice.com/2017/11/21/metoo-to-address-sexual-assault-among-disabled-people-need-to-stop-desexualizing-segregating-us.

21. Emily Flores, "The #MeToo Movement Hasn't Been Inclusive of the Disability Community," *TeenVogue*, April 24, 2018, https://www.teenvogue.com/story/the-metoo-movement-hasnt-been-inclusive-of-the-disability-community.

22. Erika Harrel, "Crime Against Persons with Disabilities, 2009–2015—Statistical Tables," Bureau of Justice Statistics, July 11, 2017, https://www.bjs.gov/index.cfm?ty=pbdetail&iid=5986.

23. Kuppers, *Disability and Contemporary Perspectives*, 17.

24. Imani, "#MeToo?"

25. Kuppers, *Disability and Contemporary Perspectives*, 46.

26. Maayan Agmon, Amalia Sa'ar, and Tal Araten-Bergman, "The Person in the Disabled Body: A Perspective on Culture and Personhood from the Margins," *International Journal for Equity in Health* 15, no. 147 (2016): 4.

27. Renu Addlakha, Janet Price, and Shirin Heidari, "Disability and Sexuality: Claiming Sexual and Reproductive Rights," *Reproductive Health Matters* 25, no. 50 (2017): 5.

28. Meadours and Davis, "#MeToo Survivors with Disabilities."

29. Yates, "Disability and Sex."

30. Margaret Wright, "The Disability Community's Long-awaited #MeToo Moment," *NM Political Report*, February 26, 2018, http://nmpoliticalreport.com/2018/02/26/the-disability-communitys-long-awaited-metoo-moment.

31. Shapiro, "Abused and Betrayed."

32. Yates, "Disability and Sex."

33. Shildrick, "Sexual Citizenship," 140.

34. Shildrick, "Sexual Citizenship," 144.

35. smith, "Disability Should Be Integral."

36. Imani, "#MeToo?"

37. Anne Wafula Strike, "Disabled Women See #MeToo and Think: What about Us?" *Guardian*, March 8, 2018, https://www.theguardian.com/commentisfree/2018/mar/08/disabled-people-metoo-womens-movement-inclusion-diversity.

38. Agmon et al., "Disabled Body," 2.

39. #MeToo; @rootedinrights, *Twitter*.

40. Shildrick, "Sexual Citizenship," 154.

41. Neal, "Ignored Disabled People."

42. Tobin Siebers, *Disability Theory* (Ann Arbor: University of Michigan Press, 2008), 136.

43. Kuppers, *Disability and Contemporary Perspectives*, 7.

44. Kuppers, *Disability and Contemporary Perspectives*, 9.

45. Meadours and Davis, "#MeToo Survivors with Disabilities."

46. Flores, "Disability Community."

47. smith, "Disability Should Be Integral."

48. Pamela Stafford, "Long-Awaited #MeToo Moment," interview by Margaret Wright, *NM Political Report*, February 26, 2018, http://nmpoliticalreport.com/2018/02/26/the-disability-communitys-long-awaited-metoo-moment.

CHAPTER 7

Toxic Masculinity and Male Responses to #MeToo

"Perhaps All the Moment Requires Is for Men to Shut Up and Listen"

"My Mama Taught Me How to March." 2018 Women's March in Chicago, Illinois. *Jessica Podraza/Unsplash*

141

> I heard that if you want something done ask a man, if you want something
> said ask a woman, you think this twitter rant is enacting a change, it's a
> joke not a fight, you will need better fights than an empty eligible rant
>
> —@brazzenmirror, October 19, 2018

Despite the focus on women speaking out against the historical weight
of oppression, men and boys also suffer in silence; "the emphasis on
self-reliance and the rigidity of the way we perceive masculinity, means
that many men feel that they have no other choice but to fulfill these
social expectations."[1] Socialization teaches boys at a young age how they
must think and act in ways that reassert dominance, independence, and
aggression while suppressing emotional expressivity. Much as academic
and cultural attention followed the feminist movements, many disciplines
have emerged and developed to assess the social, psychological, representational, and cultural productions and processes of masculinities. As
these fields intersect academically and these issues attain new urgency in
the wake of #MeToo, it becomes increasingly apparent that opening up
the concept of masculinity may allow young boys and men to resist hegemonic expectations. While there are still fervent ideologies seeking to
reassert gender norms, the cultural flashpoint of #MeToo has awakened
millions to the possibilities of gender equality, collaboration, and emotional connection integral for every human.

In many cultures, boys and men are often socialized and taught that
their superiority and privilege is an entitlement. They subsequently learn
that "women and girls are inferior, are second-class citizens, or worse yet,
not worthy of being viewed as anything other than sexual objects, punch-
ing bags, or caretakers to us and our needs."[2] When "boys will be boys"
resonated as an anthem, teachers, principals, parents, community leaders,
faculty members, deans, and then the greater workforce of authority figures
looked the other way. Perhaps it was because authority figures were once
boys taught the same thing, understanding that to challenge such behavior
also meant a threat of expulsion from the club of masculinity. Perhaps it
was because authority figures were once girls socialized into this system,
resigned to the position of inferiority, doubt, and shame. Or perhaps it was
because assumptions surrounding binaried gender inform perceptions of
sexual violence and misconduct. These ideologies shape our worldviews in
terms of division rather than unison.

With the increased discourse surrounding sexual violence and misconduct in mainstream and social media, the call to action stresses the need for
men to engage with the activism and advocacy of movements like #MeToo.
Regardless of perceptions that "men must be engaged in this conversation
in order to be effective at preventing violence and changing deep-seated
patriarchal attitudes, the place of male voices in this ongoing conversation

is hotly in question."[3] There are great implications of accepting and welcoming male voices within #MeToo, especially in consideration of men as victims, bystanders, or perpetrators.

Considering the powerful U.S. and international media spotlight following #MeToo, the survivors have largely been believed—a seismic shift after centuries of victim blaming, shaming, and punishment. While recognizing the accomplishments of #MeToo, Davis notes that due process is often overlooked; the movement "has also generated a 'trial by media' where individual men are publicly 'blamed and shamed' for actions for which they often suffer severe consequences, and before having a chance to defend themselves."[4] The question of how media and the general public are called upon to judge the innocence or guilt of people instills a sense of responsibility—rewarding when the accused are brought to justice but harrowing when innocent people suffer irreparable damages. Often, by the time someone is cleared of allegations, the media focus has already shifted to the next story of accuser and accused, forgoing any resolution of the previous claims.

As marginalized individuals continue making strides in self-determination and access, white masculine privilege and authority is threatened and questioned. As Kimmel states, "just because straight white men don't feel powerful doesn't make it any less true that compared to other groups, they benefit from inequality and are, indeed privileged."[5] This creates a cross-cultural unease marked by violations as heterosexual, cis, white men often descend into defensiveness or denial regarding their cultural privilege. This can be seen in men's rights movements and online trolls denouncing feminists and gender equality, police brutality against black men, political movements against immigration, and a variety of other manifestations. Kimmel posits that the crisis in masculinity occurs because of a sense of "aggrieved entitlement": "those benefits to which you believed yourself entitled have been snatched away from you by unseen forces larger and more powerful."[6]

While it must be reiterated that we have not yet reached a utopic state of equality, there have been remarkable gains made for the visibility, representation, and acceptance of marginalized Others in the United States. For many white, heteronormative, cisgender men, this has invoked feelings of failure, humiliation, and rage—which often manifests in actions. Powell notes that "many of us men feel so incredibly inadequate in our own lives, so weak and powerless, no matter how wealthy or poor we are, that we have come, without apology, to view the abuse and control of women as central to propping up our puny egos and our punier sense of self-worth."[7] Insecurity surrounding inclusivity for marginalized Others has generated a sense of righteous defensiveness and violent hatred. This deeply ingrained sense of inadequacy demands relinquishing the power that sustains all intersecting positions of privilege.

The positions and perspectives of hetero, cis men in the #MeToo movement reveal myriad complexities and conversations including hegemonic
masculinity as a foundation for backlash; the discourse and challenge of
toxic masculinity; networked and popular misogyny that creates new online
spheres of gendered violence, misconduct, and discrimination; the negotiations of complicity; the detrimental impact of hegemonic masculinity on
mental and physical health; and the external and internal silencing of male
survivors of abuse.

HEGEMONIC BACKLASH

It is a human instinct, no need to create great drama

—@RahulMK17685404, October 16, 2018

Rooted in structural Marxist theory, the concept of hegemonic masculinity exposes the network of power in which we operate and engage. This
framework illustrates how socialization and recognition of these norms and
deviations monitor and direct identity performance and representation.
Connell and Messerschmidt reveal how hegemonic masculinity operates as
a system positioning idealized norms of masculinity while subjugating all
others in relation to that ideal.[8] When this system operates continuously, it
becomes internalized and naturalized as the norm. The discursive practices
involved in constructing and maintaining hegemonic masculinity are thus
predicated on the relational positionality of all involved in this system.

Hegemonic masculinity intersects with local, state, and global power; this
illuminates how these systems are predicated on the oppression not only
of women, but of people of color, the LGBTQ+ community, underserved
populations, developing and underdeveloped cultures, and various other
marginalized groups. Hegemonic masculinity is a culturally valued manifestation of masculinity that assumes beliefs and behaviors that continue
the justified subordination of women and marginalized groups within a
patriarchal culture.[9] Patriarchy is thus sustained by the multiple definitions
of masculinities elevating men through "positivist (what men are), normative (what they ought to be), essentialist (core features of masculinity),
and semiotic (masculinity as not femininity) qualities."[10] These systemic
oppressions are not self-sustained organisms; support of men and women
through consent and complicity becomes integral to the success and elevation of hegemonic masculine dominance. This constitutes the "matrix of
domination"[11] that constructs and affixes individuals to positions of domination and subjugation within the intersectional network of power.

Cultural narratives surrounding many of these performances and representations are often bolstered through acts "building heterosexual men,

strengthening hetero-masculine bonds, and strengthening the bonds of white manhood in particular."[12] This occurs with and against the use of oppressed and marginalized Others—through appropriation, mockery, ignorance, and exploitation of non-hetero, non-white, non-male identities and communities. It is not necessarily the absence or opposition of these identities that guides hegemonic masculinity but the unique strategy of engaging directly with these individuals and communities to both mock traditional masculinities and shore up heteronormative, classed, abled, white investments. Powell reiterated the bond of manhood and dominance, explaining how the "taste of power was totally intoxicating. . . . This real-life modeling of male privilege shaped our identity. . . . Our schools rarely bothered to include women as equals in terms of intellectual achievement or career aspiration."[13] This reaffirms the lack of education on not only what masculinity is, but how instrumental women are in building communities at the local, regional, and global levels.

Frameworks of hegemonic, subordinated, marginalized, and complicit masculinities unmask the intricate networks of performance and construction surrounding sexual violence and misconduct. Because hegemonic masculinity is dependent on the intersectional identities and oppressions of race, class, age, religion, and various other categorizations, it further delineates the ideals of masculinity among men. This system of internalized hegemony assumes "other aspects of hegemonic masculinity in recompense for lowered status in the hierarchy and applies them strategically in a constant and contextual practice of negotiation and requisition to maintain and police external hegemony."[14] Because hegemonic masculinity operates on the construction and maintenance of privileged positions throughout society, these processes uphold a status quo through sustained inequality in the system.

Within the hegemony, subordinate masculinity involves targeting "othered" men based on categorizations seen as "less than" by the hegemonic structure. Complicit masculinity—and this includes performances by men, women, and nonbinaried individuals—incorporates those much-maligned "bystanders" who do not necessarily practice hegemonic or toxic forms of masculinity yet enjoy benefits from the power of those sociopolitical structures. Enjoying what Connell calls the "patriarchal dividends" of overall oppression without actively deploying masculine dominance, these complicities embody a "slacker" hegemonic masculinity.[15] Marginalized masculinity highlights the position of men situated according to physicality, race, class, religion, age, ableism, or various forms of "Otherness" in comparison to the hegemonic hierarchy. Bolstered by cultural, political, academic, and social contexts, all of these masculinities create and maintain a structure of dominance and subordination.

According to Glick and Fiske, while the ideologies and actions of hostile and benevolent sexism are distinct, these belief systems collaboratively create and sustain the structures of gender hegemony.[16] Hostile sexism emerges from the claim that men are more capable mentally and physically than women. This position subsequently affords privilege in status and power to men while ascribing women with deploying sexuality or feminism to "steal" this status or power. Issues of control and dominance constitute this ideological system, supported by misrepresentation through damning stereotypes and reliance on tropes like "tradition." While hostile sexism remains an overt and therefore recognizable form of oppression, benevolent sexist ideologies build and sustain a more complex and inscrutable hegemonic network.

As explained by Becker and Wright, benevolent sexism manifests as protective paternalism, complementary gender differentiation, and heterosexual intimacy.[17] On the surface, these forms of benevolent sexism appear positive: protective paternalism iterates a need for men to protect women; complementary gender differentiation suggests that women are imbued with superior qualities; and heterosexual intimacy reasserts the capabilities of women to fulfill relational and romantic needs lacking in their heterosexual male partners. Digging deeper, these benevolent beliefs correlate with a patronizing system that undermines or devalues women's own sense of identity and capability. In the depiction of girls and women as "wonderful but childlike, incompetent, needing men to protect them, and therefore best suited for low-status roles, benevolent sexism justifies gender inequality."[18] Further, this pattern of benevolence might only be afforded to girls and women who comply with the hegemonic structure.

The combination of affection and dominance within benevolent sexism offers a strategic leveraging tool simultaneously diminishing acts of resistance against gender inequality and sustaining the hegemonic hierarchy of gender. While the recognition of patronizing or disqualifying strategies within benevolent sexism often incites swift and angry responses from society or individual women, there are increased chances that it will be mitigated and even accepted if the system promises benefits to girls and women. Dominant, privileged groups will continue thwarting resistance from marginalized communities and individuals through both overtly hostile practices and covertly disarming or conciliatory strategies.

Extending previous literature surrounding hegemonic masculinity and intersectionality across the discursive sites of physical space and social media, it becomes clear that within the Twittersphere, lessened surveillance permits uncontested discourse. While this works in ways that might galvanize groups toward progressive social activism and advocacy, the unpoliced sites of social media also encourage responses that "rally against feminism and modern political correctness—viewed by some men as a threat to their White Male privilege."[19] As research demonstrates the masculine use of language to reassert positions of strength and dominance, this mixed-method content analysis depicts how the discourses in media coverage, #MeToo posts, and responses simultaneously structure and dismantle hegemonic masculinity.

When sexual conquest and violent dominance become markers of swaggering manhood, the rape culture thrives. The cultural productions informing and supporting toxic masculinity start "with straight, white men and trickles down through marginalized groups, affecting the way they perceive themselves and behave."[20] To understand the gendered, racial, or sexual dynamics in all marginalized groups it is necessary to first look at where that behavior originates and how it seeps into society.

The Toxic Locker Room

> And when you're a star, they let you do it. You can do anything. . . . Grab them by the pussy. You can do anything.[21]

Following the release of the *Access Hollywood* recording of Trump boasting over his sexual assault of women, he called it "locker room talk" and the future first lady Melania Trump similarly described it as "boy talk." This language remains a central theme of hegemonic masculinity, often used to attain legitimacy in the self-surveillance and policing of other men. Yet the tradition of dismissing these actions in such a way implies "that all men act this way . . . but the 'boys will be boys' excuse, for any kind of behavior, is demeaning."[22] In relegating all aggressive, disparaging, or misogynist behaviors to "boys will be boys," boys and men are not only handed an excuse but taught that they cannot strive for better.

Despite its origins as a term coined by Shepherd Bliss in reference to the Mythopoetic Men's Movement (MMM)[23] most visible in the late 1980s and early 1990s, the phrase "toxic masculinity" has resurfaced in the wake of #MeToo, the U.S. election of Trump, and the multiple manifestations of harmful and threatening behaviors and ideologies online. The Mythopoetic Men's Movement assumed that in elevating women's voices and concerns, men's voices would be muted. The MMM believed that this led to aggressive, violent, hyper-masculinities in crisis—toxic masculinities. In the roar of #MeToo, toxic masculinity has reemerged as a phrase with complicated ties to the past and limitless implications in the current viral movement.

Kuper studied toxic masculinity as a barrier to psychosocial development, incorporating regressive misogynist, homophobic, racist, classist, ableist, and aggressive ideologies.[24] Connell and Messerschmidt suggest that these elements are not fixed traits but rather toxic behaviors men sometimes engage in, especially under sociopolitical surveillance.[25] Considering the rather narrow and oppressive description of toxic masculinity, the Good Men Project offers it as the cultural ideal "where sex and brutality are yardsticks by which men are measured, while supposedly 'feminine' traits—which can range from emotional vulnerability to simply not being hypersexual—are the means by which your status as 'man' can be taken away."[26] This encompasses the normatives, ideologies, and actions associated with specific behaviors including competition, self-sufficiency, violence, sexism, misogyny, heteronormativity, and entitlement. Cooper notes that "this unhealthy form of masculinity has been cited as the reason for everything noxious, from school shootings and climate change to racism and bullying."[27] As critics argue that this phrase unfairly generalizes all men based on the worst behaviors of a few, the majority of activists, academics, advocates, and public pundits reiterate that "toxic masculinity" is not a wholesale attack but only a description of the most violent, harmful, and oppressive aspects associated with masculinity.

Psychology has long explored the issues surrounding masculinity and mental health, with recent focus on toxic masculinity.[28] According to psychologist Eric Mankowski, toxic masculinity is built around four tenets: repressing stereotypical feminine expressions, masculine domination, aggression, and suppressing emotions (aside from anger). As these four components work together, it leads to acts of sexual or physical violence.[29] At the crux of these tenets of toxicity, serial harassers, abusers, and rapists emerge when predators believe that domination or aggression over others can both negate the presence of the feminine as person and forgo feelings of connection or empathy. Alternatively, Saad explored the hazards in pathologizing manhood, offering examples from the animal kingdom to reiterate that aggression is often part of the sexual selection process.[30] Saad suggests that toxic masculinity only becomes a pathology when categorized in gender relations. Veissière spoke about the challenges of raising sons into a manhood that can be seen as toxic, often associating, expecting, and even rewarding risk, violence, and sexual aggression. As he stated, "in the wake of the #MeToo crisis, it may be wise to remember that complementarities, rather than competition between genders, is the healthy cultural attitude to promote."[31] Much as binaried or contradicting ideals of gender exist across all cultures, there are far more complementary and fluid gendered identities that elude any one box or type.

Masculinity remains a highly contested construction, which often emerges in the language of battle: "The one who wins is the one who walks away with the manhood and the one who loses is the one who is made invisible and is feminized."[32] Processes and performances of masculinity typically stress aggression and independence; thus, bonding and kinship between men becomes limited to spaces that prize battle talk—as in conversations about sports—or "locker room talk" that objectifies women. Marche argues that our current state involves "a public conversation about male sexual misbehavior, while barely touching on the nature of men and sex."[33] While

Marche attempts to understand the allegations that led to #MeToo through a conversation about the "nature" of male desire (similarly to Saad), this suggestion of irrepressible masculine sexuality becomes problematic. As Zimmer states, "this is the kind of masculinity that also teaches men they don't have to ask permission to act on their sexual desires."[34] When social constructions teach us that emotions (aside from anger) or communicating about emotions violates masculine norms, this leads to a silencing of the conversations that might educate boys and men about healthy and respectful relationships. Toxic masculinity elevates this stifled communication and repressed emotion, suggesting that the ideal masculinity is built on sexual conquests and oppressive power.

The embattled discourse surrounding toxic masculinity reasserts certain defensive and divisive tendencies. Sculos suggests that the conversation steers many to "aggressively defend a concept of masculinity, in such a way that shows how such a debate over the normative value of a concept of masculinity is tied to the aggressive, competitive, homophobic, sexist, and misogynistic character of toxic masculinity."[35] The virulent responses to the use of the phrase are often bound to an identity that the privileged, patriarchal, hegemonic populace has been taught as the "correct" form of masculine identity and valued as such. Rather than shutting the conversation down or vilifying boys and men, using this phrase might instead create a moment to recognize the limitations of traditional masculinities. Thus, talking about toxic masculinity is an opportunity to revise and reconstruct positive and diverse models of being and identity.

Networked Misogyny

> Bravo for your intent, but many females have distorted your views. #MeToo has turned into a man-hating machine. Redirect this conversation with those in the limelight, please.
>
> —@_mrs_ladybug, August 20, 2018

The combination of masculinity studies and social media frameworks has been posited as a particularly fertile area of research known as "networked masculinities."[36] Reminiscent of the antifeminist and profeminist factions that emerged in various men's rights movements of the 1970s, the reach and access of social media platforms has opened dialogue for men's responses to feminism, gender equality, and women's rights. The discourse cultivated online has often directly rejected feminism while demanding entitlement and claiming simultaneous superiority and victimhood. This discursive production of men's rights movements online has drastically transformed and gained support across various communities, organizations, and platforms—also known as the manosphere.[37]

Reasserting the hegemonic masculine hierarchy, the digital manosphere regularly employs language of misogyny, racism, homophobia, and various other privileged rhetorical tenets to continue extending the ladder of power. Our digital world continuously expands the reach of toxic masculine discourse and ideology. Hybrid cultures of masculinities "compete with one another online to establish power within a male hierarchy, despite possessing power offline. . . . The process includes extreme bouts of racism and misogyny, while engaging in hacking and doxing."[38] These hybrid masculinities spread across platforms to reassert hegemonic masculinity through an oxymoronic rhetoric of victimhood and superiority.

Charged and vitriolic antifeminism often props up hegemonic masculinity by further deploying racist or homophobic language. These manifestations of defensive or toxic masculinities have reached greater heights in the era of social media. Banet-Weiser and Miltner refer to this phenomenon as networked misogyny, characterized by anonymity, technological developments and access, trolls and unpoliced or unenforced online policies, and the disparate relations between the speed of technological development and the methodical processes of the justice system.[39] When these forces are deeply ingrained and routine, the institutional and intersectional oppressions become naturalized and legitimized. Further, with the recognition of overwhelming engagement and support for the #MeToo movement as the latest (and most high-profile) form of feminist digital activism or popular feminism, popular misogyny has emerged as a countermovement. Popular or networked misogyny manifests as a "political and economic culture, where rape culture is normative, violent threats against women are validated, and rights of the body for women are either under threat or being formally retracted."[40] #MeToo accentuates how greater expressions and embodiments of feminism are engaged across digital platforms and in media coverage. Yet the progress made by girls and women threatens the privileged positions of boys and men in the hegemonic social structure. In response, many boys and men flock to social media to carve a space of popular misogyny and toxic masculinity.

Claiming aggrieved disenfranchisement and victimhood, these angry white men often emphasize certain aspects of hegemonic masculinity while distancing themselves from others. In a strategic move for white, hetero, cis, middle- and upper-class men to retain sociopolitical, economic, and cultural power in eras of greater support and recognition of marginalized identities, the manosphere often highlights the plight of "beta" males, "geeks," "incels" (involuntary celibates), and myriad other hybrid masculinities organizing against women, feminism, social justice projects, and alpha males. Some have argued that the question of anonymity and avatars might appear to confuse the borders of "real" and "fantasy" in social media. This is a moot point. Male sexual, political, and social dominance remains a driving force regardless of intent or impact: "That this might be achieved through exaggerated performances of misogyny and the simultaneous mobilization of tropes of victimhood is nothing new."[41] Social media platforms and virtual spaces erase, conflate, and revise our concepts of self and other, permitting a reimagining of embodiment and identity. Technological discourse also affords protection through anonymity; honest opinions are encouraged while culpability is diminished or obliterated entirely. In an era where social media opens spaces for sharing and storytelling, there is also the inevitable result of emotional impulse and information overload.

Manospheric ideologies "travel to whichever spaces they perceive as threatening male privilege and thus also exert a powerful chilling effect on the Internet's nonmanosphere spaces."[42] Shifting further from the grassroots organization of activism and advocacy, social media often creates a space not only for generous and appreciative sharing but also ad hominem attacks and threats against individual girls and women, as well as feminist allies. In addition to the death and rape threats against individual women and feminists, there have been organized antifeminist protests and support forums for murderers of women, women who criticize hegemonic oppression, and those who support these countermovements.

Manosphere machinations reiterate how united against a "common enemy" that is, feminism, gender equality, etc., the bro-code remains intact despite differences. Hybrid or intersectional masculinities in the digital era conflate or elude fixed assumptions of gender binaries and identities. Yet the hybridization involved in the manosphere continues to secure positions of privilege through the "transnational and technological affordances of social media . . . by mobilizing and reifying narratives of personal suffering to build affective consensus about an allegedly collective, gendered experience, namely men's position in the social hierarchy as a result of feminism."[43] The seemingly disparate threads of masculine identity weave into a shared tapestry; when done well, it might work for progressive aims yet in the manosphere the echo chambers instead work to threaten and exclude women publicly in order to send a warning to all women. When deployed across the social media platforms that generated these ideologies in the first place, it denotes how the hegemonic patriarchy remains intact—despite claims to the contrary.

From Bystanders to Upstanders

> For now I think part of a solution would be to get these guys that witness this type of behavior to speak up and out for the victim.
>
> —@audrey_thomason, October 29, 2017

Sexual abuse, assault, harassment, and exploitation often occurs and thrives not only in dark alleyways and unimaginable corners of the world but in the spaces where many have already encountered reasons for suspicion of a common threat. Institutions that cultivate or protect sexual violence and misconduct do not do this merely at the expense of the survivor, but at a cost to all other coworkers who are not perpetrators of the crime. The hegemonic power structure that enables sexual violence and misconduct is not a top-down system but a network impacting more than the targets of this abuse. This fosters the necessity for all to become allies and advocates of #MeToo. As many others—specifically within #MeToo—have noted, toxic masculinity is just as much about men looking away from abuse, harassment, and rape to maintain their privileged positions.

Environments where sexual violence and misconduct grow and thrive often expose the dangers of complicity. Reports of at least sixteen people directly aware of Weinstein's alleged abuses emerged amid acknowledgments that inside the Weinstein Company and Miramax, Weinstein had held a notorious reputation for exactly these types of behaviors.[44] On the *House of Cards* set, cast and crew members complained about the multiple ways that Spacey created a hostile workplace with predatory behavior including uninvited and nonconsensual touching and comments.[45] In addition to the FBI, local law enforcement, the U.S. Olympic Committee, the NCAA, and USA Gymnastics, academic institutions Penn State and Michigan State delayed, ignored, or covered up allegations against assistant football coach Jerry Sandusky and athletic trainer Larry Nassar, *nonrespectively*, despite multiple reports over decades of alleged (and convicted) abuse.[46] When accusations of sexual assault, abuse, and harassment were lobbed against famed restaurateur Ken Friedman and "celebrity chef" Mario Batali, the public also became aware of how multiple colleagues and industry insiders referred to the third floor of famed NYC establishment The Spotted Pig as "the rape room."[47] The attendant focus on #MeToo exposes not only how rampant these abuses are across diverse public and private industries, but also how often third parties or bystanders recognize, disregard, or even enable these behaviors.

Revisiting system justification, the model of protecting, defending, and bolstering a societal status quo against activism and advocacy emerges in the discussion of bystanders, toxic masculinity, and the #MeToo movement. This concept helps "explain when people will (and will not) experience a sense of moral outrage and whether moral outrage will yield collective action that challenges (vs. upholds) the status quo."[48] For men and women dependent on social, economic, and political institutions, the sense of security and stability promised by hegemonic institutions might often outweigh the sense of moral obligation or outrage. Moreover, systemic ideologies and actions might further shift into the terrain of the taken-for-granted, as articulated by Berger and Luckmann.[49] When institutions create cultures experienced as inevitable or natural, this further legitimizes the system and informs the individual's relationship to it and others within it.

Some have advocated for the legal system to provide more explicit guidance for third-party bystanders. State and federal duty-to-report laws might resonate with the millions left questioning their own responsibilities in the wake of #MeToo. As of 2018, duty-to-report laws only apply to witnesses in twelve U.S. states, yet as Kaufman suggests, these laws might now reflect "a society's revulsion at silence—treating it as a type of complicity."[50] Considering the international reach and response to #MeToo as addressed in the fifth chapter of this text, many foreign countries have explicitly mandated bystander intervention in national laws. Studying the impact these laws have for sexual violence and misconduct allegations, it becomes evident that in cases where the victims face not only skepticism but blaming and shaming, any corroboration would likely support the claims of these survivors. According to Kaufman, a strategic combination of duty-to-report laws and rewards for reporting might transform bystanders into "upstanders." In the wake of #MeToo, legal acts may cement the cultural moment, yet what might carry the message further is recognizing the essential humane response to speak for those who might not have a voice, speak against those who use power to silence their victims, and speak up to add to the chorus of #MeToo.

The Hazards of Conformity

> The metoo movement is not for us men. That's a damn lie. Women have weaponized it to use as a revenge tool to use when they want to get back at some.

> —@romeyromegaming, August 24, 2018

Despite earlier reports that women were more likely to suffer depression, that gender gap has narrowed in recent years.[51] Additionally, men are far less likely to seek treatment (which is inherently tied to masculine expectations of self-reliance, problem solving, and stoicism) yet often engage in violent behaviors to cope with destabilized emotional and psychological states.[52] The daily negotiations, performances, and surveillance strategies tied to masculine norms often have permanent and destructive impacts on mental health.[53] This evidence suggests that the unrealistic ideals set forth as normative masculinity directly increase psychological and emotional distress and disturbance for boys and men.

Synthesizing findings across seventy-eight samples of 19,453 participants, Wong and colleagues offered quantitative evidence to illustrate the link between conforming to masculine norms and the outcomes of mental health struggles. The empirical meta-analysis revealed how "conformity to masculine norms was modestly and unfavorably associated with mental health as well as moderately and unfavorably related to psychological help seeking."[54] The survey specified conformity with dominant status, power over women, and sexual promiscuity as markers of masculinity, all detrimental to mental health.

The emotional and psychological toll in straining to conform and attain the impossible goals of idealized hegemonic masculinity emerges as men are taught to regulate and inhibit emotions, exhibit tough self-reliance, and avoid any communicative correlations with femininity. As Butler articulates, performativity involves acts that if repeated enough, become natural and erode the potential for subversion.[55] Patterned behavior within the hegemonic masculine framework is thus naturalized, internalized, and idealized; these masculine normatives create paradigms for the appropriate ways that boys and men might think, feel, and behave. In constructing a hierarchy predicated upon dominance for men and subordination for women, these patterns are subsequently taught and learned to maintain the structural gender order. In addition to the hostile sexist ideologies and practices of aggression, objectification, or misogyny, it is often shown that boys and men are trained in complicity from an early age.

Conforming to or rejecting these strategic performances and representations of masculinity further impacts positive and negative outcomes. Despite critical and negative mental health consequences for boys and men failing to attain that impossible standard of hegemonic masculinity, a longitudinal study reasserts that the indicator of "Power Over Women may help them feel powerful and efficacious and maintain their desire for dominance in their intimate relationships."[56] Yet women have also been studied for their complicity in the consent and construction of hegemonic masculinity. Girls and women who learn and exhibit loyalty to and support of the hegemonic framework strengthen the system. In seeking short-term benefits, these girls and women often lose sight of the long-term damages not only to their own identified gender but to humanity.

Recognizing how sociopolitical oppressions become replicated in the microcosms of labor demonstrates how lessons ingrained about the perception and treatment of women as objects or properties can inform boys and men implicitly and explicitly. For everyone who joins the laughter over sexist jokes or participates in objectifying women, "once you connect the dots and show men how the jokes they see as harmless actually validate and fuel more harmful behavior, they are quick to change."[57] Reasserting traditional norms of masculinity becomes "associated with violence, risky sexual behaviors, and sexual and intimate partner violence against women, which in turn negatively affect the health of men, women, and children."[58] Health campaigns or social justice projects encouraging male participation should continue striving for gender-transformative language that promotes the equitable relationships between all humans.

#WEDO BELIEVE MALE SURVIVORS

I hope men who are victims are coming forward as well. Them too!

—@candiemenza, October 30, 2017

Let's change that from this moment for all women and men alike. Let's change #metoo to #wedo

—@Arvin_Chopra, October 30, 2017

The question of #MeToo and masculinities also relates directly to male sexual assault victims. While male survivors of sexual violence and misconduct constitute and deserve an entirely separate space of attention, many of the challenges they face in their survival and recognition emerge as byproducts of hegemonic, toxic, and networked masculinity. The support group MaleSurvivor, founded by Dr. Andrew Schmutzer and Dr. Richard Gartner, has worked to provide resources and counsel for the large population of male sexual violence and misconduct survivors. In addition to combating stereotypes surrounding men as survivors, advocacy groups like MaleSurvivor reiterate staggering facts: at least one in six boys is sexually abused in childhood, and at least one out of every four males experiences some form of sexual trauma in their lifetimes.[59] These findings also stress the following: female perpetrators account for 40 percent of childhood sexual abuse experienced by men, predators often know the victims, and most sexual abuse of boys is *not* perpetrated by homosexual men. Highlighting these facts challenges misconceptions and myths surrounding men as always-already perpetrators/women as always-already victims, rape and abuse as actions that occur in dark alleyways inflicted by strangers rather than zones of comfort and trust, and tired homophobic allegations that LGBTQ+ folk are always trying to "scout" or "groom" young people. This knowledge becomes especially significant in battling social stigma faced by male survivors of sexual violence and misconduct—especially whereas most male survivors delay disclosure for an average of twenty years.

> Thank you for standing up for EVERYONE. As a victim of sexual abuse by men AND women, throughout my entire life (at 3, 7, 11, and 19), it means the WORLD to be comfortable enough to confront those demons and not feel less of a man. Thank you Tarana. Thank you.

—@PetitHolland21, August 20, 2018

Shocking isn't it? That all people should be treated equal. I'm a male and also a victim of a predator. Predators exist everywhere. Equally.

—@fancyfatty, August 20, 2018

Bravo. Whether you're a man or a woman, heterosexual, bisexual or homosexual, you can potentially be either the victim or perpetrator of sexual
assault, sexual harassment, bullying or domestic abuse

—@chorlton1973, August 20, 2018

#MeToo has helped shift the (mis)representation of sexual violence and
misconduct away from the formula of powerful, hetero, cis, older men
victimizing young, cis, white hetero women. This is especially notable
when considering how #MeToo has opened a discursive space for men
to share their own experiences facing sexual violence and misconduct. As
Sian Brooke of the Oxford Internet Institute told the BBC, "One group
can be given attention and be taken seriously with regards to allegations
of rape, without it taking any of the severity or weight away from another
part of it."[60] The #MeToo movement's quickfire impact specifically helped
increase the numbers of men seeking support after suffering sexual violence or misconduct—with nonprofit groups like the Los Angeles–based
male sex abuse survivor group 1in6 seeing over 100 percent increases in
the use of online helpline services.

So much of this trend has been incidentally and actively gendered in its
framing that it's hard to be optimistic the movement at large will ever
respond to the reality of non-women victims and of women predators.

—@NerdyEnby, August 20, 2018

It's unfortunate that because of how much suffering women have gone
through, some completely discount that many men have gone through
this abuse as well.
I hope that mentality changes.

—@unkonfined, August 20, 2018

As male victims often become aligned with subordinated masculinities in
the hegemonic structure, they are further marginalized and othered. Thus,
male sexual victimization is often doubted or dismissed in institutional
practices and policies. Further, the threat to masculinity or heteronormativity emerges in the discourse of male sexual violence and misconduct survivors. When male rape and the handling of male rape or harassment cases
are called into question based on homophobic and hegemonic practices
and processes, it is important to identify and clarify these oppressive responses regardless of sexual orientation. When "male rape myths dominate
state and voluntary agencies, male rape victims are left untreated, isolated,
and sidelined."[61] This secondary victimization manifests from hostile, oppressive, biased, homophobic, and shaming beliefs and behaviors that treat
male sexual violence and misconduct survivors as less legitimate. Subse-

quently, this creates silencing strategies in which these survivors are far less likely to report these crimes.[62]

Stereotypical images and vocabularies of sexual violence and misconduct focus on a model of victim/woman and perpetrator/man. While this holds deep implications for our cultural awareness and sensitivity to the multiple and intersectional individuals and oppressions involved in sexual violence and misconduct, it also generates dire consequences for institutions dealing with survivors and perpetrators who do not fit into the typologies. According to Javaid, "state agencies deal with both female and male rape in the same way. . . . Male rape victims experience rape differently in comparison to female rape victims."[63] This becomes especially problematic because male survivors often question their own identity or orientation in the hegemonic context. Myths surrounding male survivors of sexual violence and misconduct emerge in the disbelief of male rape, the emasculation of men who could not defend themselves, the assumption that women cannot rape or assault men, and, the suggestion that "real men" should welcome all sexual interaction.

Yet other public faces have called this into question. NFL athlete turned actor Terry Crews documented his own sexual harassment experience. The perpetrator—Hollywood agent Adam Venit—has since offered public and private apologies and resigned as head of his department at the William Morris Endeavor agency. Yet Crews's motivation from #MeToo bears the most import on transforming the notion of heteronormative and gendered language: "I saw my social media and men specifically were calling these women gold diggers and opportunists. . . . I'm reading all these guys calling these women all these names and I was like: 'I can't let this happen.'"[64] Crews has been acknowledged as one of the most prominent male voices of #MeToo and has helped shift the representation of heteronormative or gendered thinking surrounding #MeToo's perpetrators and survivors.

#MeToo has helped shred the tightly woven cultural tapestry protecting hegemonic masculinity and systemic oppressions. This reveals the intersection of toxic masculinity, networked misogyny, bystander complicity, and the harrowing and silenced experiences for male survivors of sexual violence and abuse. The #MeToo movement incites drastically varied responses from these disparate communities of boys and men. In attempting to move past these dynamics of oppression, #MeToo can provide lessons for participation in a progressive and accepting humanity.

FRAGILE STRENGTH

Psychological undercurrents in gendered ideologies hold sociopolitical implications with far-reaching and long-lasting impact. Hegemonic and networked masculinity affects everyone—yet it is significant to note the differences in how communities and cultures receive and interpret this ideology. Sculos's insightful exploration of the concept states that "Both the Left and the Right view toxic masculinity as a threat, whether it is the material and ideational realities that the concept refers to (this is what the Left opposes) or the concept itself (this is what the Right fears)."[65] Rather than focusing on the oppositional or binaried arguments surrounding #MeToo, Sculos emphasizes how "toxic masculinity" is a threat shared by everyone.

Studying the trending hashtag #MasculinitySoFragile of 2015, Banet-Weiser and Miltner illustrate the precarious nature of gender construction in the social media era. The initially lighthearted hashtag trend confronted the typically hetero, cis masculinity threatened by any link to femininity. Rather than engage with the discourse in a positive or humorous way, many men "conflated this attack on the construct of masculinity with an attack on maleness and responded, rather ironically, in a macho and violent manner."[66] Exemplifying this, Banet-Weiser and Miltner cited one particularly defensive tweet from @mechofjusticewz that read: "I challenge any female tweeting unironically with #MasculinitySoFragile to last three rounds against me in a fight. We'll see who's fragile." The rabid defensiveness of many men reasserts the divisive nature of gender relations in this sociopolitical moment. Much as Trump was more concerned with defending the size of his hands during his campaign than being caught boasting about committing sexual assault, the verbal violence aimed at women across social media reiterates the very fragility noted by the hashtag.[67] The surveillance that creates anxiety and defensiveness regarding potential emasculation reinforces toxic masculinity, popular misogyny, and rape culture. These intersectional oppressions prioritize illusions of hegemonic masculinity over experiences of survivors.

In addition to multiple workshops and support groups dedicated to revising cultural constructions of masculinity including ReThink, Collective Action for Safe Spaces, and A Call to Men, several colleges are offering courses to guide men in examining their own actions, emotions, and biases. These strategies help open communication and prevent misogynistic perspectives and sexual violence. As misogyny and violence are ingrained and systemic forces, these types of courses may not transform a Weinstein or Cosby into an enlightened human being. Yet these conversations and education for boys and men might be a compelling first step in the process of continuing the power of #MeToo for us all.

When boys or men fail at or reject hegemonic ideals, they often face punitive social measures from bullying to exclusion. Underserved and racial/ethnic minority men are often specifically targeted for performances and representations of appropriate maleness. For example, in her piece on "toxic machismo," Ferreira writes that cultural norms create an additional layer of oppression and surveillance on masculinities: "While none of this is exclusive to race or ethnicity, the idea that men need to be hyper masculine in order to be men is very much reinforced in Latino culture."[68] For the black community, oppressive stereotypes perpetrated by media and culture in addition to internal policing of masculinity continually reassert a hypersexual and heteronormative black masculinity. Sociohistorical stereotypes generate and maintain assumptions about black boys and men as dangerous and sexually threatening while negating these men as potential survivors. This reasserts the significance of Crews's public sharing of his own trauma and subsequent revision of stereotypes surrounding white, hetero, cis women as #MeToo survivors.

When rapper 50 Cent posted a meme of Crews that read: "I got raped My wife just watched" on Instagram, it generated a discussion about the nature of abuse perpetrated against boys and men within the context of cultural, racial, and gendered oppressions. This dialogue demonstrated the intersectional forces constraining experiences and support for male survivors.

> Shit like this is the reason men don't come forward as victims of sexual assault often. 50 Cent is publicly mocking Terry Crews, allowing Russell Simmons @UncleRUSH to openly laugh at him.[69]
>
> —@wlymcln, June 26, 2018

> As a survivor advocate who has accompanied two men during their sexual assault forensic exams, it's so disheartening to see male survivors of sexual assault like @terrycrews be mocked. 1 in 6, y'all. 1 in 6.
>
> —@TowardsLessHarm, June 26, 2018

> Just as men need to say "We believe you" to the female survivors, women need to say "We believe you" to the male survivors. We believe you, @ terrycrews. Glad you are sharing your story.
>
> —@MainLineSpy, June 27, 2018

Forces of cultural expectations both external and internal to those from underserved or ethnic/racial minority groups perpetuate a cycle of self-surveillance and policing of others to detect any deviation from these gendered normatives. These oppressive patterns stifle the narrative of sexual violence and misconduct for all male survivors.

As an exaggerated performance of normative masculine hegemony, toxic masculinity might reflect the difficulties in all socially constructed expectations of gender. When boys and men are taught to stifle emotions and communication, they are also shutting down any empathetic discourse that could effect cultural change. As an activism born of social media, #MeToo can and has opened a space for communication where boys and men can engage in the greater conversation and learn from it in valuable ways. When men refuse to be defined by one standard of stereotypical masculinities, all those within society benefit. Douglass claims that "as soon as you betray the idea that you can't be a strong man without punishing everyone who isn't toxically masculine, we'll all become stronger for it."[70] The growing participation of men in the conversations of #MeToo, #IHave, or #Timesup illustrate the power of educating oneself beyond previously defined limits of identity.

As Gramsci suggests, the "ideological struggle" emerges as the aspiring group adopts a principle that opens the possibilities for the inclusion and assimilation of beliefs and behaviors from the discourse of all marginalized groups. Women and men who have "looked the other way" may now realize that consent creates hegemony. The fundamental group exercises leadership of sociopolitical, intellectual, and cultural import within the hegemonic structure already locked into place through shared ideologies. Yet transformative possibilities exist when group leadership and participation expand to address previous ideological structures, unify subordinate Others, and commit to collective agency.

Societal expectations for boys and men to be assertive, aggressive, and even violent often reasserts itself in dynamics of sexuality. Homophobic statements might be strategies to prove heterosexuality; unchecked verbal abuse often culminates in physical or sexual violence. Similarly, hypersexual or misogynist statements—or the "bystander" laughing at the jokes—is dismissed as "locker-room talk." Rather than accept language and actions that devalue women and marginalized communities, #MeToo has forced many to question how historical constructions of competitive masculinities based on "physical power, risk-taking and sexual prowess and promiscuity . . . are damaging to both men and women, and society at large."[71] In the ideological struggle for dominance, the hegemonic productions motivated by consent unveil the more comprehensive cultural imperative toward revolution.

Although the return to essentialist thought has created greater unrest, division, and activist responses in U.S. culture, the educational system hosts a specific divide in thinking about gender. Boys and young men "falling behind" in education are often used to legitimize resurging claims for essentialism. In academia, it is notable that the increased attention to gender-based advocacy in education often rejects biological essentialism to challenge gender bias and address cultural oppressions against girls and women. In recent years, this has led to active campaigns to increase self-esteem for young girls and women and encourage participation in traditionally male-dominated fields like STEM programs.[72] Although this educational advocacy has expanded opportunities for girls and women, research also suggests that "boys' advocates . . . foreground approaches that emphasize biological sex differences when addressing the widely reported gender gap in academic achievement and other indicators that boys are falling behind girls in school."[73]

Much of masculinities studies and scholarship emphasizes the flaw in this system insofar as male behaviors presumably return to essentialism— or "boys-will-be-boys" excuses—and subsequently form a critical component of the socialization process. Regarding the socialization and education of youth, "it is in discussions of girls that we most often encounter a transcendent rhetoric of possibility . . . we are much more likely to be warned of the damaging effects of pushing boys beyond biologically-determined cognitive and emotional limits."[74] Even as this upends the traditionally oppressive dialogue surrounding gender biases against women throughout history, this shift in thinking stops short at dismantling the hegemonic hierarchy. Considering the sociopolitical embrace of biological essentialism to construct normative gendered roles, it becomes clear that when boys or men fail, the immutable laws of biology can be blamed. As gender and feminist scholars and activists fought for decades against the limitations of biologically defined roles for girls and women, it now appears they might need to take up the mantle to battle this appropriation of essentialized masculinity for boys and men.

Career opportunities valuing emotional intelligence and collaboration have drastically increased over the past three decades.[75] Yet narrow definitions of masculinity have traditionally stunted these softer communication skills for boys and men in socialization. This renders boys and men much more vulnerable to social pressures and role models. Social justice projects and activist movements have often failed to address these intricacies of identity formation. The representations central to #MeToo may have similarly overshadowed or eroded the discourse of gendered performance and production. In these complex negotiations, there must be a refocus on "what kind of masculinities are offered as ideals to boys and young men, and how to make them not just aware that sexual harassment is simply unacceptable, but also to recognize it and act in the situations in which they see other men do it."[76] This returns to the impact of socialization and need for expansive and positive models of humanity.

The #MeToo movement offers a message to boys and young men that the falling icons of wealth and fame are not merely impotent role models— they are inept as human beings. Yet the movement also stresses that there are boys and men who are superior role models and remarkable human beings. In this way, #MeToo helps distinguish between these male role models and "the 'grab-her-pussy' types who do it with an absolute sense of entitlement. And we also have to look at men who sit on the fence."[77] Additionally, #MeToo creates a pivotal warning that not only will these actions no longer be tolerated but the powerful, visible men and women who act and think in this way will be called into question. The movement calls for bystanders to become "upstanders" who end the hegemonic chain of command that silences accusations against the most privileged members of communities and culture. Finally, #MeToo draws attention to the notion that the perpetrator/man victim/woman binary has imploded, especially whereas more men have spoken up about their own experiences with sexual violence and misconduct.

The sociopolitical influences on gender norms include familial and peer-based socialization, educational opportunities, economic status, group membership, career goals, and institutional policies and practices. Social justice projects using these constructions often fail to recognize that they may be creating and contributing to complex ideologies surrounding gender. Gender-transformative language in activism and advocacy challenges the limited definitions of masculinity, builds toward gender equality, and furthers collaboration between women and men. This generates a larger population working toward shared and equitable goals. These approaches resist and reject harmful gender normatives, challenging the inequitable institutions that perpetuate these binaried and limited definitions of gender. Any "gender-transformative interventions address the gender and power structures at the root of a host of harmful behaviors and therefore can effect positive changes."[78] Social justice projects like #MeToo can take major steps to create and use gender-transformative language in promoting inclusivity and equality.

The Wake-Up Call

Ultimately, toxic masculinity serves as what Veissière calls the "worst-case ideal type: a fairy tale with some basis in biology and broad cross-cultural relevance. The TM myth serves the useful purpose of promoting socially desirable behavior among males."[79] This is evocative of many discussions within feminism regarding a junction between essentializing gender and denying those essences as anything but a social construct. Zimmer describes witnessing a man yelling obscenities at a passing woman on the street. She turned and threw her milkshake at him as everyone applauded and laughed at the offending man. As Zimmer says, "this was a man who needed a wake-up call that the woman he was shouting at was a person, not an object for him to dominate. Maybe the #MeToo moment will be just that for a lot of men."[80] Rather than continue a dialogue built on binaried language of toxic or deep masculinities, or returning to Freudian concepts of a natural, brutal, undeniable desire available exclusively to men, the greater conversation surrounding men who are waking up to #MeToo marks a new beginning.

It must be noted that it is not the responsibility of women to teach men not to harass, exploit, or abuse them. It is not the responsibility of people of color to explain racism, nor is it the duty of the LGBTQ+ community to educate anyone on sexuality. In the wake of #MeToo, #BlackLivesMatter, or #ItGetsBetter, white, heteronormative, cisgender men are going to need to do this work on their own. Or in the case of the emerging positivist men's movements, together. Godwin notes that "not one of us has a clue what he's doing. I think it's one reason many men are finding this moment so hard: we are perceived to have the power, yet most of us feel powerless in relation to our own lives, emotions, relations."[81] Change is possible when we critically assess ourselves and all of our toxic, complicit, and abusive behaviors and language. This includes "all the things that toxic manhood sets out furiously to deny: our imperfections, our vulnerabilities, our easy lapses into male privilege."[82] As a new conversation begins, men might admit these feelings of powerlessness and hear them echoed.

While it is true that the dominant voices have held the stage for far too long, there are opportunities for men to learn from those who finally have a turn at the microphone. In his experience with the men's group Rebel Wisdom, Godwin spoke about the need for a new men's movement to embrace the current crisis in masculinity and create something positive. When speaking with the group and his male friends, he articulated #MeToo as confusing, shaming, but most necessary and liberating. As Godwin wrote, "I've begun the sentence: 'You know, not all men . . .' only to recall that that in itself is seen as a dick move . . . perhaps all the moment requires is for men to shut up and listen . . . but watching the hashtags accrue— #menaretrash, etc.—it's often hard to discern any positive role for men."[83] Even among the men horrified by the actions of a Louis C.K. or Charlie Rose, many feel disoriented, shamed, and scared by the thought that they may be categorized similarly. The current moment for a potential new men's movement might in fact come from demonstrating and communicating that masculinity, despite its privilege, is not a monolithic oppressor. Along with the current cultural awakening, boys and men stuck in spirals of emotional repression, frustrated alienation, and constant surveillance might shut down completely or deploy power over others.

Stoltenberg claims that as divisive camps grapple with the use of the term "toxic masculinity," it is more significant to note that the allegedly nontoxic aspects are not gender-specific.[84] To claim these ideologies or behaviors as masculine further oppresses women and reifies rigid gender binaries. Stoltenberg advocates instead for individual character to be separated from gender. This contributes to the ways in which we all respond to the #MeToo movement and progressive era of gender equality and acceptance. Despite systemic surveillance, punishment, and threats to security against the status quo of oppression, boys and men must be encouraged to recognize sexual violence and misconduct as perpetrated and experienced by multiple people—despite the stereotypical man/woman dynamic. #MeToo and our responses to the notions of popular and networked misogyny has engendered substantive discourse surrounding the ethic, moral, and cultural strategies of masculinity. This has also strengthened conversations surrounding how human beings in general might elude the most harmful and limiting aspects of hegemonic masculine identity that drove privilege and oppression throughout much of history.

Through education, advocacy, and activism, boys and men can learn the ways that their roles and expectations are shifting for the better of all humankind. As White suggests, "Sex as shared instead of sex that is taken is something that too many adult men are now understanding is the acceptable way to sexually engage."[85] While these are behaviors and beliefs that have taken far too long for the collective conscience to address, #MeToo has pushed the agenda forward with renewed urgency for all survivors sharing their stories. The onus does not fall back on women—nor are sexual or physical violence and misconduct "women's issues." The privileged protection afforded predators for too long is eroding and it is now the responsibility of boys and men to find new ways of being in the world apart from a tradition of toxicity.

NOTES

1. Ruth C. White, "Toxic Masculinity as a Mask for Anxiety," *Psychology Today*, December 22, 2017, https://www.psychologytoday.com/us/blog/culture-in-mind/201712/toxic-masculinity-mask-anxiety.

2. Kevin Powell, "Re-Defining Manhood," *Baffler*, October 31, 2017, https://thebaffler.com/latest/weinstein-masculinity-powell.

3. Karen Crawley and Olivera Simic, "Telling Stories of Rape, Revenge and Redemption in the Age of the TED Talk," *Crime, Media, Culture*, May 14, 2018, https://journals.sagepub.com/doi/abs/10.1177/1741659018771117?journalCode=cmca.

4. Dubravka Zarkov and Kathy Davis, "Ambiguities and Dilemmas around #MeToo: #ForHow Long and #WhereTo?" *European Journal of Women's Studies* 25, no. 1 (2018): 6, https://doi:10.1177/1350506817749436.

5. Michael Kimmel, *Angry White Men: American Masculinity and the End of an Era* (New York: Nation Books, 2013), 250.

6. Kimmel, *Angry White Men*, 78.

7. Powell, "Re-Defining Manhood."

8. Raewyn W. Connell and James W. Messerschmidt, "Hegemonic Masculinity: Rethinking the Concept," *Gender and Society* 19, no. 6 (2005): 829–59.

9. Connell and Messerschmidt, "Hegemonic Masculinity," 832.

10. Michelle Smirnova, "Small Hands, Nasty Women, and Bad Hombres: Hegemonic Masculinity and Humor in the 2016 Presidential Election," *Socius: Sociological Research for a Dynamic World* 4 (2018): 2.

11. Patricia Hill Collins, *Black Feminist Thought: Knowledge, Consciousness, and the Politics of Empowerment* (New York: Routledge, 2000), 221–38.

12. Jane Ward, *Not Gay: Sex Between Straight White Men* (New York: New York University Press, 2015), 4.

13. Powell, "Re-Defining Manhood."

14. Nathian Shae Rodriguez and Terri Hernandez, "Dibs on That Sexy Piece of Ass: Hegemonic Masculinity on TFM Girls Instagram Account," *Social Media and Society* 4, no. 1 (2018): 2, https://doi:10.1177/2056305118760809.

15. Raewyn W. Connell, *Masculinities* (Berkeley: University of California Press, 2005), 79.

16. Peter Glick and Susan T. Fiske, "The Ambivalent Sexism Inventory: Differentiating Hostile and Benevolent Sexism," *Journal of Personality and Social Psychology* 70, no. 3 (1996): 491–512, https://doi:10.1037//0022-3514.70.3.491.

17. Julia C. Becker and Stephen C. Wright, "Yet Another Dark Side of Chivalry: Benevolent Sexism Undermines and Hostile Sexism Motivates Collective Action for Social Change," *Journal of Personality and Social Psychology* 101, no. 1 (2011): 62–77, https://doi:10.1037/a0022615.

18. Becker and Wright, "Dark Side of Chivalry," 63.

19. Rodriguez and Hernandez, "Dibs," 9.

20. Ryan Douglass, "More Men Should Learn the Difference Between Masculinity and Toxic Masculinity," *Huffington Post*, August 5, 2017, https://www.huffingtonpost.com/entry/the-difference-between-masculinity-and-toxic-masculinity_us_59842e3ce4b0f2c7d93f54ce.

21. David A. Farenthold, "Trump Recorded Having Extremely Lewd Conversation about Women in 2005," *Washington Post*, October 8, 2016.

22. Claire Cain Miller, "What Our Sons Are Learning from Donald Trump," *New York Times*, October 18, 2016.

23. Shepherd Bliss, "Mythopoetic Men's Movements," in *The Politics of Manhood: Profeminist Men Respond to the Mythopoetic Men's Movement (and the Mythopoetic Leaders Answer)*, ed. Michael S. Kimmel (Philadelphia: Temple University Press, 1995), 292–307.

24. Terry A. Kuper, "Toxic Masculinity as a Barrier to Mental Health Treatment in Prison," *Journal of Clinical Psychology* 61, no. 6 (2005): 713–24.

25. Connell and Messerschmidt, "Hegemonic Masculinity," 829–59.

26. Harris O'Malley, "The Difference Between Toxic Masculinity and Being a Man," *Good Men Project*, June 27, 2016, https://goodmenproject.com/featured-content/the-difference-between-toxic-masculinity-and-being-a-man-dg.

27. John Stoltenberg, "All Masculinity Is Toxic, According to John Stoltenberg," interview by Wilbert L. Cooper, *Vice*, July 26, 2018, https://www.vice.com/en_us/article/zmk3ej/all-masculinity-is-toxic.

28. *Psychology Today* has revisited the topic of toxic masculinity often, with multiple writers contributing their perspectives. In Dr. Gad Saad's article "Is Toxic Masculinity a Valid Concept?" he explored the hazards of pathologizing manhood. In an earlier issue, Dr. Samuel Veissière advocated the counterpoint that our culture needs nuanced gender archetypes.

29. Olivia Campbell, "The Men Taking Classes to Unlearn Toxic Masculinity," *Cut*, October 23, 2017, https://www.thecut.com/2017/10/the-men-taking-classes-to-unlearn-toxic-masculinity.html.

30. Gad Saad, "Is Toxic Masculinity a Valid Concept?" *Psychology Today*, March 8, 2018, https://www.psychologytoday.com/us/blog/homo-consumericus/201803/is-toxic-masculinity-valid-concept.

31. Samuel Veissière, "The Real Problem with 'Toxic Masculinity,'" *Psychology Today*, February 16, 2018, https://www.psychologytoday.com/us/blog/culture-mind-and-brain/201802/the-real-problem-toxic-masculinity.

32. Stoltenberg, "All Masculinity Is Toxic."

33. Stephen Marche, "The Unexamined Brutality of the Male Libido," *New York Times*, November 25, 2017, https://www.nytimes.com/2017/11/25/opinion/sunday/harassment-men-libido-masculinity.html.

34. Tyler Zimmer, "Men Aren't Monstrous, But Masculinity Can Be," *Slate*, November 29, 2017, http://www.slate.com/blogs/better_life_lab/2017/11/29/men_aren_t_monsters_the_problem_is_toxic_masculinity.html.

35. Bryant W. Sculos, "Who's Afraid of 'Toxic Masculinity'?" *Class, Race and Corporate Power* 5, no. 3 (2017): 3, https//doi:10.25148/CRCP.5.3.006517.

36. Ben Light, "Networked Masculinities and Social Networking Sites: A Call for the Analysis of Men and Contemporary Digital Media," *Masculinities and Social Change* 2, no. 3 (2013): 245–65, https://doi: 10.4471/MCS.2013.34.

37. Ian Ironwood, *The Manosphere: A New Hope for Masculinity* (Otto, NC: Red Pill Press, 2013).

38. Rodriguez and Hernandez, "Dibs," 3.

39. Sarah Banet-Weiser and Kate M. Miltner, "#MasculinitySoFragile: Culture, Structure, and Networked Misogyny," *Feminist Media Studies* 16, no. 1 (2016): 171–74, https//doi:10.1080/14680777.2016.1120490.

40. Banet-Weiser and Miltner, "#MasculinitySoFragile," 172.

41. Debbie Ging, "Alphas, Betas, and Incels: Theorizing the Masculinities of the Manosphere," *Men and Masculinities* (2017): 11.

42. Ging, "Alphas, Betas, and Incels," 16.

43. Ging, "Alphas, Betas, and Incels," 16.

44. Ronan Farrow, "From Aggressive Overtures to Sexual Assault: Harvey Weinstein's Accusers Tell Their Stories," *New Yorker*, October 23, 2017, https://www.newyorker.com/news/news-desk/from-aggressive-overtures-to-sexual-assault-harvey-weinsteins-accusers-tell-their-stories.

45. Chloe Melas, "'House of Cards' Employees Allege Sexual Harassment, Assault by Kevin Spacey," *CNNMoney*, November 3, 2017, https://money.cnn.com/2017/11/02/media/house-of-cards-kevin-spacey-harassment/index.html.

46. David Crary, "Some Male Sexual Assault Victims Feel Left Behind by #MeToo," *MSN.com*, April 19, 2018, https://www.msn.com/en-us/news/us/some-male-sexual-assault-victims-feel-left-behind-by-metoo/ar-AAw2Kpq; Zachary D. Kaufman, "When Sexual Abuse Is Common Knowledge—But Nobody Speaks Up," *Boston Globe*, August 3, 2018, https://www.bostonglobe.com/ideas/2018/08/03/when-sexual-abuse-common-knowledge-but-nobody-speaks/bL0DyTfmKAO9yYxf1VE6zO/story.html.

47. Greg Morabito, "Things Are Falling Apart in the Ken Friedman/April Bloomfield Empire," *Eater*, May 25, 2018, https://www.eater.com/2018/5/25/17394632/ken-friedman-april-bloomfield-dissolve-partnership-salvation-taco.

48. John T. Jost, Julia Becker, Danny Osborne, and Vivienne Badaan, "Missing in (Collective) Action," *Current Directions in Psychological Science* 26, no. 2 (2017): 101, https://doi:10.1177/0963721417690633.

49. Peter L. Berger and Thomas Luckmann, *The Social Construction of Reality* (London: Penguin Books, 1966).

50. Kaufman, "Common Knowledge."

51. Paul R. Albert, "Why Is Depression More Prevalent in Women?" *Journal of Psychiatry & Neuroscience* 40, no. 4 (2015): 219–21; Robynn Zender and Ellen Olshansky, "Women's Mental Health: Depression and Anxiety," *Nursing Clinics of North America* 44, no. 3 (2009): 355–64.

52. Simon M. Rice, Barry J. Fallon, Helen M. Aucote, and Anne Maria Möller-Leimkühler, "Development and Preliminary Validation of the Male Depression Risk Scale: Furthering the Assessment of Depression in Men," *Journal of Affective Disorders* 151, no. 3 (2013): 950–58, https://doi:10.1016/j.jad.2013.08.013.

53. Ronald F. Levant and Katherine Richmond, "The Gender Role Strain Paradigm and Masculine Ideologies," in *APA Handbook of Men and Masculinities*, ed. Joel Y. Wong and Stephen R. Westers (Washington, DC: American Psychological Association, 2017), 23–49.

54. Y. Joel Wong, Moon-Ho Ringo Ho, Shu-Yi Wang, and I. S. Keino Miller, "Meta-Analyses of the Relationship between Conformity to Masculine Norms and Mental Health-Related Outcomes," *Journal of Counseling Psychology* 64, no. 1 (2017): 80, http://dx.doi.org/10.1037/cou0000176.

55. Judith Butler, "Performative Acts and Gender Constitution: An Essay in Phenomenology and Feminist Theory," *Theatre Journal* 40, no. 4 (1988): 519–31; Judith Butler, *Gender Trouble* (New York: Routledge, 1990).

56. Derek K. Iwamoto, Jennifer Brady, Aylin Kaya, and Athena Park, "Masculinity and Depression: A Longitudinal Investigation of Multidimensional Masculine Norms Among College Men," *American Journal of Men's Health* 12, no. 6 (2018): 1878.

57. Rebecca Seales, "What Has #MeToo Actually Changed?" *BBC News*, May 12, 2018, https://www.bbc.com/news/world-44045291.

58. Paul J. Fleming, Joseph G. L. Lee, and Shari L. Dworkin, "'Real Men Don't': Constructions of Masculinity and Inadvertent Harm in Public Health Interventions," *American Journal of Public Health* 104, no. 6 (June 2014): 1029, https://doi: 10.2105/AJPH.2013.301820.

59. Michele C. Black, Kathleen C. Basile, Matthew J. Breiding, Sharon G. Smith, Mikel L. Walters, Melissa T. Merrick, Jieru Chen, and Mark R. Stevens, "National Intimate Partner and Sexual Violence Survey (NISVS): 2010 Summary Report," Atlanta, GA: National Center for Injury Prevention and Control, Centers for Disease Control and Prevention.

60. Seales, "Actually Changed?"

61. Aliraza Javaid, "The Unknown Victims: Hegemonic Masculinity, Masculinities, and Male Sexual Victimisation," *Sociological Research Online*, February 28, 2017, https://journals.sagepub.com/doi/pdf/10.5153/sro.4155.

62. Claire Cohen, *Male Rape Is a Feminist Issue: Feminism, Governmentality and Male Rape* (London: Palgrave Macmillan, 2014).

63. Javaid, "Unknown Victims," 3.

64. Jonathan Bernstein, "Terry Crews: Marvel, Toxic Masculinity and Life after #MeToo," *Guardian*, May 22, 2018, https://www.theguardian.com/culture/2018/may/22/terry-crews-marvel-toxic-masculinity-and-life-after-metoo.

65. Sculos, "Who's Afraid of 'Toxic Masculinity'?" 3.

66. Banet-Weiser and Miltner, "#MasculinitySoFragile," 171.

67. Smirnova, "Small Hands," 12.

68. Johanna Ferreira, "Why We Need to Talk About Toxic Masculinity & Machismo," *Hip Latina*, May 10, 2018, https://hiplatina.com/need-talk-toxic-masculinity-machismo.

69. It should be noted here that Simmons was a friend of Crews's abuser Venit and he tried to convince Crews to drop the allegations. Over a dozen allegations of sexual assault and misconduct against Simmons have since been made public. He has since stepped down from his multiple corporate roles.

70. Douglass, "More Men."

71. White, "Mask for Anxiety."

72. Science, Technology, Engineering, and Mathematics.

73. Juliet A. Williams, "Girls Can Be Anything . . . But Boys Will Be Boys: Discourses of Sex Difference in Education Reform Debates," *Nevada Law Journal* 13, no. 2 (2013): 533.

74. Williams, "Girls Can Be Anything," 546.

75. David J. Deming, "The Growing Importance of Social Skills in the Labor Market," *Quarterly Journal of Economics* 132, no. 4 (2017): 1593–640, https://doi:10.3386/w21473.

76. Zarkov and Davis, "Ambiguities and Dilemmas," 7.

77. Zarkov and Davis, "Ambiguities and Dilemmas," 7.

78. Fleming et al., "'Real Men Don't,'" 1035.

79. Veissière, "Real Problem."

80. Zimmer, "Men Aren't Monstrous."

81. Richard Godwin, "Men after #MeToo: 'There's a Narrative That Masculinity Is Fundamentally Toxic,'" *Guardian*, March 9, 2018, https://www.theguardian.com/world/2018/mar/09/men-after-metoo-masculinity-fundamentally-toxic.

82. Powell, "Re-Defining Manhood."

83. Godwin, "Men after #MeToo."

84. Stoltenberg, "All Masculinity Is Toxic."

85. White, "Mask for Anxiety."

Final Thoughts

"The Future Is Female." *Nicole Adams/Unsplash*

The seeds for the #metooMVMT were planted more than 20 years ago. The words were crystalized over a decade ago. A year ago the world finally understood their power. And we'll never be the same. #metoo

—@MeTooMVMT, October 15, 2018

One year ago today, you shared with me your #MeToo stories.
Our collective pain became our collective power.
#MeTooOneYearLater
Thank you @TaranaBurke for being a force for good.

—@Alyssa_Milano, October 15, 2018

#MeToo—in addition to many recent hashtag activist campaigns—has imploded the notion of a public persona insofar as social media itself has transformed us all into public selves. #MeToo has become an equalizer through a shared platform; it does not insist on the same status or experience but welcomes all in a collective narrative for change. In telling similar stories across public and private spheres, #MeToo drains the symbolic meaning of elitism and elevates the commonality of sexual harassment, abuse, assault, and exploitation. This enables a return to the mass mobilization of grassroots force.

Grassroots activism by and for marginalized communities often becomes viewed purely as an academic site of study. As Hill Collins notes, this "creates a false dichotomy between scholarship and activism, between thinking and doing."[1] Focusing on the activists, scholars, and citizens who experience social injustice and intersectionality, this project aimed to engage with voices often silenced and learn from those lived experiences. Activists like Burke use practice as philosophy to reclaim the simultaneous forces of knowledge and activism. This serves as a model to comprehend intersectional voices as subjects rather than objects of study. The #MeToo movement thus provided a compelling framework to understand identity politics at the intersection of sexual violence and misconduct, survival and support.

#MeToo—in addition to the other forums illustrated in this book—creates a space for individual stories of anger, frustration, sadness, courage, joy, and liberation. There remains great risk in disclosing many of these experiences, especially as these narratives build into a larger collective movement of such massive viral and visible impact. I applaud and appreciate all the voices willing to participate and strengthen the network of survival across marginalized communities and intersectional experiences. Additionally, I remain painfully aware that there are still so many marginalized communities, intersectional oppressions, and relational experiences that deserve more pages in this text—or entire volumes. Looking forward, I hope that in extending this work, we can follow movements like #MeToo to learn from the spectrum of experience, identity, and marginalized forces of activism and advocacy everywhere. I am so grateful for social media movements like #MeToo and the multiple, intersectional, and international voices that have contributed to its viral roar. This book would not be possible without each and every one of you.

NOTE

1. Patricia Hill Collins, *Black Feminist Thought: Knowledge, Consciousness, and the Politics of Empowerment* (New York: Routledge, 2000), 17.

Index

Aalbæk, Peter, 108
AAU. *See* Association of American Universities
abuse: experiences of, 2; pipelines of, 59–60; psychological responses to, 90; sexuality and, 129; spectrum of, 81. *See also* sexual abuse
activism: advocacy and, 11–12; alliances in, 14–15; anti-discrimination, 107; black women and, 54–56; collective, 15, 22; culture and, 30–31; digital, 21–22; discourse of, 17; discursive, 12; of everyday survival, 55–63; expansion of, 116–17; grassroots, 15, 170; international, 12; intersectionality for, 20–21; rise in, 10; "slacktivism," 5; social drama in, 25n49; structuralist approaches to, 9–10; success of, 8; on Twitter, 5, 14–15. *See also* hashtag activism; social media activism
Adam, Karla, 113
advocacy: activism and, 11–12; of celebrities, 30; single-identified, 14
anti-discrimination, 13, 107
Arnault, Jean-Claude, 115
Association of American Universities (AAU), 72–73

Baca Zinn, Maxine, 50, 53, 57–58
Barak-Erez, Daphne, 102
Bates, Laura, 3–4
Becker, Julia, 11
biological determinism, 86–87
biphobia, 76
black women, 48; activism and, 54–56; identity politics and, 56; influence of, 55–56; "maternal politics," 56
Booth, William, 113
Brockington, Dan, 28–30
Burke, Don, 105–6
Burke, Tarana, 2–3, 7, 18–19, 47, 57

"call-out" strategies, 11
campaigns: #BlackLivesMatter, 8; #BringBackOurGirls, 100; #DisVisibility, 138n2; #EverydaySexism, 3–4; #IAmNotAfraidToSay, 113; #IBelieveHer, 111; #IHave, 4; #MeTooInChina, 107; #TimesUp, 18; #WhyIStayed, 8; #YesAllWomen, 3–4
capitalism, 30, 63–64
Carby, Hazel, 57
CDC. *See* Centers for Disease Control and Prevention

celebrities: accusations of, 70–71; advocacy of, 30; Brockington on, 28; "charitainment," 31; class and, 57; criticism of, 31; by culture, 29; machine of, 29–42; performativity of, 39–40; power of, 31–32, 57; study of, 28–29
censorship, 98
Centers for Disease Control and Prevention (CDC), 71–72
Chouliaraki, Lilie, 32, 39
Chuang, Lei, 107
citizens, 28, 40–41
citizenship, 133–34, 137
Clark-Parsons, Rosemary, 4, 8–9, 12
collective action: definition of, 9; history of, 9–11; models toward, 10
collective understanding, 100–102
Collins, Patricia Hill, 15–16, 51–53, 58–59, 170
Committee on the Elimination of Discrimination Against Women, 104
Communist Party, 107
community, 2–3, 42, 90
confession, 39
conforming, 85, 153–54
Conley, Tara L., 8
consent: of disabled persons, 136–37; language around, 126–27; nature of, 19; statistical, 102–5
consumerism, 32–34
content analysis, 17
corporate discourse, 7
Cosby, Bill, 6
Crenshaw, Kimberlé: on discrimination, 54; on identity, 55–56; on intersectionality, 12–13; on oppression, 21; on rape, 16; on women, 59
Crews, Terry, 19, 42, 157, 168n69
Crimes Against People with Disabilities, 129
critical consciousness, 55–56
critical mass, 31–36
Crouch, Colin, 29
culture: activism and, 30–31; celebrities by, 29; growth of, 10; of hegemonic

masculinity, 158–59; marginalized, 7, 62–64; rules of, 56; of victim-blaming, 110–11; of women's rights, 98–99. *See also* disability culture

Davis, Angela, 49, 52–53, 59
Department of Justice, U.S. (DOJ), 132
digital activism, 21–22
digital communication, 8
digital technology, 14
digital world: WOC and, 60–63
Dill, Thornton Bonnie, 50, 53, 57–58
disability culture, 19–20; consent in, 136–37; justice for, 132–33; perceptions of, 131–32; representation of, 127–30; rights in, 127; sex education for, 131–32; sexual abuse of, 124–38; sexual activity in, 127–28; solidarity for, 138; studies of, 136; vulnerability of, 130–31
Disability Visibility Project, 124
discrimination, 54
DOJ. *See* Department of Justice, U.S.
dominant hierarchy structures, 13
Dorsey, Jack, 60–61
Dunham, Lena, 63
Duterte, Rodrigo, 112
Dutta, Tanushree, 110

education: inclusive sex, 87; responsibility of, 163; sex, 131–32; value of, 79; of women, 60
educational justice, 131–35
Edwards, Haley Sweetland, 28
Engdahl, Horace, 115
Equal Employment Opportunity Commission, U.S., 41
Equality Now, 103
European Court of Human Rights, 104
existential motivation, 10–11

Facebook, 2, 6
Fallon, Michael, 109
Fang, Jenn, 8, 64
feminism: academic, 101; anti-, 150; capitalism and, 63–64; forms of,

11–12; hashtag, 8, 12; majority, 64; multiracial, 57–58; phases of, 58; popular, 65; scholarship models in, 57–59; social media and, 11–12; standpoint, 15–16; waves of, 22; white, 19
Flores, Emily, 128–29, 138
Ford, Ashley C., 60–61
Fraser, Nancy, 63–64
"The Future Is Female," *169*

Gehrig, Karolyn, 127
gender: cisgender, 20; communication between, 19; equality of, 7, 143–44; identity of, 56–57; sociopolitical influences on, 162. *See also* men; women
Gilbert, Sophie, 4–5
Girls for Gender Equity, 2
global responses: in Australia, 105; in Brazil, 106–7; in China, 107; in Denmark, 108; in England, 108–9; in France, 109; in India, 110–11; in Ireland, 111; in Japan, 111–12; in Kenya, 109–10; to movements, 105–16; in Philippines, 112–13; in Russia, 113; in South Korea, 113–14; in Spain, 114; spectrum of, 117; in Sweden, 115–16
Godwin, Richard, 163
Goetz, Anne Marie, 100–101
Goodwin, Jeff, 9–10
Google Trends, 98
Graham, Ruth, 5
Gramsci, Antonio, 16, 160
Green, Damian, 109

Hartsock, Nancy, 15–16
hashtag activism, 4–6; benefits of, 31; criticism of, 7–8, 31; for visibility, 64
hegemonic masculinity: backlash of, 144–54; cultural revising of, 158–59; fragile strength of, 157–64; hierarchy in, 150; impact of, 157–58; literature on, 146; in locker rooms, 147–49; manospheric ideologies in, 151; networked misogyny of, 149–51;

subordination in, 145–46. *See also* toxic masculinity
Henson, Spensor, 29–30
"her-meneutics," 102
heteronormativity, 82–83, 90
Hill, Anita, 47–48
Hill, Jemele, 60–62
Hutchinson, Darren Lenard, 13, 21

identity politics, 3, 8; appropriation of, 18; black women and, 56; oppressions in, 13; power and, 14
ignorance, 83–84
International Women's Day March, *123*
intersectionality: activism for, 20–21; approaches to, 15–17; blank boxes and, 135–38; Crenshaw on, 12–13; definition of, 17; oppression in, 63; principles of, 55; purpose of, 15–16; recognition of, 22; social media and, 11–15; strategic, 57; structure of, 13; theories of, 16; value of, 54–55; voices of, 82
intimate partner violence (IPV), 72, 85–86, 110
Ito, Shiori, 111–12

Jackson, Michael, 6
Jasper, James M., 9–10
Ji-eun, Kim, 113–14
Jones, Leslie, 61–62
Jost, John, T., 10
Just Be Inc., 2
justification: gender-specific, 11; system-justification theory, 10

Kaletsky, Kim, 75–76
Kelly, Robert "R.," 62–63
Kermani, Sheema, 100
Khoja-Moolji, Shenila, 22, 100
Kilroy, Debbie, 4

language: bias in, 82; binaried, 81–82; of change, 116–18; changes in, 105, 162; around consent, 126–27; heteronormative, 83; of inclusion, 87; value of, 87–88

Lauer, Matt, 6
Lawrence, Jennifer, 41
legal system, 101; impact on, 104–5;
    international, 104
LGBTQ+ community, 16;
    bisexuality, 76–77; challenges
    for, 85–88; internalization of,
    80–81; participation of, 74; sexual
    violence in, 19, 71–74; silence
    of, 71–73, 80–81; statistics of,
    19; stigmatization of, 79; trans
    community, 77–78; visibility of,
    70–71; youth in, 78–79
Lu, Wendy, 81

Maas, Heiko, 104
mainstream discourse, 82–83
MaleSurvivor, 155
Mankowski, Eric, 148
"manosphere," 6, 150–51
margin mapping, 17–20
mass mobilization, 29–30
McCool, Nanine, 6
McDormand, Frances, 41
McFarland, Daniel, A., 12
McGowan, Rose, 60–61
men: bonds of, 144–45; feminine
    traits of, 147–49; growth of, 164;
    masculinity destabilizing of, 18;
    "networked masculinities," 149–50;
    oppression of, 142–44; participation
    of, 151–53; psychology of, 147–49;
    rape of, 156–57; socialization
    of, 142; societal expectations for,
    160–61; as survivors, 155–57; white
    privilege of, 143, 146–47. *See also*
    hegemonic masculinity
mental health, 153–54
"Me Too Rising," 98
Milano, Alyssa, 1–2, 27, 51–52, 81, 169
Miltner, Kate M., 65
misogynism, 6
#MeQueer, 82–85, 92n16
MMM. *See* Mythopoetic Men's
    Movement
moral outrage, 11

movements: blind spots in, 28;
    challenges of, 6; collective, 102;
    counter-, 8–9; criticism of, 116;
    definition of, 20–22; development
    of, 1–2; discourse between, 102;
    exploitation in, 7; genealogy
    of, 17–18; global responses to,
    105–16; goals of, 2–3, 48, 101–2;
    grassroots, 3; hashtag, 22; impact
    of, 2, 96; international, 95–96;
    leadership of, 49–50; liberation in,
    7; negotiations in, 97; networks in,
    48; phases of, 101–2; politics of,
    7; publicity of, 42; public opinion
    in, 6; reach of, 19–20, 98; value of,
    170; voices of, 3–15; as witch-hunts,
    109; worldwide, 97–116. *See also*
    campaigns
Muller, Sandra, 109
Mythopoetic Men's Movement (MMM),
    147–48

National Public Radio (NPR), 132
National School Climate Survey, 78
Neal, D'Arcee, 124
"Nous Voulons L'égalité" (We Too), 95
NPR. *See* National Public Radio

Obado, Okoth, 110
O'Connor, Amy, 111
Onwuachi-Willig, Angela, 49, 54, 61
oppression, 58, 63; Crenshaw on, 21;
    in identity politics, 13; institutional,
    13; of men, 142–44; multifaceted,
    73–75; networks of, 97; power and,
    14; systemic, 104
Otieno, Sharon, 110

personhood, 128–31
post-humanitarianism, 40
Presidents Club Charity Dinner, 109
privilege, 49
protest participation, 11

racism: "whitewashing," 49, 64–65;
    women and, 48

rape, 16; "corrective rape," 75; definition of, 104; evidence of, 103–4; marital, 103–4; of men, 156–57; "real rape," 105; reports of, 103
Rebel Wisdom, 163
rights: civil, 48–49; in disability culture, 127; human, 99–100, 117. *See also* women's rights
Robbins, Tony, 6–7
Roger, Elliot, 3–4
Rose, Charlie, 6

Sandberg, Sheryl, 6–7
Sarkar, Raya, 110–11
Savile, Jimmy, 6
Schiappa, Marlène, 109
Schrewe, Hartmut, 83
Scott, James C., 32
Scott, Ridley, 70
Scott, Vahiri, 42
self-interested altruism, 40
sexism, 11, 146
sexual abuse: acceptance of, 113–14; awareness of, 83; in colleges, 72–73; common global standard of, 101; of disabled community, 124–38; evidence of, 5–6; frequency of, 96–97, 110; as moral crime, 103; statistics of, 40–41, 71–73; stereotypical representations of, 85
sexual citizenship, 20, 125–35
sexual fetishization, 75–76, 130
sexual harassment, 2; degrees of, 5–6; online, 61; in public, 109
sexual misconduct, 5, 18
sexual orientation, 73–74
sexual predators, 88, 164
sexual stereotypes, 58
sexual violence, 3; discourse around, 142–43; as enabled, 152; heteronormative gendered framing of, 85–86; legislation on, 103; in LGBTQ+ communities, 19; patterns of, 103; resources for, 82; same-sex, 19; visibility of, 18
Shah, Sonali, 125–27

Shapiro, Joseph, 127, 133
Shaw, Frances, 12–13
"The Silence Breakers," 18, 43n2
SIMCA. *See* social identity model of collective action
Smith, Dorothy, 15–16
Smith, Savannah, 84
social engagement, 15
social identity model of collective action (SIMCA), 10
social justice, 3; criteria of, 14; criticism of, 21; evolution of, 10
social media: censorship against, 107; criticism of, 5–6; feminism and, 11–12; #Intersectionality and, 11–15; impact of, 4; power of, 11–12; roar of, 17–18, 170; trial by, 6
social media activism, 1–2; challenges of, 6; debates on, 5; merits of, 9
social order, 12
sociopolitical history, 14–15
sociopolitical interests, 11–12
sociopolitical transformation, 8
sociopsychological models, 10
Solnit, Rebecca, 5
Spacey, Kevin, 19, 70
Spicer, Tracey, 105–6
Stache, Lara C., 4
Stafford, Pamela, 132, 138
Stoltenberg, John, 163–64
Strike, Wafula, 135
structuralism, 9–10
subjugation, 56
Supreme Court, U.S., 48
Surviving R. Kelly, 63
survivors: challenges for, 18, 159–60; of color, 48; differently abled, 19–20; disabled, 19–20, 124–26; group, 16, 55–56; imperatives of, 8–9; men as, 155–57; pressures of, 102; trust in, 143
system justification, 152–53

Telegraph, 105–6
Thomas, Clarence, 48
Time, 18, 27–28

toxic masculinity, 147–49, 162–64, 165n28
Trump, Donald, 43n2, 147
Turner, Victor, 12
Twitter, 2; activism on, 5, 14–15; impact of, 14–15; #MeQueer and, 92n16

United Nations Entity for Gender Equality and the Empowerment of Women, 102–3
United States (U.S.), 61, 101

Valdes, Francisco, 14
Valenti, Jessica, 21–22
victim-blaming, 48, 62–63, 110–11
victimization, 87–88
Violence Against Women Act, U.S., 82

Weinstein, Harvey, 1–2
We Too ("Nous Voulons L'égalité"), 95
Wildman, Stephanie M., 49
Williams, Wendy, 62–63
WOC. *See* women of color
women: Asian, 58–59; bisexual, 76–77; Crenshaw on, 59; education of,

60; inequality of, 15–16; minority, 3; misrepresentation of, 101; oppression of, 58; racism and, 48; silence of, 3, 56–59; stereotypes of, 58–59; truth of, 97–98; in underdeveloped countries, 19–20; in U.S., 61. *See also* black women; feminism
women of color (WOC), 2–3; digital world and, 60–63; girls of color, 59–60; Native American, 60; sexualization of, 59–60; stereotypes of, 59–60. *See also* black women
Women's March, *69, 141*
women's rights, 96; cultural dialogue of, 98–99; as discredited, 100–101; in Egypt, 99; in India, 99–100; in Iran, 98–99; in Latin America, 99; in Nigeria, 100; in Pakistan, 100; in U.S., 101
World Health Organization, 103
Wright, Stephen C., 11

Yamaguchi, Noriyuki, 112
Yiannopoulos, Milo, 61

Made in the USA
Columbia, SC
05 September 2021